Virginia Woolf as Feminist

Other works by the same author:

Social Feminism
Canadian Women: A History (coauthor)
Feminist Politics on the Farm (coauthor)
Shakespeare Head Press edition of Virginia Woolf's *Three Guineas* (editor)

Virginia Woolf as Feminist

NAOMI BLACK

Cornell University Press

ITHACA & LONDON

For information, address
   Cornell University Press,
   Sage House
   512 East State Street
   Ithaca, New York 14850.

First published 2004 by
Cornell University Press
First printing, Cornell Paperbacks, 2004

Printed in the United States of America

Library of Congress
Cataloging in Publication Data

Black, Naomi, 1935–
   Virginia Woolf as feminist / Naomi
Black.
      p. cm.
Includes bibliographical references and
index.
   ISBN 0-8014-4177-3 (cloth : alk. paper)
— ISBN 0-8014-8877-X (pbk. : alk. paper)
   1. Woolf, Virginia, 1882–1941—Views on
feminism. 2. Feminism and literature—
England—History—20th century. 3.
Feminism—England—History—20th
century. 4. Woolf, Virginia, 1882–1941
Three guineas.   I. Title.
   PR6045.O72Z558 2004
   823'.912—dc21

                        2003011988

Cornell University Press strives to use
environmentally responsible suppliers and
materials to the fullest extent possible in
the publishing of its books. Such materials
include vegetable-based, low-VOC inks and
acid-free papers that are recycled, totally
chlorine-free, or partly composed of
nonwood fibers. For further information,
visit our website at
www.cornellpress.cornell.edu.

Cloth printing   10 9 8 7 6 5 4 3 2 1
Paperback printing   10 9 8 7 6 5 4 3 2 1

In memory of MAX BLACK

Contents

Acknowledgments

Because this project has taken so long to complete, I can thank only a few of the many who helped gather resources for it. In particular, Ann Pelley at Mount Saint Vincent University continues to bring all the libraries of the world within my reach in Halifax. The Women's Library staff in London have been wonderfully helpful, particularly Wendy Thomas and Lisa Giffen; I also owe special thanks to David Doughan, formerly at the Fawcett Library (before it was the Women's Library), who has over the years generously shared with me his detailed knowledge of British feminism. The photograph of the bust of Virginia Woolf by Stephen Tomlin that appears on the title page was supplied by the Pratt Library of Victoria University, Toronto, whose staff I thank also for facilitating my use of their microfilms of Virginia Woolf manuscripts. B. J. Kirkpatrick scanned even more suffragist journals for me, Jean Gaffin provided information about the current situation of the Co-operative Women's Guild, and Kalyani Menon kindly wrote me her recollections of the Women's Employment Federation. James M. Haule helped me repeatedly in many ways; I must also thank Isaac Gewirtz of the New York Public Library and Sylvia Asmus of the Deutsche Bibliothek of Frankfurt am Main for their role in laying to rest the myth that a *Three Guineas* manuscript was sold "for the refugees" and then to the Berg Collection.

The assistants who worked on my edition of *Three Guineas* laid the groundwork for this book, and I want to thank them again: Louise Carbert, who did all the initial tedious sorting and identification of the books and periodicals that Virginia Woolf consulted, as well as Cindy Kleiman, Jacqueline Vukman, Liz Millward, Tamara Barclay, and Elizabeth Hutchinson. As I was completing the manuscript, the efficient and intelligent work of Anna Nomiko (in Sussex) and April F. Carter (in London) saved me a trip to England.

Identifying the subjects of the photographs was possible because of the much appreciated help of the following in 1997: Mrs. S. K. Hopkins (head of the Department of Uniforms, Badges, and Medals at the National Army Museum), Thomas Woodcock (Norroy and Ulster king of arms), Lieutenant Colonel (ret'd) Jim Oliver (Household Cavalry), Major Kersting (curator, Household Cavalry Museum), Professor Mary Jane Mossman (Osgoode Hall Law School), The Honourable Sir Stephen Sedley, Father Edward Black (chaplain, Trinity College, University of Toronto), and Melanie Barber (deputy librarian and archivist, Lambeth Palace Library). The identifications were later confirmed by information in the Hogarth Press archives in the University of Reading library; I thank the staff there for their assistance, as also the staff in the library of the University of Sussex.

The editorial committee of the Shakespeare Head Edition of Virginia Woolf encouraged me to write this book by their enthusiasm for the introduction to the edition of *Three Guineas* that I prepared for them. Among the editors I must particularly thank S. P. Rosenbaum, who helped me continue to feel that this work is worth doing. Dear Pat, this book is dedicated to my father—it is time for me to honor him—but it is really for you.

NAOMI BLACK

Halifax, Nova Scotia

Abbreviations

Works by Virginia Woolf

3G

Three Guineas. Ed. Naomi Black. London: Shakespeare Head Press for Basil Blackwell, 2001.

D1–5

The Diary of Virginia Woolf. 5 vols. Ed. Anne Olivier Bell, assisted by Andrew McNeillie. London: Hogarth Press, 1977–84.

L1–6

The Letters of Virginia Woolf. 6 vols. Ed. Nigel Nicolson and Joanne Trautmann. London: Hogarth Press, 1975–80.

N1–67

Brenda R. Silver. Virginia Woolf's Reading Notebooks. Princeton, N.J.: Princeton University Press, 1983.

"WMW"

"Women Must Weep" and "Women Must Weep—Or Unite against War." *Atlantic Monthly Magazine* 1621.5 (May 1938): 585–94; 1621.6 (June 1938): 750–59.

Other Abbreviations

FIL

For Intellectual Liberty

L&NSWS

London and National Society for Women's Service

NUSEC

National Union of Societies for Equal Citizenship

NUWSS

National Union of Women's Suffrage Societies

PSF

People's Suffrage Federation

WCG
  Women's Co-operative Guild
WEF
  Women's Employment Federation
WFL
  Women's Freedom League
WSPU
  Women's Social and Political Union

Note on Editions of *Three Guineas*

There are numerous versions of *Three Guineas* available in libraries and bookstores. The text of the first English edition has been used for all of Hogarth Press's clothbound editions of the book (although the photographs were missing from the 1968 and 1977 reprints of the Uniform Edition, as they have been from many of the paperback editions). The Harbinger book that was the first paperback edition in 1963 used the text of the first American edition that had been published by Harcourt Brace in 1938, but the next paperback editions, published by Penguin (1977) and Hogarth (1986), used a text that had been reset from the first English edition. Other paperback editions copy the first English edition with minor standardization or corrections. These include the most easily available paperbacks as I write, the double volumes combining *A Room of One's Own* and *Three Guineas* (Oxford University Press, 1992; Penguin Books, 1993). American readers often use a clothbound or paperback version of the first American edition. All of these versions, including the two first editions, include some errors.

For this book, all references to *Three Guineas* are keyed to the Shakespeare Head edition that I prepared for Blackwell's in 2001. It is a standardized and slightly emended version of the first English edition. (For details of the emendations, see Appendix A of the Shakespeare Head edition.) The two first editions of *Three Guineas* were both published in 1938, in England by the Hogarth Press (London) and in the United States by Harcourt Brace (New York).

The Shakespeare Head edition text of *Three Guineas* is 166 pages long, just about half the length of the first English edition. For readers who must rely on other editions, the following table shows pagination for markers in the Shakespeare Head (SH), Hogarth Press (IE), and Harcourt Brace (IA) texts.

Virginia Woolf as Feminist

Finding Feminism in Virginia Woolf

"I have already said all I have to say in my book Three Guineas," wrote Virginia Woolf at the end of November 1938. This is a stunning comment about a book that is certainly now recognized as feminist but usually not seen as central to Woolf's work. Woolf herself did not undervalue the book or what it had to say; she had already called it her "Credo" a month earlier (*D5* 169).[1] *Three Guineas* is most often read as a book opposing war. In fact, this book is the best, clearest presentation of Woolf's feminism. It is about war because it is about the better, nonsexist, and therefore peaceful world that feminism envisages. "Living differently" is how Woolf described her feminist goals.[2] And living differently is what we all desperately need to know about.

In the abstract, the solution to war is easy: pacifism, the refusal to prepare for or to engage in armed conflict. Woolf herself, like many others confronted with the monstrous and aggressive fascist regimes of the interwar years, finally concluded that evil must sometimes be countered forcefully. Survival once ensured, the solution to a militaristic and hierarchical world is more difficult, but it is to be found in feminism. All of which is, of course, an excessively simple summary of a complex theory embodied in a book that has provoked more hostility and more misunderstanding than anything else in Virginia Woolf's large body of work. The theory itself is, today, more worth attention than ever. The patriarchs, the tyrants petty and huge, the devastations both public and private—they are still with us after the succession of wars and postwars that have followed Virginia Woolf's death. So too, more fortunately, is the writing Woolf left, of which the much maligned *Three Guineas* is the central focus of this book.

Any writer's texts differ, and texts themselves develop as they are written. But there is likely to be a sort of skeleton or armature of belief underneath them all. Virginia Woolf's writings demonstrate a constant and consistent pattern that is both feminist and recognizably the same over time. She shared the specific humanism of her friends and relatives in the Bloomsbury Group, but she differed from them in a number of ways, including in her views about women, about feminism, and therefore about how best to change the world. These dimensions of her feminism can be found in her diaries and letters, as early as the first of the so-called world wars. They are present in her fiction, though they have to be teased out of complex and subtle narratives. In *Three Guineas* they are front and center, explicit. For *Three Guineas* is the piece of published writing where Woolf demonstrated, deliberately, that her feminist analysis applied to war as well as, more importantly, to all varieties of hierarchy.

This book's goal is twofold: to elucidate Woolf's feminism, focusing on its presentation in *Three Guineas*, and to show how that feminism is relevant today. By examining those publications—nearly all nonfiction—in which Woolf presented a feminist position, by looking at the occasion and logic of each such statement, and by looking at how she expressed her beliefs in each particular piece of writing, I outline the feminism that, present in all her work, is also sometimes more explicitly set out.

I

A frequently cited entry in Virginia Woolf's 1935 diary can serve as a starting point, though we must be wary of how much weight we put on what Woolf wrote for herself rather than for a wider audience. She was to process such material elaborately before it became a considered statement of her beliefs. Still, her initial, raw responses provide useful signposts.

In 1935, as usual, Virginia Woolf had a number of writing projects in hand. Central, as it was to be for two more long, frustrating years, was the future best-seller *The Years*. But she was also already collecting material and ideas for a sequel to *A Room of One's Own*, to be called, perhaps, "On Being Despised." The result would be *Three Guineas*, published in 1938. As the thirties wound down, she recorded, fuming, the encounters and remarks that fueled her feminism. On 9 April 1935 she recounted a particularly revealing episode.

"I met Morgan [E. M. Forster] in the London Library yesterday & flew into a passion," she begins. He said to her: "And Virginia, you know I'm on the Co[mmittee] here . . . and we've been discussing whether to allow ladies." Woolf writes down her response:

It came over me that they were going to put me on: & I was then to re-fuse: Oh but they do—I said. There was Mrs. Green . . .

Forster then said:

Yes yes—there was Mrs. Green. And Sir Leslie Stephen said, never again. She was so troublesome. And I said, havent ladies improved? But they were all quite determined. No no no, ladies are quite impossible. They wouldnt hear of it.

And Woolf writes, "See how my hand trembles. I was so angry." The diary passage goes on to imagine that a woman friend is offered some honor usually reserved for men. It ends as follows:

You didnt tell them what you thought of them for daring to suggest that you should rub your nose in that pail of offal? I remarked. . . .

The veil of the temple—which, whether university or cathedral, was academic or ecclesiastical I forget—was to be raised, & as an exception she was to be allowed to enter in. But what about my civilisation? For 2,000 years we have done things without being paid for doing them. You cant bribe me now.

"Truth is only to be spoken by those women whose fathers were pork butchers & left them a share in the pig factory," the daughter of Leslie Stephen, the distinguished editor of the *Dictionary of National Biography* ended her indignant diary entry about how women like her were treated. "This little piece of rant wont be very intelligible in a years time," she re-flected three days later, "yet there are some useful facts & phrases in it" (*D4* 297–98).

This episode has, understandably, received considerable analysis, in-cluding as it does opinions attributed to Woolf's father as well as some memorable statements about the nature of male domination. On occasion her reaction has even been given a significant role in producing *Three Guineas*. Yet it is a mistake to take the entry simply at face value, as an ex-ample of anger with direct literary consequences. To begin with, *Three Guineas*, though not yet called that, was well under way by the beginning of 1935; that project was far more than a riposte to immediate provocation. In addition, the reality of the injury should be questioned. We have only Virginia Woolf's report of Forster's claim that there was a policy, originat-ing with her father, against appointing more women to the committee. Perhaps Forster was being mischievous: it seems unlikely that Leslie

Stephen would have taken such a position, for, as his daughter knew, he was supportive of women's education and their professional activity even though he opposed any immediate granting of the vote to them.[3]

Woolf's diary notes about the London Library Committee are nevertheless worth attention. Certainly they express deeply felt views. In addition, they include a number of features found throughout her feminist writing. For one thing, this diary entry demonstrates how Woolf uses and possibly distorts situations in her own life, and how contextual information can clarify the process. For another, the dismissive reference to "Mrs. Green" hardly conveys the reality of the first woman to serve on the London Library Committee. Alice Stopford Green—who was reelected to the London Library Committee five times between 1894 and 1916—was herself a respectable scholar as well as a good friend of Leslie Stephen, who edited in 1910 the letters of Green's deceased husband, the eminent historian J. R. Green.[4]

In addition, this diary entry includes the dramatizing creation of fictional characters who embody feminist responses and both are and are not Virginia Woolf, such as the imaginary friend who is to refuse honors but far less politely than Woolf did herself. The archetypal daughter of the elite so central to *Three Guineas* has already made her appearance, cherishing her own experience and traditions as a woman, resenting her relative powerlessness and lack of recompense or recognition. The primary audience of *Three Guineas* is foreshadowed—the women who might be in the situation of the wife of J. R. Green or the daughter of Leslie Stephen. The diarist recognizes that such a woman nevertheless has the power to speak freely as most women do not; she is aware of the women whose fathers do not own actual or metaphorical factories. In *Three Guineas* the pork butcher's daughter will be identified as the daughter and sister of "educated men," and an Outsiders' Society will articulate the quite considerable resources available to her. Finally, in her reflection three days later, Woolf comments that both "facts" and "phrases" will be saved for future use; just such procedures will be noted in her published feminist works. To round out the story, we should note that Professor Eileen Power was elected to the London Library Committee two years later, and in 1940 Woolf had the pleasure of refusing, politely, an offer by Forster to propose her for it (*D5* 337).

In a way, the literal accuracy of the account in Woolf's diary is beside the point, as is the case for quite a lot of the "facts" provided in *Three Guineas*. Woolf's response, as she reports it, effectively represents the sort of indignation that women are likely to feel in a male-dominated world, even, perhaps especially, those women who, if they were men, would have access to privilege and power. Feminists are more likely than other women to share Virginia Woolf's indignation, yet that episode can bring out feminist responses in women not previously radicalized. That is, it can make them angry at Mrs. Green's having been made the stand-in for a whole class of human beings who are seen as unfit to do what men do as a matter of course. *Three Guineas* is, among other things, an attempt to provoke in women just such an irritated awareness of the structures of sexist exclusion. One of the tasks of *Three Guineas* is to document the details of continuing sexism. Woolf would like to make every woman conscious of the existence of "my civilisation" and the reasons to refuse any offers of joining the boys. These are central themes of Virginia Woolf's feminism.

Finally, what the book demonstrates is that sexism itself is both the root and the flower of the male-dominated hierarchies that, when it was written, were leading the world into global conflict. The image of the father who is a pork butcher associates blood and brutality with patriarchy. Contemptuous of influential and successful men, Woolf describes them as owners of the slaughterhouse. *Three Guineas* was to make explicit the connection to the butchery of war.

II

Three Guineas has always had a mixed reception, and frequently a hostile one. When it was first published in the year leading up to the Munich Agreements, that last, futile attempt at appeasing Hitler's Germany, the book's ostensible subject was war. That fact, and that it was by that famous (woman) writer Virginia Woolf, made attention to it unavoidable. Nevertheless, alienated critics, disappointed friends and relatives, and unhappy biographers recoiled from the book precisely because it was really about feminism and therefore about systemic change. Many women and a few men welcomed the feminist project that it represented. But most other readers dismissed it as a personal, emotional response to oncoming renewal of war. Thus, Virginia Woolf's first biographer, her nephew Quentin Bell, was firmly insistent that *Three Guineas* was an irrational cry of feminine anguish. Yet he also admitted that it was feminist. And though he believed that what he considered to be feminism was already outdated by the 1930s, he noted bemusedly in 1979 that feminism had apparently continued to be—become?—a significant social movement, and one for which his aunt was some sort of emblematic figure. "Twenty years ago . . .

no one would have seen Virginia Woolf as a maker of political ideologies comparable with the great anti-imperialist or the prophet of deficit budgeting," Bell wrote plaintively, comparing her to Forster and Keynes. He still found *Three Guineas* "a saddening and exasperating production."[5]

It is a fact that many readers dislike *Three Guineas*. Certainly it is a difficult book, not nearly as accessible or as charming as *A Room of One's Own*. Men in particular are likely to find the photographs baffling and the text and notes frivolous, and to question whether a book at least ostensibly about war should even try to be amusing. And then there are the sentiments—an old-fashioned word for a book that some find old-fashioned, self-conscious, even arty. The book's central argument, linking fascism with the status of women, has been attacked ever since it was first published on the eve of World War Two. Irrelevant, said those frantic to halt Hitler and Mussolini. Like some among later feminists, they backed off from a possible evocation of what we would now call essentialism, a definition of women as somehow intrinsically—biologically?—more peaceful and virtuous than men.

And yet, and yet—apparently neither *Three Guineas* nor Woolf's feminism is a topic that can be relegated to the dustbin. Only a few years ago a hugely successful biography of Woolf approvingly made *Three Guineas* a central part of the account of Woolf's feminism, part of her political work that "tended to be misunderstood and undervalued."[6] Then in the year 2000 another biography of Virginia Woolf appeared, written by the son of Woolf's dear friend Vita Sackville-West, and its author felt obliged to spend five pages on *Three Guineas*, trying to refute an argument that he described as "neither sober nor rational" but which he identified as Woolf's "profoundest convictions on a subject central to her life."[7] Early in the year 2002, a lengthy review of a new edition of *Three Guineas* described the book as a passive "sublimation" of "feelings of helplessness and self-hatred"; six months later, another literary essay used the book to attack Woolf and "the triumph of narcissism." Both were cover reviews with hideous cartoons of Virginia Woolf.[8]

The explanation of the continuing acclaim and rejection of *Three Guineas* is both straightforward and complicated. Most importantly, most simply, Virginia Woolf's feminism is of a sort still not easily accepted today. In addition, *Three Guineas* has a complex history, a unique form, and a dense, allusive style, none of which has yet been fully explicated.

In this book, I bring together what can be known about *Three Guineas*—its context in Woolf's writing and in feminist activism, its composition, its contents, its predecessors, its versions, the responses to it, its form—in order to draw from them and from the book itself an account of Woolf's feminism. She would, I think, approve of this effort, for in *Three Guineas* she carefully, deliberately, put together documented accounts of women's lives in order to argue for changes that would transform society. Being Virginia Woolf, she also labored to make the result something that was aesthetically coherent as well as (and therefore?) persuasive. Here, as always, she sets a standard for those who study her work.

The nature of Woolf's feminism is crucial to assessment of her writing, especially in *Three Guineas*. Many women thought, when they became women's movement activists, that the case they had to make—what had persuaded them—was, simply, obvious. Once understood, it would be accepted by everyone. However, most feminists in North America did not make the arguments Woolf did. Many of them repeated familiar (and surely plausible) claims that women, if given the chance, were as rational as men. Give women that chance, treat them fairly and educate them as well as men, and they would make their way. Alternately, contemporary feminists followed Continental thinkers and adjusted the analyses and claims of Marxism to include the situation of women, with an emphasis on how relationships of production were affected by gender.

By contrast, Woolf presents a deeply radical sort of feminism. Her feminism was original, yet firmly rooted in the women's movement of her time. Incorporating a vision of a completely changed society, *Three Guineas* is more radical than most of us yet recognize. And even those who fully appreciate, even cherish, the book are far from knowing all that could be known about it.

If *Three Guineas* were indeed just a war book or merely a polemical pamphlet, but one written by Virginia Woolf, it would be well worth our attention. But it is more; it is the clearest, most explicit statement of Woolf's feminism. In this book, war is not Woolf's main target; in this her critics are correct. For her, war is only one of the products, admittedly one of the worst products, of a system of power and domination that has its roots in gender hierarchy. That hierarchy, and all others, are the targets of her feminism.

To understand the book we need to understand Woolf's feminism, and to understand Woolf's feminism, we need to understand the book. Both goals are important. Woolf's feminism is tough and sophisticated, and it has transformative implications that are quite staggering. Q. D. Leavis, possibly the most hostile critic of *Three Guineas* at the time of its publication, understood its message very well. Her review of *Three Guineas* has the contemptuous title "Caterpillars of the Commonwealth Unite!" In it she writes that she pities "the unfortunate men who are to marry these daughters of educated men [and who] must from the start share the work of tending their offspring," including hurrying home every four hours to give the baby its bottle. This would represent, she says, "a thorough-going revolution . . . a regular social reorganisation." The tone of the review is apocalyptic: Woolf's feminism would be the end of civilization as we know it.[9] To which, again, the radical and political feminist who is Virginia Woolf replies: And what about my civilization?

III

Virginia Woolf herself is now such a massive figure in cultural as well as literary studies that it may seem foolish to make any claims about what she said, let alone believed.[10] Yet there is a paradox in the refusal to continue analysis, for it amounts to a bias toward certain sorts of interpretation. Thus a recent critic usefully reminds us that we who read Woolf, read her in accord with our own interests. Certainly, feminist critics have constructed and reconstructed a variety of versions of Woolf's feminism. The indeterminism about it all, she then concludes, is an indeterminism that reflects a major feature of Woolf's beliefs. With this, she too constructs her own version of Woolf's feminism.[11] But why should we accept hers rather than any other?

In fact, we can do better. There is, after all, something linking or sustaining the accretion of interpretations of Virginia Woolf, an identifiable body of work that endures. However complex and fluid its intent or meaning, an identifiable person wrote it at an actual point or location in history. Virginia Woolf's writing is real. So too is the feminism central to it. In spite of iconization, this is a feminism—a radical and political feminism— that is significant. This feminism mattered even in its own time, in an era that was bound to misunderstand it. It is even more important today when our understanding of feminism is less constrained but our understanding of Woolf's beliefs is clouded by accumulated attempts at interpretation.

Feminism itself remains a much disputed notion, a "contested" term in the philosophical sense. As claims to define it have diversified, so too has the intensity, even bitterness, of the competing identifications. However, this barrage of claims and counterclaims often amounts to not a lot more than assertion of ownership. A rock-bottom definition of feminism, one that is descriptive rather than pejorative or rhetorical, needs to capture all those who, often bravely, say they are feminists, as well as those who sub-scribe to feminist beliefs while doubting or even rejecting the identifica-tion. And such a definition of feminism is certainly possible.

Feminism must start with the observation that women are categorized in terms of their gender. That is, they are contrasted to men and also nearly always subordinate to men. In addition, women share, in a complex fashion, a range of distinctive history, experience, and values.[12] We can disagree about the extent to which all this is socially constructed, how per-manent or desirable (or ephemeral, or undesirable) the distinctiveness of women is, and how best to improve conditions or benefit from the conse-quences. But feminists necessarily agree that women are different from men, and also—this is crucial—that women should not therefore be judged inferior to men or treated in ways that disadvantage them. How to measure "disadvantage" presents a number of theoretical problems. In practical terms, however, women's deprivation is usually easy enough to identify, for most societies still have significant gender-skewed differences in access to whatever that society most values.[13] A United Nations formu-lation from 1980 put the situation of women in terms not much changed today: "While they represent 50 per cent of the world adult population and one third of the official labor force, they perform nearly two thirds of all working hours, receive one tenth of the world income and own less than one per cent of the world's property."[14]

It now seems obvious that women have enough in common to be dis-cussed as a category, if only for analytic and strategic reasons. At the same time, importantly, they are both heterogeneous and heteronomous (to use Teresa de Lauretis's useful terms). That is, women are diverse, but as a group they are subject to regulations made not by themselves but by men. Heterogeneity is inevitable and to be celebrated; gender-based control by male authority is to be deplored and combated.[15] Again, fem-inists are likely to disagree about the reasons for women's subordination, and unlikely to agree on the priority of improvements and how auton-omy, the opposite of heteronomy, is best to be achieved. But they will necessarily insist that women not be treated as subordinate, second rate, or simply complementary in terms of some prior, superior masculine standard.

I do not want to give Woolf's feminism a label. When I insist that Woolf's feminism is radical, this does not mean I am identifying Woolf as a radical feminist in the sense that the term has been used by analysts of twentieth-century feminism. The term *radical feminism* itself has a specific history that makes it seriously anachronistic when applied to a theorist writing in the 1930s. It was used first by the American women activists who broke away from the student movement in the 1960s and then, again mostly in North America, by those feminists who discarded a class-based Marxist or socialist analysis in favor of one linking the oppression of women to masculinity or sexism.[16] Contemporary studies of what came to be called the second wave of feminism then delineated theoretical differences among groups. None of the main categories—liberal, Marxist, socialist, or radical feminism—corresponds to the beliefs expressed by Virginia Woolf, though radical feminism, in its focus on women's specificity, is the closest. The still emerging "identity" feminisms, distinctive by their adherents and their context, are a bit closer to Woolf, because each draws on women's experience. But each necessarily has specific history and priorities, as well as its own theoretical articulations.[17]

Another, more helpful way of sorting forms of feminism has placed on one side the many sorts of *equity feminism* derived from preexisting theoretical systems. Such feminisms draw on women's similarities to men, in order to argue for their receiving the same treatment as men. Here we find liberal, Marxist, and socialist feminism, and additional categories such as anarcha-feminism. By contrast, *social feminism*, based on women's differences from men, is derived from women's distinctive experience and characteristics. The goal is more than just equality or equal treatment. Virginia Woolf belongs among the social feminists, because of her valorization of women's "civilisation" as a basis for social and political transformation.[18] It seems increasingly unhelpful, however, to limit analysis by categories whose chief value has been for organizations justifying their separate existence. Women require full access to economic and political rights in order to promote reforms that will use women's history and experience as a basis for reconstruction of the world shared by all human beings.

Radical remains a useful adjective for feminism to the extent that it means drastic or thorough-going rather than membership in some self-identified group. And Woolf's feminism is indeed drastic, basic, transformational. *Political*, the other adjective I would apply to Woolf's feminism, is also helpful, for it indicates relevance to the public world and its structures of domination.[19] But in the end, categories have to be jettisoned for the project of mapping the feminism of a given writer or activist—in this case, of Virginia Woolf.

We will never, in any simple sense, fully understand either *Three Guineas* or the feminism it presents. Both have a richness and an inherent ambiguity that help to explain their continuing interest. At the same time, we will understand them better if we know more about them. We need to understand how and why *Three Guineas* was written, we need to examine the text of the book and the different versions of *Three Guineas* itself, and we need to examine the responses to *Three Guineas*. I began this process in my edition of *Three Guineas*, where the interested reader can find a full annotation of the text as well as detailed lists of the books and periodicals that Woolf cited in it. Here I present a discussion that is less closely tied to the requirements of a scholarly edition and more directed toward understanding Virginia Woolf's feminism.

The problem is where to find that feminism. It is now reasonable, I think, to accept that all of Woolf's writing, separately as well as collectively, was influenced by an underlying feminism. That is, recognizable and continuing features of Virginia Woolf's feminism can be traced in all her writing. Although by no means the whole of Woolf's beliefs, this was an important and an omnipresent one that has been acknowledged, if not usually seen clearly, by both Woolf's greatest admirers and her most hostile critics. *Three Guineas* is special, because in it the feminist perspective becomes an explicit argument. *Three Guineas* also has the virtue of being a deliberately planned, completed text. We may have trouble interpreting the author's meaning, but at least we know that the words and their arrangement are what she intended to have read by an undifferentiated public (though I argue that there was also a specific intended audience for *Three Guineas*, even if not limited to a personally known one). Difficult, confusing, teasing, elusive, *Three Guineas* nevertheless is in the form that Woolf wanted. If we understand *Three Guineas*, we understand a good deal about what she believed.

All readers of English now have available authoritative editions of Woolf's novels, longer nonfiction books, and shorter fiction, as well as a substantial portion of her essays. We also have available in print more of Virginia Woolf's own "private" writing than of any other modern writer: published diaries, letters, manuscripts. No doubt she would find it comic; we can hope she would also find it flattering. Any of us can dive into this wondrous ocean of text and emerge with treasures, nuggets of information, new monocausal explanations, our own readings of the published writing that was central to Woolf's working life. So I have hesitated to launch (to continue the metaphor) this study of *Three Guineas*, one more small effort to make sense out of too much material, one more small effort to read with plausibility even one among the multiple products of Woolf's creativity.

The difficulty of the present enterprise seems the greater because we have come to doubt the authenticity of any single account, to become increasingly aware of the role of interpretation and context in the changing and multiple understandings of any work of art. *Three Guineas* is such a work of art. It deserves the same care appropriate for any of its author's creations. Interestingly, even those critics who couple Woolf's perceptions and interpretations most insistently with the form of her fiction tend to read *Three Guineas* as simply an attempt at a straightforward, documented argument. Thus, a recent study uses *Three Guineas* merely to establish Woolf's concern for the impact of "gender identity, war, imperialism and Englishness," even though the author notes that "it exemplifies the experiences of women and records the social conditions that obstruct them— employing mockery, satire, fantasy, irony." Insistent about the fluidity of discourse and narrative in Woolf's fiction, he feels no need to analyze such aspects of *Three Guineas,* or to discuss its feminism. Can we speculate that this is because his "cryptanalytical" discussion seeks hidden messages? As a result, he cannot deal with Woolf's feminist writing, which, in spite of the complexities of its form, has its ideological constructs pretty much on the surface.[20] And if, for a variety of reasons, feminism is not presented overtly in Woolf's fiction and most of her nonfiction, yet in *Three Guineas* it is.

There is no need to "decode" *Three Guineas*, dense and complex as it is, nor to seek in it what is not clearly evident. I intend rather to describe the feminism that is there and to use evidence of related texts to trace Woolf's perspectives and concerns. There is not an infinite number of—what shall we call them, mistress themes?—in Woolf's writing. But there are many, and I do not aspire to identify all of them. I would insist only that feminism is among them, and important. After Virginia Woolf's death, E. M. Forster said that there were "spots of [feminism] all over her work, and it was constantly in her mind." He did not like feminism, and thought the "cantankerous" *Three Guineas* the worst of her books. In fairness to Forster, we must note that he also generously insisted that the young women of future generations should have the final word on Woolf's feminism, instead of elderly men like himself.[21] He was correct in seeing that feminism was everywhere in Woolf's writing, and most obviously and clearly in *Three Guineas*.

In any analysis of Virginia Woolf's writing as a body of work, her novels must be central, for they were Woolf's most absorbing and carefully designed creations. Scholars have now discussed at great length the place of feminism in Virginia Woolf's novels.[22] In fiction, Woolf was highly original and radically innovative. This was, however, a radicalism unrelated to politics or to feminism in the normal senses of the words. Overturning (transcending?) the existing literary canon is not feminism as such, even if the canon was created by men; James Joyce did as much or more. *The Years*, perhaps the most conventional in form of Woolf's mature fiction, is nevertheless closest to the fullest statement of her feminism in *Three Guineas*.[23] Nor are traces of a distinctly feminine autobiography, such as can be found, for example, in *To the Lighthouse*, feminist as such.

Novels are, in fact, the least appropriate source for someone seeking to delineate a writer's belief system. In fiction, as Woolf stated frequently, the demands of the form and medium are preeminent. Politics must be subordinated to art: "Art is being rid of all preaching: things in themselves: the sentence in itself beautiful." She was writing about D. H. Lawrence's novels, comparing him unfavorably to Proust: "What I want is to be made free of another world. . . . And the repetition of one idea. I don't want that either. I don't want a 'philosophy' in the least; I don't believe in other people's reading of riddles" (*D4* 126). Such a passage ought perhaps be enough to stop the investigation of Woolf's ideas, not just in her novels but anywhere in her writing. Yet the ideas and idea systems are there, variously transmuted. The question is how—and where—best to find them.

I am convinced that, to start with, we should limit ourselves to work prepared for publication by their author. For biographers or for those interested in the creative processes in general or as they relate to Virginia Woolf more specifically, her letters and diaries are invaluable (and whatever our doubts about the details of some transcriptions, we can all be grateful not to have to struggle with Woolf's difficult handwriting or her erratic typing). It is certainly appropriate to use these sources, as I do repeatedly, citing Woolf's relevant statements, especially about feminism, and documenting how *Three Guineas* was written. But such ephemera must be distinguished with care from considered statements deliberately laid out for all to see, the finished work of an author who sometimes wrote as many as seven or eight drafts of what she intended for the public.

Woolf's adult diaries, now published in six volumes, are a wonderful, rich source of her views, but they are most centrally a writer's sketchbooks and a record of progress in writing. Never intended to be a complete or consistent chronicle, this body of material is strongly affected by mood and circumstances. Like letters, the diaries include reported conversations and reflections on the processes of reading and writing and living, jokes and gossip and domestic concerns, all edited for the intended recipient, whether the diarist herself or a correspondent. As with letters not written for publication but put down on paper for the eyes of a particular individual, there is something troublesome about leaning too heavily on a private journal.

In Woolf's diaries and letters, events to be recounted are selectively included, and even accounts of the same event are differently presented in different contexts. Thus, in 1922, Virginia Woolf mocked Margaret Llewelyn Davies' speech to a Co-operative Union congress in a letter to a friend who needed amusing in the wilds of Spain, though even to him she reported that she had been in tears (*L2* 533). At the same time, to her former teacher Janet Case she wrote, in a long descriptive letter, that "it was all the greatest success imaginable" (*L2* 534). Davies, a longtime friend of both Case and Woolf, retired in 1921 after thirty-two years of leading the Women's Co-operative Guild; she was the first woman ever to preside over a Co-operative Union congress. But the event did not make its way into Woolf's diary. We know from other sources Woolf's ambivalence about societies and ceremonies, including even the guild's own congresses. In spite of much recorded praise and admiration, diary entries also show that Davies, in her long retirement that lasted more than twenty years, came instead to inspire regret and pity (e.g., *D2* 142). In this case, for Woolf's views on the Women's Co-operative Guild, we are able to turn to a published source, her "Introductory Letter" to a collection of memoirs by guildswomen, *Life as We Have Known It*. For her views on other subjects also, we are best off relying centrally on considered statements in public form.

Virginia Woolf's literary remains include a large number of manuscripts at different stages of completion. More than one feminist critic has argued that the unfinished earlier "versions" of published texts have greater authenticity because they were not constrained by the demands of publication. But Leonard and Virginia Woolf founded their Hogarth Press precisely to escape such constraints, and it seems strange to equate an author's own choices to some sort of marketplace tyranny or even self-censorship. Students are usually instructed that notes for examination essays will not be graded; writers should be able to expect as much. Such material is, again, useful for understanding how a piece of writing was developed. However, it should also be remembered that we rarely if ever have available all stages of the creative process. The manuscript of *A Room of One's Own* was pieced together only some seventy years after the book was written, and no more than fragments of *Three Guineas* manuscripts are known. Nor do we often have the proofs of Woolf's work, a stage at which, we know, she still made significant revisions. For *Three Guineas*, for example, we have exactly two pages of proof, marked not for book publication but for the serial.

Nor am I persuaded by efforts to find meaning in the patterning of the reading notes and other print material that Woolf collected throughout her professional life in preparation for writing various publications. This material, collected in notebooks or homemade booklets, looks most like ad hoc reference libraries, sources for the telling quote. Thus, Woolf, who had read Proust in French, took notes on the English translation for use in reviews and essays (N13 82; N14 87; L5 297, 304). She copied and recopied material in the notebooks, arranging and rearranging it during the writing of various texts. *Three Guineas* in particular drew in many places on material originally recorded for quite other purposes. Even the three loose-leaf scrapbooks from which material went into *Three Guineas* contain many items Woolf never cited and omit much that is included in the book. For example, there are many satirizable photographs in the scrapbooks, including the pope in all his glory, but they are not among the five that appear in *Three Guineas*. Such material is worth some attention, for it shows what Woolf found interesting, and certainly the various notebooks and manuscripts document both the ways in which Woolf worked and her sources. An annotator or biographer will find them invaluable, as I did. But someone hoping to explicate Woolf's beliefs must look elsewhere for anything other than interesting examples.

Relatively little feminist attention has been directed to Woolf's main and substantial body of nonfiction, her literary essays and reviews, and understandably so.[24] Here subject matter (not always of her own choice, especially early in her career), as well as formal demands of the publication sites, mediated beliefs to a considerable extent. It is possible to pick out those items that have recognizably feminist topics or concerns, such as a moving essay on Mary Wollstonecraft, and a number of anthologists have done so.[25] Essays and reviews include many illustrations of points made in *Three Guineas*, particularly about women writers—that Charlotte Brontë died young after having been rendered miserable by her father, that Mrs. Carlyle seems to have benefited less than Mr. Carlyle from their rather peculiar marriage. But with a few exceptions, such as reviews of books about activists such as Emily Davies, the feminist dimension is subdued in Woolf's essays. Her own feminism is certainly there, if only as coloring or shading, but it is not central as theme or image.

V

By contrast, the underlying structures of belief are close to the surface, even explicit, in Woolf's feminist publications, a cluster of works including and related to *Three Guineas*. *Polemical* is not quite the right word for this material, though it is often used for the best-known examples, *A Room of One's Own* and *Three Guineas*. In a diary entry dated 23 January 1931, Woolf herself supplies a useful pair of terms in a discussion of how the earliest stages of the future *Three Guineas* were interfering with work on her current novel-in-progress: "The didactive demonstrative style conflicts with the dramatic" (*D4* 6). These words—*didactive*, *demonstrative*, contrasted with *dramatic*—can serve to identify intention as well as, to a certain degree, style.

Woolf's didactive, demonstrative writings are not easy to describe. Although none is a novel—"dramatic"—all have some fictional element. Here *Three Guineas* is characteristic in its rather strange combination of fiction and nonfiction and the difficulty encountered in trying to classify it: pamphlet, polemic, epistolary essay? All the same, the didactive, demonstrative category makes sense intuitively, and within it is found work that is also feminist. It consists of published writing by Woolf that either appeared in feminist publications or, in other locations, was directed unmistakably to topics central to *Three Guineas*. The most important of these are the articles Woolf wrote for the feminist journal the *Woman's Leader*, an exchange of public letters with Desmond MacCarthy in the *New Statesman*, a short piece titled "A Society," *A Room of One's Own*, the "Introductory Letter" to *Life as We Have Known It*, and the 1940 essay "Thoughts on Peace in an Air Raid." This body of writing shares analyses, arguments, and even actual examples. Appearing from the beginning of the 1920s to shortly before Woolf's death, these publications demonstrate a consistent pattern of beliefs that has its fullest, most explicit statement in *Three Guineas*. The earlier feminist writings can be thought of as ancestors or predecessors of that book. To return again to the marine metaphor, we may say that feminism is not submerged in *Three Guineas* as it is elsewhere in Woolf's published writing, where it is to be found underwater everywhere. A number of relatively shallow reefs and islets of feminist writing are connected. But *Three Guineas* is the central piece of dry land, and therefore the focus of an analysis of Woolf's feminism.

Virginia Woolf's feminism is not just about war, nor is *Three Guineas*. Instead, they are about social and political structure. For Woolf, the oppression of women is both the central example and the key cause of those tyrannies that produce war but are evil in themselves apart from that outcome. She also believed that women would be the most important agents of the necessary social transformations that would, among other things, end war. *Three Guineas* reflects Woolf's feminism as a whole. Its subject is peace, not war.

Organized around imagined letters and responses to them, *Three Guineas* is presented as a single long letter. The president of a peace society has written to the (fictional) narrator asking for financial and other support. Her answer turns into a reflection, over two hundred pages long, initially upon what a woman like herself can do to prevent war. Nested within the narrative are eleven more letters or draft letters either received or composed by the narrator. Among these are two further requests for donations; lengthy draft and formal responses justify contributions to organizations supporting women's education and work. It becomes clear that, for the narrator (and also for Virginia Woolf), peace means much more than avoidance of armed international or civil conflict. Instead, it is necessary to end the patterns of oppression and exclusion, nearly always embodied in men, that extend from the family through educational, economic, and political systems everywhere. Fascism, Nazism, and world politics, including war itself, are the furthest extensions of patriarchal power, but they are not different in kind from what happens in the family. It is the basic hierarchical structures of society that constrain, psychologically deform, and often kill both women and men.

Most importantly, *Three Guineas* gives substantial attention to the role of women as actual and potential agents of change. The title of the book directs the reader's attention to three charitable donations that the narrator will make in the course of the book. The guinea, so baffling to a non-English reader, is the unit of money that a middle-class person would have used in the 1930s for, among other things, a donation to a good cause. Ten years earlier, *A Room of One's Own* had suggested that, with autonomy ("a room of one's own") and a reasonable income, a woman could hope for professional success. Given that, says *Three Guineas*, she can influence civil society and the wider public world. The guineas therefore represent women's use of economic and cultural resources to produce social change, and *Three Guineas* tells them just why and how to do so. Women are both the worst sufferers from current conditions and also the best prospect for societal change. Partly because women have remained relatively powerless, they have developed practices and attitudes that can counter the tyrannies we all suffer from. Women activists have demonstrated that the private virtues imposed on them, brought deliberately into public life, can generate hopeful results and, above all, more peaceful and productive procedures. Drawing on the lessons of their enforced seclusion, they have, in some few cases, shown that it is possible to enter public life without being corrupted by it.

Even women of the elite—identified as "the daughters of educated men"—have been denied access to the education as well as the economic and political power available to men like themselves. The narrator therefore intends to support two organizations that help provide the intellectual, economic, and psychological resources needed for women to overturn masculine tyranny without replacing it by any corresponding feminine one. A women's college and a group that assists professional women each receive long explanations of their appropriate role along with a symbolic donation of a guinea. The letter writer also proposes to support the peace society in its goal of protecting intellectual liberty. Without intellectual liberty, women will be neither educated nor economically autonomous; we may be reminded of the way in which fundamentalist regimes of our time exclude women from schooling and paid labor. The third guinea therefore goes to the peace society. However, instead of joining it, the narrator proposes an alternative, an Outsiders' Society that will eschew leaders and formalities but instead represent a number of ways in which individual women and women's groups can transform public life. Men will support such action, she hopes. However, it is women who are expected to have the most significant impact in the public sphere; there is some implication that the domestic setting is where men's actions will be most important. In any case, the private tyrannies that support public ones have to be ended, beginning in the family. The usual attempts to end war are attacking symptoms of a deranged social order; they should be refocused on causes.

VI

The feminist-inspired quest for world peace was central among the explicit goals of the first-wave women's movement and Virginia Woolf herself. More generally, among the feminists whom Woolf most respected, it was a well established belief that women would, as voters and activists, be able to make the world more peaceful and therefore better. At the time of the Franco-Prussian War (1870), Woolf's aunt Anne Thackeray Ritchie wrote in a letter, "if all women set their faces against wars, it would do more than all peace conventions." She also commented, as Virginia Woolf was to in *Three Guineas* and her later "Thoughts on Peace in an Air Raid," on the role of women as supporters of war: "women who tacitly encourage fighting are the real mitrailleuses [gunners]."[26] In 1916 Woolf wrote to her friend, the feminist activist Margaret Llewelyn Davies, "I become steadily more feminist, owing to the Times, which I read at breakfast and wonder how this preposterous masculine fiction [the war] keeps going a day longer—without some vigorous young woman pulling us all together and marching through it" (*L2* 76). At this early date, when she is still calling herself a feminist, Woolf already assumes that there is some connection between masculinity and war, a situation that feminism can remedy. War, it seems, is fomented—bungled? as it certainly was by 1916—by men, and response from women activists is therefore required. We can see here a foreshadowing of the arguments of *Three Guineas*, a book that develops the mandate of women not just to oppose violence but to eliminate its causes.

All through the interwar period, the women's groups with which Virginia Woolf had a connection continued their efforts both to expand women's rights and to transform domestic and international political conditions. By contrast, Woolf's male friends and associates (and some of the women she knew) endorsed a liberal feminism that supported women's entitlement to equal opportunity; they were inclined to believe that the battle for equality had been won by the 1930s, when women in the United Kingdom were fully entitled to the vote and visibly moving into the professions. Although Woolf's closest male friends and associates opposed war and warlike activities, and had avoided fighting in the First World War, they saw no connection between pacifism and feminism.[27] As the interwar period wore on, Hitler's Germany became more of a threat, the League of Nations demonstrated its impotence, and most of Woolf's male relatives and friends, like other leftist intellectuals, abandoned their objection to the use of military force.

Woolf herself remained indignantly pacifist until well after she wrote *Three Guineas*. In that book she extended the general feminist arguments of her time to insist that the oppressive hierarchies of the public world were grounded in those of the private one. The true nature of fascism was demonstrated by its exceptionally sexist response to the situation of women, but she argued that even liberal systems like England's were tyrannical, to the point of being fascist, in their treatment of women. By making this argument, she lost most of her nonfeminist audience and also many feminists, whether male or female. She then added an argument not much accepted even today, that the public structures of domination and oppression can best be combated by elimination of the private ones. Therefore war and the other horrors of the public world must be fought through opposition to that most basic subjugation, the subjugation of women. The enemy, even at home, was, she said, "the creature, Dictator as we call him when he is Italian or German, who believes that he has the right, whether given by God, Nature, sex or race is immaterial, to dictate to other human beings how they shall live; what they shall do" (*3G* 50).

Such tyranny must always be resisted. In December 1939 Woolf wrote to her niece Judith Stephen, then a student at Newnham College, Cambridge, "I'm more and more convinced that it is our duty to catch Hitler in his home haunts and prod him if even with only with the end of an old inky pen" (*L6* 372). She was justifying her refusal to lecture at Cambridge until women had equal status with men there, part of her personal, largely symbolic resistance to patriarchy.[28] In the summer of 1938 she wrote in similar terms to Margaret Llewelyn Davies, responding to Davies' excitement about *Three Guineas:* "I felt it great impertinence to come out with my views on such a subject; but to sit silent and acquiesce in all this idiotic letter signing and vocal pacifism when there's such an obvious horror in our midst . . . finally made my blood boil into the usual ink spray" (*L6* 250).

When, slowly but inevitably, the war began, Woolf looked ahead to the days when positive action would be possible. Shortly before despair and suicide engulfed her, she wrote to Shena Simon (an enthusiastic admirer of Virginia Woolf and of *Three Guineas*),

> What the Americans want of me is views on peace. Well, these spring from views about war . . . do cast your mind further that way: about sharing life after the war: about pooling men's and women's work: about the possibility, if disarmament comes, of removing men's disabilities. . . . Mustn't our next task be the emancipation of men? (*L6* 379)

The language echoes Woolf's statements in the 1931 speech that was the earliest version of *Three Guineas*. When, reluctantly, she became convinced of the necessity of resistance to Hitler, she still felt she must do it differently. *Three Guineas* represents her most considered effort at resistance.

In the next chapter, "Feminism and the Women's Movement," I look at Woolf's own explicit statements about feminism, her relevant background, and her contacts with the suffrage movement, in the form of the People's Suffrage Federation and the National Union of Women's Suffrage Societies. I also outline Woolf's connections with the Women's Co-operative Guild as well as the National Union's successors, including the London and National Society for Women's Service. The next two chapters then present what we know about *Three Guineas* itself. In chapter 3, "The Evolution of *Three Guineas*," I trace the fairly direct if complex process that began with a lecture given by Virginia Woolf in January 1931 and produced first *The Years*, then *Three Guineas*, and finally the essay "Professions for Women," which was published posthumously. Chapter 4, "The Argument in *Three Guineas*," presents the book's argument in detail through its presentation as twelve letters and letter drafts that are cited or referred to. The discussion thus framed, in chapter 5, "Other Feminist Publications by Virginia Woolf," I assess Woolf's feminist writing that preceded, foreshadowed, and in one case, followed the book. Chapter 6, "Versioning Feminism," compares the different versions of *Three Guineas*, centering on the serial "Women Must Weep" in an effort to delineate degrees of feminism. Chapter 7, "Scholarship and Subversion," discusses responses to Woolf's feminism as she presented it in *Three Guineas;* it also looks at how Woolf undercut the apparatus of masculine scholarship in her use of endnotes and photographs. The last chapter, "Feminism in the Third Millennium," is concerned with the relevance of Woolf's feminism for the twenty-first century.

In September 1938, just before the Munich Agreements sold out Czechoslovakia to Hitler and ended the immediate threat of German mobilization, Virginia Woolf wrote in her diary, reflecting on *Three Guineas:* "A good piece of work that, for it leaves me free to go on my way in silence. . . . Peaceful if depressed: anyhow a week or 2 without war" (*D5* 169). She anticipated "a hopeless war this—when we know winning means nothing . . . 1914 but without even the illusion of 1914." The only comfort she could find was that she and Leonard could survive on fruits and vegetables in the country, and "I feel I said what I wanted in 3

Gs" (*D5* 170). Her book about war, her book against war, was finally a consolation as the war approached—perhaps because it could help to prevent another war if it were taken seriously? Now, in the next century and millennium, the "good piece of work" continues to speak to all who are willing to listen.

2

Feminism and the Women's Movement

Understanding Virginia Woolf's feminism is made more difficult by the fact that, at various times in her life, she herself declared her hostility to the label. Most famously, in *Three Guineas* she wrote that the word *feminist* should be destroyed. According to Woolf, nineteenth-century activists such as Josephine Butler, who had been called feminists, ought to be recognized as something more. Once the label was discarded by contemporary women, men would feel comfortable joining them, as they had joined Butler, to struggle for a goal that Woolf drew from Butler's own writings: "the rights of all—all men and women—to the respect in their persons of the great principles of Justice and Equality and Liberty." In fact, in a dramatic gesture to celebrate women's economic independence, which made feminism redundant, the word *feminism* should be written on a piece of paper and publicly burned. Condemning the f-word to the bonfire on the grounds that it was "a vicious and corrupt word that has done much harm in its day and is now obsolete," Woolf contributed to views of herself as antifeminist and also, unfortunately, helped to discredit the key term itself (*3G* 93, 131).[1]

Playing with matches as a means of joyous expression is startling here, as are the other repeated, even more freighted examples of burning in *Three Guineas*. It is disturbing to find Woolf burning words at a time when Hitler's followers were burning books; we find it even harder to accept such a joke after the flames of the war that Woolf saw only at its beginning. Here is a useful reminder of the extent to which Woolf's expression of her views is colored by when she wrote as well as by who she was. When we interpret and extend her feminism, we must always be wary of anachronism.

Woolf also helpfully supplies what she called a dictionary definition of a feminist as "one who champions the rights of women."[2] The rights of women no longer needed pursuing, she asserts, for now women have acquired the one essential right, "the right to earn a living" (*3G* 93). As Woolf lays it out initially, the point appears simple and clear: feminism was a very limited and on the whole not particularly admirable quest, alienating to men and now successful; we are past it because women have the economic means to do anything they want to do. For the attentive reader, however, alarm bells begin to ring. Woolf has implicitly condemned all the activists whose efforts were focused on women, not just the suffragists but also those pursuing women's access to employment and education, as well as activists contemporary to her who were still concerned with such issues as status, access, and political influence for women. But she praised such campaigners in *Three Guineas* and elsewhere. In addition, she herself had substantial involvement with groups that have to be identified as feminist, and she supported a number of them in practical ways. We need, it seems, to look more closely at how she used the word, and at her experience with organizations that the word might describe.

It is worth noting, if only in passing, that Woolf also rejected the term *emancipation of women*, still current in the interwar period. It was "inexpressive and corrupt." Like feminism, she added once more (*3G* 125).[3]

I

In *Three Guineas* Woolf does indeed not so much reject as reach beyond a certain narrow definition of feminism, one that still corresponds remarkably closely to the common understanding of the term. Usually the concept has two parts: activism (by women) and a focus on equal rights (for women). As a myriad of public opinion surveys document, even after the twentieth century's "second wave" of feminism, the term *feminist* tends to be reserved for militants concerned solely with the status of women.[4] Activists (and not just feminist activists) are viewed with ambivalence by most people who are not themselves involved in public life: such people may be necessary, but they are thought likely to be extremists. In addition, what is identified as feminism draws the major part of the hostility that continues to be directed against attempts to improve the situation of women. Accordingly, even today, many women who favor such feminist goals as equal pay or improved access to politics dissociate themselves from the organized women's movement with the statement "I'm not a feminist but . . ."

Which is not to say that Woolf was one of those fence-sitters. Nor did she avoid what we would see as feminist responses. Thus, she asked "why the woman question was ignored" in an antifascist exhibition that she was asked to support two years after Hitler's takeover. The reply by the organizer, Elizabeth Bibesco, recognizes—and dismisses—Woolf's concern: "I am afraid that it had not occurred to me that in matters of ultimate importance even feminists could wish to segregate and label the sexes. It would seem to be a pity that sex alone should be able to bring [women] together" (D4 273; N59 292). Bibesco's phrase "even feminists" is a reminder of how the term tends to be stigmatized, and also of the hostility provoked by any consideration of women as a group. In the twenty-first century, feminists are still often identified as a pressure group with limited relevance to any encompassing policy issues (Bibesco's "matters of ultimate importance"). Woolf's response to Bibesco, however she herself might have labeled it, referred to something larger than the right of middle-class women to become professionals. Her criticisms of patriarchy were far more extensive, and fascism's reactionary policies related to women were, for her, intimately connected to its militarism.

As early as 1922, Virginia Woolf indicated that she herself would not want to be one of those who were activists on behalf of women. She noted in her diary that she had told her friend Molly MacCarthy, "But the Lady Rs. ought to be feminists . . . & you must encourage them, for if the rich women will do it, we neednt; & its the feminists who will drain off this black blood of bitterness which is poisoning us all" (D2 167). Money was needed, and money she gave: two of the three symbolic donations in *Three Guineas* were destined for women's groups like ones she supported in the real world. But the other necessary element was psychological stamina of a sort she did not possess. Women like "Lady R" did: she was Margaret Haig, Viscountess Rhondda, the battling peeress who had failed to assert her right to a seat in the House of Lords. Formerly a member of the militant Women's Social and Political Union, she became the proprietor and editor of the feminist *Time and Tide* and a supporter of the Six Points Group that had as one of its purposes an increase in the number of women in Parliament. These were not the sort of things Woolf wanted to do with her life, or felt she could do well. The Lady Rhonddas should do it. But note the feeling of obligation: only if they do it can we not feel we ought to. Her one other, later diary use of the term in relation to herself is in 1924, when she writes, "If I were still a feminist . . . I should make capital out of the wrangle [leading to the fall of the Labour government]. But I have traveled on" (D2 318). Here we see again the feeling of obligation to take political action, in this case using evidence of the incompetence of public men. But the obligation is no longer personally binding.

Josephine Butler, whom Woolf presents as a nonfeminist, discusses in her memoirs the relationship that we now encapsulate in the slogan "women's rights are human rights." Her best-known feminist activism was opposition to the Contagious Diseases Acts, passed in 1864, 1866, and 1869, which authorized military police to require any woman suspected of prostitution to submit to a physical examination, under threat of imprisonment. The rationale for these laws was the spread of venereal diseases in British garrison towns. It all has a familiar ring today, when concern for military efficiency also on occasion overrides concern for freedom.[5] From combating the Acts, with final success after a long campaign, Butler and her associates moved on to equally unpopular and, in Victorian terms, distasteful struggles to combat prostitution itself, particularly the sale of underage women and the low current age of consent.[6] Woolf refers approvingly to all of these efforts in *Three Guineas*.

In a book cited by Woolf in *Three Guineas*, Butler responds as follows to characterization of her activities as antimale; it was too early for her to be accused of feminism:

> Our early conflict in this cause was . . . much less of a simple woman's war against man's injustice, than it is often supposed to have been. . . . It was as a citizen of a free country first, and as a woman secondly, that I felt impelled to come forward in defence of the right.

Note that she also came forward "as a woman" in her defense of civil liberties. Butler continues:

> At the same time, the fact that this new legislation *directly* and shamefully attacked the dignity and liberties of women, became a powerful means in God's Providence of awakening a deep sympathy amongst favoured women for their poorer and less fortunate sisters.[7]

The result of such an analysis is a wide-ranging feminism: the rights of women are part of the rights of citizens, and the battle for rights specifically of women is crucial to the battle for larger social goals. Our campaigns "consolidated the women of our country, and gradually of the world, by the infliction on them of a double wrong, an outrage on free citizenship, and an outrage on the sacred rights of womanhood," Butler concludes. Around such causes, women of different degrees of privilege could unite. While "combatting the State Regulation of vice," women must also "work against all those disabilities and injustices which affect the interests of women."[8] *Three Guineas* is full of examples of the way that women, usually in the face of men's hostility or indifference (although on occasion with male support, as Butler documents), organized to achieve necessary social changes. Both Butler and Woolf were insistent that such battles must be carried on without egotism or personal advantage, incorporating the virtues that women had acquired in their constrained domestic lives; Woolf noted approvingly that Butler refused to have a "Life" written of her.

Among improvements in the situation of women, the one that Woolf singles out as crucial—the "right to earn a living"—is not as straightforward as it might seem, even for the middle-class women with whom Woolf is most concerned. References in *Three Guineas* to "the sacred year 1919" point to the Sex Disqualification (Removal) Act of that year, which meant that women could no longer be barred from public activities on grounds of sex (*3G* 23). With formal access to the professions, women now had legal entitlement to acquire the power previously monopolized by men.[9] However, as the book amply demonstrates, entitlement does not mean acquisition. When Woolf looks closely at the relevant sections in Whitaker's *Almanack* for 1936, she reports accurately that women are absent from all the higher grades of the civil service.[10] In addition, the women are remunerated in such a way that their highest salaries are at or below men's lowest. Related discrimination continued more widely: even Cambridge, the university closest to Virginia Woolf's heart, meanly denied to its women students the formal credentials necessary for jobs.[11] Opportunities to "earn their living" thus remained strictly limited. As to married women, Woolf notes that they are completely absent from Whitaker's lists because of the "marriage bar" in the civil service.[12] Under the Married Women's Property Act that was the fruit of a "collateral movement" to Butler's own campaigns, married women, more generally, had acquired by 1882 the full right to their wages, but in the 1930s they had still no expectation of equal or fair wages; nor could they expect any sort of maternity leave or stipend.

Woolf's use in *Three Guineas* of the notion of women "earning their living" displays a typical strategy used in the book. She creates a useful shorthand reference, in deceptively commonplace language, to the formal right to economic self-sufficiency. She then demonstrates its practical inadequacy, marshaling concrete evidence of its shortfalls. Yet she emphasizes its importance: like the other rights that women were gradually acquiring in Woolf's lifetime, it is the means to other ends. The first necessity is, always, the establishment of the practical conditions for the enjoyment of rights (and, as can be seen in the example of the civil service, *Three Guineas* devotes considerable attention to spelling out their continuing absence).

What the burning of the word *feminism* celebrates ("a new ceremony for this new occasion") is the ability of women like the writer to use their newly acquired economic autonomy not to advance their own rights, narrowly described, but to advance the larger goals that subsume their own needs. "The giver" of a donation to the peace society, "does not claim in return . . . admission to any profession; any honour, title, or medal; any professorship or lectureship; any seat upon any society, committee or board." She does not need to, for women have won—and *won* is the word used—"the one right of paramount importance to all human beings" (*3G* 93). This is not to say that she does not want, or at least expect other women to want, all those other things and a good many others that they are still acquiring only with difficulty. *Three Guineas* in fact praises by implication all such personal and career objectives. But even if now within reach, they are merely the means to larger ends. Imagine, writes the narrator of *Three Guineas*, what we could do if we had even one rich woman, "a woman motor-car manufacturer who, with a stroke of her pen, could endow the women's colleges with two or three hundred thousand pounds apiece" (*3G* 64). She speculates about the consequences if rich women were as common as rich men: there would be no need of a society such as those supporting professional women, there could be a women's party in Parliament, a truly free daily newspaper, financial support for unmarried women, equal pay for equal work, childbed anesthesia. "Money is the only means by which we can achieve objects that are immensely desirable," she tells her interlocutor (*3G* 64).

The argument then continues, examining how money can be earned without corrupting women as it has corrupted men, and the Outsiders' Society will finally encapsulate the principles necessary to reform public life. But here we may note that the goals of the feminists who have now lost their stigmatized name are described as "immensely desirable." The word itself has been burned because the goals of what we would still call feminism need no longer be sought by entreaty to those on whom women are economically dependent; the goals have not been abjured, even though identified as instrumental and liable to be distorted.

Such enablements in turn would make it possible for women to pursue the radical, transformative goals that Woolf had praised in Butler and her associates: liberty, equality, respect for everyone. "They were fighting the tyranny of the patriarchal state as you are fighting the tyranny of the Fascist state," writes Woolf (*3G* 94). This we may translate as the abolition of all hierarchies of entitlement, whether based on gender or on other conditions such as race or religion. The implication is the complete abolition of tyranny, both local and domestic and international, and of war. Today, we would see those larger goals, as well as the instrumental changes in the situation of women, as the goals of feminism. They are Woolf's goals in *Three Guineas*. They are feminist, first of all, because of their initial focus on women.

The goals of *Three Guineas* are also feminist because of their (realistic) reliance on women's efforts to produce change. The narrator of *Three Guineas* will contribute the third of her guineas to support the peace society whose request is used as the excuse for her reflections, but she will form her own group instead of joining his. The reasons given for not joining the peace society are central to the argument made in *Three Guineas*:

> Different we are, as facts have proved, both in sex and in education. And it is from that difference, as we have already said, that our help can come, if help we can, to protect liberty, to prevent war. But if we sign this form which implies a promise to become active members of your society, it would seem that we must lose that difference and therefore sacrifice that help. (*3G* 95)

This does not seem to be a separatist argument, as some commentators suggest, but rather one for coalition, "men and women working together for the same cause":

> it seems both wrong for us rationally and impossible for us emotionally . . . to join your society. For by so doing we should merge our identity in yours; follow and repeat and score still deeper the old worn ruts in . . . society. (*3G* 93–94, 97)

The educated man's daughter can give disinterested support to her brother because she no longer needs to beg him for her rights. Women have been freed far enough to seek larger goals and to work in concert, autonomously, with men. It is an argument that relies on women's difference. One of the major tasks of *Three Guineas* is to demonstrate that difference, and also to show that it has desirable consequences.

To return to what we might call the bonfire of feminism—that conflagration is itself more complicated than it appears, for there is also another, second burning of words envisaged in *Three Guineas* as well as suggestions of arson, burning not paper but buildings housing women's organizations. All these flames are significant, if in different ways.

The second burning of words is to celebrate the assurance of the peace society representative that his organization is "fighting with us, not against us." That is, we are to celebrate the existence of the other half logically needed for a coalition: the willingness of men to, at the least, not oppose the liberation of women in the concrete and specific forms spelled out in *Three Guineas*. So let us do so by disposing of some more dead words, such as "Tyrant, Dictator" (*3G* 94). Unfortunately, the narrator notes, these words are not yet obsolete, neither as they describe men's relationship to women nor more widely. Presumably she then goes off to celebrate more conventionally.

So far, so good, if a bit depressing. If women and men work together, eventually it will be possible to get out the paper and matches again. There is a problem here, however, a certain lack of parallelism. The terms "Tyrant, Dictator" are by no means misnomers; they accurately designate the men of evil who are terrorizing the world. But when these monsters' power has ended, surely the words no longer needed would be positive ones. It will then be time to burn something like *liberator*, or *freedom fighter*—what would the 1938 equivalent be? Or is it *feminist* that will finally, definitively, become obsolete, since the principles of feminism, understood more broadly, are those that will end tyranny?

Well, it is only a metaphor; it can be allowed some inconsistency. And it is part of a bouquet of fiery images. In draft letters present in *Three Guineas* there are also suggestions of more concrete, even dangerous flames. Not just words but actual buildings are to be destroyed because they have not been useful means to the ends that feminism sought. First, there is a suggestion to burn down the building that the women's college wants to rebuild (*3G* 32, 34). Unwittingly, the women's colleges, being part of Oxbridge, have helped to propagate the masculine values that facilitate war. The ground must be cleared in order to build instead an entirely new sort of college, unaffiliated, without professional standards or goals, without old curricula or requirements. Second, perhaps the building belonging to the society for professional women should be burnt down because the women's movement, which at this point the society represents, has not succeeded in ending war (*3G* 42). The use of petrol, rags, and matches is specified in both cases (use my donation to fuel the blaze, the narrator writes in her draft letters). Women—feminists—will dance around the fires, in a celebration rather more drastic than burning bits of paper. There is an echo here of a private letter by Virginia Woolf, when she was still Virginia Stephen (who took her husband's last name when she married Leonard Woolf in 1912). Caroline Emelia Stephen died in 1909, and her niece Virginia wrote about the service at Golder's Green Crematorium: "the whole ceremony was very thin and prosaic. . . . A bonfire in the garden would have done equally well. We might have danced around it" (*L1* 391).

The passage about the possible dance around the burning building belonging to the society to aid professional women is noteworthy, for it is the only place where Woolf refers to women as daughters not of educated fathers but of uneducated mothers. The "mothers" she then chooses to incorporate into her text are identified as the unpopular campaigners who supported women's rights in the nineteenth century. It is sad to think that the uneducated Julia Stephen, given her hostility to women's education and professional activity, does not belong among those who would laugh from their graves, encouraging their activist daughters. The burning buildings themselves appear only in draft letters. The narrator of *Three Guineas*, her anger and frustration once expressed in images of arson, turns back to the more mundane goals of feminism and its various embodiments in women's organizations. Symbolic bonfires of stigmatized language and unsuccessful organizations thus leave untouched the larger meanings of feminism.

The concept of feminism reappears twice more in Woolf's diaries in the 1930s. These brief references nevertheless make clear her views about the topic and the concept: they are stigmatized, limited—and necessary. In 1932 she wrote in her diary that the title "Men are like that" would be "too patently feminist" for her little book, the future *Three Guineas* for which she had "collected enough powder to blow up St Pauls" (bombs now join flames, we note) (*D4* 77). The explosive and transformational nature of the enterprise must be kept hidden; the confrontational label of feminism has to be avoided. Later, thinking excitedly about *The Pargiters*, the draft "essay-novel" that was to evolve into *The Years* and also *Three Guineas*, Woolf writes that the book is to include "millions of ideas but no preaching . . . a summing up of all I know, feel, laugh at, despise, like, admire hate & so on." The topics are to be "history, politics, feminism, art, literature" (*D4* 152). Feminism, it seems, ranks in importance with public life and with creativity.

II

The focus of this book is the particular feminism that was Virginia Woolf's. Its logic is not so much to show the development of Woolf's feminism—which does not seem to have changed significantly over time—as to demonstrate its content by looking at the different ways in which it was articulated. *Three Guineas*, its most explicit embodiment, is central, but I also look at the other feminist texts that Woolf published. I argue that Woolf's feminist beliefs are already visible in publications in the 1920s and then respond to changing contexts, as can be shown in their different presentations during the remaining decades of her life.

Contexts has two general meanings here. First there are the diverse settings and the audiences for all versions of the texts, which influenced the particular form they took. Some of Woolf's feminist nonfiction appeared only in periodicals, some only in book form; *Three Guineas* appeared in both. Some of these sites of publication were feminist but most were not. On occasion her letters or brief articles were provoked by other publications; on other occasions they were commissioned, sometimes by close friends, sometimes by others. Her two best known feminist publications grew out of lectures to very different women's groups—for *A Room of One's Own*, students at the two young colleges for women at Cambridge, and for *Three Guineas*, one of the activist descendants of the nonmilitant women's suffrage movement. In a third key feminist document, her 1931 introduction to a collection of memoirs by working women, Woolf reflected upon a women's organization's convention she had attended. This variety of situations necessarily shaped the presentation of her beliefs, as did her vocation, and her skills, as a creative writer. The resulting different formulations do not correspond to shifts in views, nor is the radicalism of the views to be gauged by how they were presented in different contexts. That is, the relative straightforwardness of early articles and letters to the editor do not indicate that their argument is different from that of the complex and artful *Three Guineas*, any more than the skillful subversion of scholarly method in *Three Guineas* makes its ideas more radical than those found in earlier writings. As I examine Woolf's various feminist publications in chapter 4, we will see how the argument becomes wider, as its implications are drawn further out—but it is the same argument.

The second meaning of *contexts* is the larger contemporary political situation, beginning with the status of women in England at the time of each of Woolf's feminist texts and, most specifically, *Three Guineas* itself. It is important to notice the changes that occurred in the interwar period that is the context of her work. Woolf's earliest identifiably feminist publications appeared in the early 1920s, when women in England had only recently, with difficulty, secured a restricted franchise and minimal legal entitlement to access to professional life. At this point, the impact of women's new rights could only be guessed at. Her last feminist publications were written at the end of the 1930s under conditions of full adult franchise and expanded legal rights, but when it had become obvious that women's educational, economic, and political opportunities were still far less than men's.

Also important, when the focus is on Woolf's feminist writings, are Woolf's own experiences and contacts with the women's movement of her day. During this same time span, the women's movement was able to discard the battle for the vote, fully achieved in 1928, and to direct its attention to the changes for whose sake the vote had been sought. Such contacts also—of course—influenced the details and the expression of Woolf's feminist beliefs. But, to repeat, not the beliefs themselves.

More generally, the expression of Woolf's beliefs was necessarily responsive to the ongoing events in the larger world that she wanted so much to change. None of us can be unaware of the impact of the First World War on English intellectuals, as on all others. A painful peace then led into a brutal depression and, in the 1930s, the failure of the League of Nations, the rise of fascism, and a belated and reluctant rearmament in England. Shortly after the publication of *Three Guineas* came the long-feared outbreak of a second—or perhaps a resumed—genocidal world war. Woolf lived among people acutely aware of politics and actively engaged in them; her diaries and letters record her own attention to the public world. Her collection of material for *Three Guineas* in the 1930s increasingly reflects arguments about fascism and war and draws out the implications for her feminism. The book itself appeared in the last prewar lull, before the Munich Agreements of 1938. The last feminist publication by Woolf in her lifetime ("Thoughts on Peace in an Air Raid") responded directly to the German aerial attacks on England in 1940 as she experienced them in Sussex in the final year of her life.

In the remainder of this chapter I look at the relationship of Virginia Woolf with the organized women's movement of her day, and in chapter 3 I trace the impact of surrounding conditions on the evolution of *Three Guineas*. But we should note that biographical interpretations of anyone's writing are always limited. We have all been miserable, we have all been elated, and many of us have tried to express in writing either our emotions or our illuminating visions. Most of the results are, if important to the writer, instantly forgettable. And who cares why they wrote it, or how? But sometimes emotions or ideas that in other hands would be uninteresting become important or are importantly expressed. Then, in the attempt to understand the final product fully, the reader would like to know the source of the material that was transformed into something of lasting value. Two images: a piece of grit generates an oyster's pearl, a caddis-fly grub arranges fragments of crystal that make its case a delight to the eye. What the grit was, and what the crystals, and how they became beautiful—these pieces of information can tell us more about the final jewels than any question about why that piece of grit got inside the shell, and what personal/generic compulsions led the bivalve and the bug to labor.

However—to drop the analogies—when we are looking at a writer, it is often biography that guides us to the source of ideas and images. Something may be in *l'air du temps;* it most likely got to the transformative author in some direct and traceable way—or ways, for all such transmissions are overdetermined. Feminism was certainly, in various versions, mostly unidentified as such, available to interested English women at any time after the middle of the nineteenth century. Any individual woman could work out her own notions about it, ranging from rejectionism on up. But certain women's groups that were feminist asked for certain things, and in particular ways. It was, for example, simply not possible to confuse the militant and the nonmilitant suffragists. Virginia Woolf was to muddle up their financial situations in *Three Guineas,* misled by what looked like reliable sources, but she could not possibly have made the same mistake about their worldviews. In addition, Woolf had personally a series of specific involvements with activist women's organizations whose impact can be seen in her feminist writings. We shall now look at these groups and her contacts with them.

III

I do not want to exaggerate Virginia Woolf's own involvement with the women's movement. But neither should we minimize it. When her first biographer, Quentin Bell, wrote about the topic, a quarter of a century ago, it was generally assumed that Woolf had little contact with feminist activism. The women's movement was seen as mainly concerned with the vote, and in this connection she had merely worked briefly addressing envelopes and sitting on a platform for a relatively obscure suffrage group. Thus, her brother-in-law and close friend Clive Bell wrote (inaccurately) in a memoir: "I do seem to remember that once or twice she and I went to some obscure office where we licked up envelopes for the Adult Suffrage League."[13] Her involvement with women's groups was noticed only insofar as it could be seen to have directly produced some written outcome. That is, the Women's Co-operative Guild (WCG) was the subject of the "Introductory Letter" of *Life as We Have Known It*, while lectures to women's colleges became *A Room of One's Own* and a speech to a postsuffragist society run by a Strachey became *Three Guineas*.

We are now aware of a more substantial series of contacts between Virginia Woolf and women's organizations, but their importance still tends to be underrated. In general terms, Woolf grew up in an environment that nurtured beliefs in the value of education, professional opportunity, political equality, and organized political effort for and by women. Other women of her background and generation were among early professional women in England and the pioneering students at Cambridge and Oxford colleges for women. In the twentieth century their daughters and nieces, such as Woolf's own nieces Ann and Judith Stephen at Newnham College, went to university as a matter of course, while friends and relations were heads of the women's colleges. Pernel Strachey headed Newnham from 1923 to 1941, preceded by Woolf's cousin Katherine Stephen; Janet Vaughan, Woolf's second cousin, made her way into *A Room of One's Own* as a model for the laboratory work of "Chloe" and "Olivia" when she was a medical student at Somerville College, Oxford, of which she was to become principal in 1945.[14]

All her life Woolf had connections and contacts with leaders and members of the suffrage movement as well as with women involved in the organizations actively involved in developing educational institutions for women and seeking access to the closed world of male professions. In England from the mid-nineteenth century on, such associations were led by women of the intellectual and political elite to which Leslie Stephen and his daughter Virginia belonged. The list of feminist daughters, sisters, and wives of that group of "educated men" is long even if we include only women mentioned in *Three Guineas:* Emily Davies and her niece Margaret Llewelyn Davies, Anne Jemima Clough and her niece and biographer Blanche Athena Clough, Florence Nightingale and Sophia Jex-Blake, Lady Stanley of Alderley (grandmother of Bertrand Russell), Josephine Butler and Barbara (Leigh Smith) Bodichon, Harriet Martineau and Octavia Hill, Millicent Garrett Fawcett and her sister Elizabeth Garrett Anderson. Nearest to Virginia Woolf's time and experience, the women of the Strachey family, always close friends of the Stephens and of Virginia Woolf herself, were active in the suffrage movement and also in its successors. Lady Strachey had been the first signatory of the suffrage petition presented to Parliament by John Stuart Mill in 1867 and had a long involvement in the Women's Local Government Society (founded in 1866 to promote women's participation in politics, beginning with the local level), as well as in support of Girton College. Vice president of the National Union of Women's Suffrage Societies, she participated, along with her daughters, in the famous Mud March of 1907. But most of this occurred well before the young Virginia Stephen was involved in the women's suffrage effort; in 1918 she recorded hearing Lady Strachey's reminiscences of an "ancient world" and noted that "talk of womens votes doesn't move her much" (D1 108). The next generation of Strachey women made up Woolf's feminist contacts; Lady Strachey's daughter Pippa and her daughter-in-law Ray Strachey both played major roles in the National Union of Women's Suffrage Societies and its daughters, the London and National Society for Women's Service and the Women's Employment Federation.[15]

Yet no one in Woolf's immediate family was directly involved in feminist activism, and her mother was unusual in her opposition to change in the situation of women; Julia Stephen even signed the notorious "Appeal against Female Suffrage" published in the *Nineteenth Century* in 1889 and disapproved of formal education for women. Woolf's father, Leslie Stephen, was opposed to immediate grant of the vote to women, though he supported education and professional activity for women.[16] It seems to be the case that it was because of her delicate mental and physical health, rather than any preferences on the part of her mother (who died in 1895, when her daughter was only thirteen), that Woolf herself never attended school or university.[17] But there can be no doubt that she grew up as a nonparticipant in the public world in which activist women were beginning to play a role. She was an outsider, a nonjoiner, always fully conscious of the excesses, even absurdities, of the organizations she nevertheless supported. At the same time, by her middle years, Woolf was a professional writer and public figure, regularly earning her share or more of her household's income, able to influence public opinion if she cared to. Furthermore, as an adult, Woolf had more than just personal contacts with organized feminism, and not just suffragist activism but other women's groups, including ones we would not now hesitate to see as part of the women's movement.

Woolf's earliest direct connection with women's activism seems to have been in 1910, when she did some work for an "extremely shadowy organisation" called the People's Suffrage Federation (PSF).[18] Although it had some individual members, the PSF was basically an umbrella organization for the women's auxiliaries of the British Labour movement, as well as the Women's Co-operative Guild, whose general secretary, Margaret Llewelyn Davies, was among its founders.[19] Virginia Stephen was not yet acquainted with Davies when, in January 1910, she wrote to offer her services to Janet Case, her former Latin teacher and dear friend, who was on the PSF executive board. Asked to do some writing or research for the "People's Suffrage," Stephen noted that she ended up addressing envelopes.[20] By April she was ill and taken off to Dorset to recover, and there is no indication that she ever picked up her PSF connection as such again. There are fragmentary traces of other contacts with the suffrage movement, however. Thus, in November 1910 she wrote in a letter, "my time has been wasted a good deal upon Suffrage," reporting sardonically on her attendance at two suffrage meetings at the Albert Hall (*L1* 421, 426, 438).[21] Ray Strachey's daughter quotes a letter dated December 1910 in which Ray refers to Virginia Stephen coming to hand out suffrage handbills in the street, and in October 1912 Strachey recorded that the Woolfs had been over for dinner and a suffrage bazaar.[22] In March 1918 the Woolfs went to the great Kingsway Hall rally to celebrate the grant of the limited suffrage to women; she sought in vain an eloquence appropriate to "the triumph" (*D1* 125).[23]

The People's Suffrage Federation is the only group that we can identify with any probability from such scrappy, incomplete evidence. The PSF seems to have been remembered only as an adult suffrage group, but it was in practice a woman suffrage group that used the desirability of full adult suffrage as an argument for the inclusion of women in any measure designed to expand the franchise. After 1912 there are some scattered references to the PSF in the records of the Women's Labour League, and then silence.[24] Involvement with the PSF, however brief, can hardly have avoided increasing Woolf's awareness of the activities of the suffragists, especially the nonmilitant or constitutionalist groups in which such a large role was played by the Strachey women whom she already knew. In a memoir written in 1939–40, Virginia Woolf included "the Vote" among the major influences on her; she recorded the final approval of the suffrage bill in January 1918 with her usual ambivalence: "I don't feel much more important—perhaps slightly so. It's like a knighthood; might be useful to impress people one despises." She concluded: "But there are other aspects of it naturally" (*D1* 104). In an important draft letter written in 1940, Woolf explicitly identified "working for the vote" as one of her "political" activities (*L6* 419).[25]

In addition, the PSF introduced Stephen as well as, later, her husband to Margaret Llewelyn Davies and thus to the Women's Co-operative Guild and the Co-operative movement more widely. The Davies family was squarely within the intellectual elite of the day. Thoby Stephen, Virginia's brother, knew at Cambridge both Theodore and Crompton Llewelyn Davies, as did Leonard Woolf. But neither they nor Virginia Stephen knew the men's younger sister before 1910, and Stephen met Davies in a context of a form of activism most importantly associated with women's organizations. Clearly, she was not close to Margaret Llewelyn Davies at the time when she offered her services to the People's Suffrage Federation. Somewhere toward the end of that year, in a letter by Virginia Stephen to Janet Case, it is still "Miss LL. Davies" seen "at a lighted window in Barton St with all the conspirators round her," and Stephen adds that she "cursed under my breath"; in this letter she talks about "the inhuman side of politics and how all the best feelings are shrivelled." It is, as so often, a jokey letter, in which Woolf's ambivalence about conventional politics, even in the best of its nonprofessional exemplars, is evident (L1 441–42). By the time of Virginia Woolf's serious illness in 1913, the year after her marriage, Davies was a friend of both of the Woolfs, a collaborator and a major emotional support for Leonard Woolf, who himself had become much involved with the Co-operative movement.[26]

The women's groups that belonged to the PSF were all feminist and also all organized on a cross-class basis. The Women's Co-operative Guild, composed of wives of slightly more prosperous working men, usually women who themselves had had experience in the paid labor force before their marriages, was led from 1889 to 1921 by the distinctly upper-middle-class Margaret Llewelyn Davies.[27] Virginia Woolf's later and continuing involvement with the guild was in no way anomalous.

IV

At this point, in examining the political activities of Virginia Stephen, soon to become Woolf (in 1912), we move from a shadowy and ephemeral mixed-membership coalition to significant, long-lasting women's organizations that can be shown to have had a direct impact on her feminist writings. Even if now probably best remembered for its association with Virginia Woolf, in the early years of the twentieth century the Women's Co-operative Guild was already a major suffrage and reform organization. It grew steadily through the interwar period, reaching the considerable membership of 87,000 by 1939. Woolf clearly had enormous respect for both the middle-class leaders and the working-class members of the group, though she knew that she was different from the first in her discomfort with activism and organizations, and different from the second in her secure, superior class and economic situation. She shared many of their beliefs and goals, though without accepting the full ideology of consumer co-operation.[28] Most importantly, she seems to have drawn from the group some doctrinal and organizational support for pacifism. Perhaps she also drew from the guild itself the idea of the potential power of a group of "outsiders," the married working-class women who were additionally marginalized by their links to a male-dominated organization. The group's strength rested on its members' and leaders' integrity and their disdain for praise or money. Woolf was to praise and recommend just such independence in *Three Guineas*.

From a number of references in Virginia Woolf's published letters and diaries, we can piece together a quite extensive series of Co-operative movement involvements in the years 1913–33 on the part of the supposedly apolitical member of the Woolf family, including attendance at congresses and a role in publications of the Women's Co-operative Guild. Perhaps because her involvement was primarily concerned with what was considered the women's auxiliary, neither Woolf nor others seem to have seen her involvement as either political or important. When Leonard Woolf was educating himself about industrial conditions and Co-operation in 1913, his wife accompanied him to Manchester, Liverpool, Leeds, Glasgow, and Leicester, as well as to Newcastle for what her writing would make the most famous of the Women's Co-operative Guild's annual congresses. When she was recovering a year later from illness and a suicide attempt, she was studying Co-operative manuals, and in December she read the bundle of letters that became the WCG publication *Maternity: Letters from Working Women;* she urged Davies to publish them, as in fact happened the next year. G. Bell was the publisher; the Hogarth Press was not yet in existence. In 1916 both Woolfs attended the guild congress in London. For several years Virginia organized meetings and speakers for the Richmond branch of the WCG; in 1919 she noted that she had been "till lately" the president of a guild branch, and in 1923 she was still seeking speakers for guild meetings and reported having been doing so for four years.[29]

Woolf's account of the 1922 Co-operative Union Congress for Janet Case indicates her familiarity with the Women's Co-operative Guild and its history. This was the congress presided over by Margaret Llewelyn

Davies. Davies had been presented to the group with a remark about what an honor it was for her, as a woman, to be invited to preside: "Whereupon up gets Margaret: and says that the honour is not hers but ours (so I feel it myself)—women's in general." Later, the guild leader was given roses and praise by the city and the Co-operative Union leaders, who said her name would always be remembered among the movement's great. Margaret's reply, says Woolf, was "Not my name, but the names of Mrs Laurenson, Mrs Reddish, etc." And Virginia Woolf knew enough to pass on Davies' compliment to the founders of the guild (*L2* 535).[30] In 1925 came the first mention of the letters that were to become *Life as We Have Known It*; by 1929 an introduction by Virginia Woolf to the letters became a definite project, and in 1930 and 1931 she published two different versions of it. Her last record of personal involvement refers to her attendance at the guild's Jubilee Congress in 1933, about which she grumbled characteristically that she had wasted a morning on "a very ugly thing, a ceremony. I detest them more and more."[31] Her friendship with Margaret Llewelyn Davies continued; then, in a letter to Davies in 1938, there is one additional, important note of approval of the WCG's pacifism.

The Women's Co-operative Guild started as a women's auxiliary to the English Consumer Co-operative movement, but it rapidly developed a surprising degree of autonomy. It was envisaged by the male leaders of the group as a way to encourage wives of co-operators to patronize the relatively expensive co-operative stores. For the women founders, who were wives, sisters, and daughters of the movement leaders and active in the movement themselves, another important motive was adult education for the group's barely literate women members. In addition, from the start, one of the WCG's four goals was the ambitious intention "to improve the condition of women all over the country."[32] After Davies became general secretary, the WCG pushed for a more extensive and egalitarian role for women inside the Co-operative movement and also in the larger society. Amazingly, it supported legalization of access to both divorce and abortion. The guild sacrificed its Co-operative Union subsidy for four years when Catholic co-operators objected to guild support for easier conditions of divorce.[33]

The WCG's support of woman suffrage grew out of its basic beliefs about the nature and importance of women's domestic roles. So did its commitment to pacifism. In an undated pamphlet, "Why Women Should Have the Vote," the guildswomen were told:

Politics is nothing but the art of helping the life of the people. . . . Employment, the wages question, housing, education, old-age pensions, temperance, public health in all its branches, public economy—everything in one way or the other touches the purse-bearer and homemaker in her daily work, her spending power, and her care for the members of the family, young and old.[34]

Extending such arguments, the questions singled out for women's attention and expertise included the working-class issues of wages, the economic concerns that follow from a commitment to the Co-operative movement, and, eventually, the problems of war and peace. In the 1930s the last category came to dominate the WCG's activities, as its members insisted on a completely pacifist response to world conflict.

The guild's stubborn and consistent opposition to the use of armed force was based on a fairly simple belief in women's maternal obligation to oppose war; it lacked Virginia Woolf's analysis of the impact of male domination and hierarchy more broadly understood. The group's opposition to militarism was a more extreme version of the position of other antiwar women's groups; they condemned not just the Boy Scouts and the Girl Guides (with their military origins, uniforms, and structure) and military tattoos, but also the Church Lads' Brigades, Armistice Day celebrations, and the League of Nations' sanctions policy. They even invented their own, quite successful white peace poppy to be worn along with the red poppy commemorating war dead; it has reappeared in Britain and North America in recent years.[35] The guild congress passed a resolution undauntedly opposing rearmament at the late date of July 1938, when war was visibly approaching. Woolf's approval of their act was unqualified: "The Co-op; women as usual were magnificent," she wrote to Davies. "They beat the Labour Party hollow" (*L6* 251). Unlike other sections of the labor movement, unlike Virginia Woolf herself, the WCG never gave positive endorsement to the Second World War. As late as March 1939, the group was calling for the repeal of the Conscription Bill. During the war, the group was split by the issue of whether to give even indirect support to the war by assisting in evacuations and in supplying meals to those sheltering in the subways from the Blitz. Afterward, it continued, at the far left of the Labour Party, as pacifist, antinuclear, anti-NATO, anti-American, uneasy about communism and any international organizations except Co-operative ones.[36]

V

Virginia Woolf's reference to "the Vote" also directs our attention to the National Union of Women's Suffrage Societies (NUWSS) and its successors, most significantly the London and National Society for Women's Service. Integrity and, in a different way, outsider status were also exemplified by this coalition of nonmilitant suffrage groups that worked so patiently for more than half a century to gain access to political influence. Its middle-class women members had resources of education and class that the members of the WCG could not aspire to, but they too had to face a political world that considered their concerns marginal and nonpolitical. From the NUWSS and its successors, Woolf seems to have drawn notions about process and also about specific policies that she was to recommend in *Three Guineas*.

Unaffiliated with any male group, the NUWSS had the straightforward goal of acquiring the vote for women on the same terms as it was exercised by men. The members' greatest pride was their retention of decency and democracy within their organization; they felt that this was one of the most important contributions women could make to public life. The association had its origins in the first women's rights societies started in England in the 1860s; in their heyday more than four hundred constituent groups of the National Union were able to hold as many as fifty public meetings at the same time, and mustered parades and demonstrations of 10,000 to 15,000 women. Martin Pugh's recent "revisionist analysis of the campaign for women's suffrage" validates the belief held by the members of the NUWSS that they were the group basically responsible for Parliament's approval of the vote to English women.[37]

In *Three Guineas*, Woolf presents a NUWSS perspective on women's activism in England, a perspective that focused on the vote but was by no means limited to it. For her account of suffragism (and also for a good deal of her information about the development of women's education) she relied on Ray Strachey's book *The Cause*.[38] Several Stracheys had been central to the National Union; as its former parliamentary secretary, Ray was in a privileged position to write about it. In her words, the issue for suffragists in the NUWSS was "hardly even a matter of 'rights' at all." They sought the vote in order to provide "an extended power to do good in the world."[39] The NUWSS suffragism was close to that of the WCG, lacking only the explicit Co-operative movement coloring and the emphasis on women as housewives and consumers.

Virginia Woolf, it should be repeated, did not join or work for any suffrage group except, briefly, the People's Suffrage Federation. But it is plausible that the large union of moderates, headed by Millicent Garrett Fawcett and actively participated in by the women of the Strachey family, had some impact on Woolf's perception of the suffrage struggles and also on her writing about the relationship between women and war. The NUWSS supported the First World War, but reluctantly. When, shortly before her death, Virginia Woolf finally agreed that armed resistance to Hitler was necessary, she might have echoed the arguments by which the French feminist Maria Vérone finally persuaded a deeply divided NUWSS in 1914: "The more pacifist we are, the more we should demand today the destruction of German Militarism."[40] But Woolf would have added that all militarism must be destroyed, even if its more aggressive forms demanded the most immediate attention.

The NUWSS consciously put suffrage agitation on hold for the duration of the First World War and proceeded to organize women's civilian support of the war effort as a demonstration of their general competence and entitlement to a voice.[41] We can see a direct link to *Three Guineas* in a statement that the organization issued in 1914 to justify its support of the war:

> Suffragists will be unworthy of the political power which they have claimed . . . if they do not now . . . strive with all their mind and soul to understand the causes of this recurrent madness, so that they may heal it. . . . until women learn to *think* as women (and not merely *feel* as women), they will not effect much. "Men must work and women must weep" wrote Charles Kingsley in his poem *The Three Fishers*. . . . The modern woman must drive back her tears; she has work to do.[42]

When Virginia Woolf published a version of *Three Guineas* in serial form in the *Atlantic Monthly*, it was titled "Women Must Weep." Even without those pointers, Woolf's views are to be found here: women's distinctive experience and perspective as a basis for ending militarism. In addition, the NUWSS provided the example of a group of organized activist women and a model in procedural terms.

Two suffrage groups besides the NUWSS are mentioned briefly in *Three Guineas*. Woolf seems to have had no personal contact with militant suffragists during their heyday, though she can hardly have missed the many colorful newspaper accounts of their activities. In 1930 she became friendly with composer Ethel Smyth, a former member of the Women's Social and Political Union (WSPU) that Emmeline Pankhurst and her daughters had organized. Mrs. Pankhurst herself appears flatteringly in *Three Guineas* in a comparison with Antigone; she is described as a martyr who "broke a window and was imprisoned in Holloway" (*3G* 154).[43] *Three Guineas'* positive comment about the WSPU leader may reflect the influence of Smyth, also imprisoned in Holloway, who admired Pankhurst extravagantly.[44]

The Women's Freedom League (WFL) is also present in *Three Guineas*. This small group was organized by former members of the Women's Social and Political Union who had left the WSPU at the early date of 1907 because they wanted greater internal democracy, more attention to working-class women, and less violent tactics.[45] In the course of a rather muddled discussion of the finances of suffrage groups, Woolf mentions by name both the WFL and the WSPU, misstating their income but adding correctly that they were "of course, opposed" (*3G* 145).[46] In 1938, replying to one of the many letters sent to her by readers of *Three Guineas*, Woolf expressed regret at not having known earlier about the role of the Pethick-Lawrences, key early leaders of the militant WSPU who were expelled by the Pankhursts and then became central to the Women's Freedom League.[47] Emmeline Pethick-Lawrence's memoirs, which Woolf read after the publication of *Three Guineas*, describe the distinctiveness of the WFL as its commitment to full "democratic equality"; its "undeviating purpose" was to win "not only political equality but complete social and economic equality for women."[48] The ex-militant WFL was in fact very like the NUWSS.

After the war the NUWSS produced a number of successor groups, several of which have some relevance to Woolf's feminism. The most important of these was the cumbersomely named London and National Society for Women's Service (L&NSWS). After the grant of the first installment of the vote to women, NUWSS continued as the National Union of Societies for Equal Citizenship (NUSEC). A decade later, Millicent Garrett Fawcett, who went from the presidency of NUWSS to the presidency of NUSEC, left the group along with some followers, including Ray and Pippa Strachey, because of disagreement over mothers' allowances. The London branch of the NUWSS had already changed its name to the London Society for Women's Service and its major attention to issues around women's employment. It then added the "national" dimension explicitly and became the London and National Society for Women's Service; Pippa

Strachey was its secretary. The group still survives as the Fawcett Society, an English lobby group for feminist issues.[49]

The Society for Women's Service, as it was sometimes called for short, kept control of the NUWSS journal, retitled *The Woman's Leader* under Ray Strachey's editorship; in it Virginia Woolf published three essays and a letter. The group also retained what had been the International Women's Suffrage Association library, the Marsham Street or Women's Service Library, later renamed the Fawcett Library and in 2001 transformed into England's national Women's Library. Virginia Woolf drew on this library for her research for *Three Guineas* and solicited support for it from her friends, writing, "I think its almost the only satisfactory deposit for stray guineas, because half the readers are bookless at home, working all day, eager to know anything and everything, and a very nice room, with a fire even, and a chair or two, is provided" (*L6* 232). From March 1938 to her death, she had a standing arrangement with the library to purchase books they wanted; in addition, she donated a number cited in *Three Guineas*.[50]

Woolf also had what begins to look like a quite substantial continuing connection with the L&NSWS. Almost two years after the speech that eventually became first *The Years* and then *Three Guineas*, she became a paid member of the organization. Leonard Woolf had joined the year before and paid the obligatory one pound minimum membership fee; she paid one guinea. Certainly *Three Guineas* incorporates the policy goals of the L&NSWS, summed up by Ray Strachey, one of its founding members, as "the economic equality of women and . . . both practical work and propaganda on equal pay and opportunity."[51] In the 1920s the group was concerned to obtain the vote for those women under thirty who in 1919 had been barred; this issue was moot by the time Woolf was speaking and writing about professions and about being despised. By the 1930s, major campaigns of the L&NSWS were for equality of treatment in the civil service—an issue that was prominent in *Three Guineas*—for pension rights, and for adequate press coverage of women's issues. There is evidence both in *Three Guineas* and in letters that Woolf was informed about these campaigns, and we can assume that after she became a member of the organization, she heard about others.[52]

In addition, Virginia Woolf had some contact with a sort of granddaughter of the NUWSS, the little-known group called in the 1930s the Women's Employment Federation (WEF) and closely associated with the L&NSWS. Founded in 1933 by Ray Strachey, with Pippa Strachey as the honorary treasurer, the WEF took over the placement and service activities in relation to women's employment that the L&NSWS had performed earlier, and it became the liaison for a much larger group of women's organizations concerned with women's employment.[53] The WEF may have been the model for the organization that sent out the third letter supposedly answered in *Three Guineas*, the "society to help the daughters of educated men to obtain employment in the professions." Commentators on *Three Guineas* have tended to assume that the recipient of Woolf's second guinea is some fictionalized version of the L&NSWS itself.[54] But it seems more likely that Woolf is writing about appeals coming from the WEF but forwarded by the L&NSWS; Pippa Strachey was central to both and always represented the women's movement for Woolf. In the WEF's list of members for 1938, "Mrs. Leonard Woolf" appears as an individual subscriber, who would have paid either one or two guineas for the privilege.[55]

The larger, politically activist descendant of the NUWSS, the National Union of Societies for Equal Citizenship (NUSEC), developed a "new feminism" in many ways close to Woolf's own beliefs. There is no evidence that Woolf had any contact with or interest in NUSEC, but it is hard to imagine that the Woolfs did not know of it and of its leader, Eleanor Rathbone, one of the very few women in Parliament during the interwar period and a prominent public figure.[56] In a book edited for the Woolfs' Hogarth Press by Ray Strachey, Rathbone summed up NUSEC's views: women should avoid being assimilated into the masculine version of society but should instead concentrate on their qualities as women. "Now that we have full possession of the tools of citizenship," she wrote, "we intend to use them not to copy men's models but to produce our own."[57] Virginia Woolf certainly knew of this book, first proposed by Ray Strachey in 1935.[58]

In any case, Woolf recommended in *Three Guineas* precisely the policy that split the NUWSS's successors and indeed the whole English women's movement in the interwar period. Supported by the NUSEC and also advocated by the Women's Co-operative Guild, the "national endowment of motherhood" was finally enacted in a much reduced version after the Second World War as mothers' allowance. The underlying argument for this policy was that women should be supported by the state in the social services that only they performed, bearing and rearing children.[59] Like the National Woman's Party in the United States, a significant segment of the English suffragists, including Millicent Garrett Fawcett herself, was strongly opposed to such measures because it amounted to treating women differently from men.

The recommendation to subsidize mothers is prominent in *Three Guineas*, rather surprisingly so given the general absence of discussion of sexual and reproductive issues. In a list of injunctions relating to women's economic self-sufficiency, "outsiders" are instructed "above all" to "press for a wage to be paid by the State legally to the mothers of educated men." Professional women are told severely that "this measure is of such importance directly to yourselves, in your own fight for liberty and equality and peace, that if any condition were to be attached to the guinea it would be this: that you should provide a wage to be paid by the State to those whose profession is marriage and motherhood" (*3G* 101). In *Three Guineas* as well as the "Introductory Letter" to *Life as We Have Known It*, Woolf notes the heavy and continuous labor required of domestics and working-class housewives; she cites an article about "the average housewife" washing acres of dirty dishes and scrubbing miles of floor yearly (*3G* 160). But the argument at this point seems concerned less with wages for housework than with constraints created by women's responsibility for childrearing. At issue are the practical measures necessary to provide autonomy for women who otherwise would be economically as well as psychologically dependent on their, possibly educated, husbands and fathers.

VI

Virginia Woolf declared herself a visionary, unable to work out details. "A living wage" for wives was "to use a convenient word supplied by the politicians, 'impracticable,'" she concluded after presenting its desirability (*3G* 102). "But then of course I'm not a politician," she wrote to Ethel Smyth in 1941, "so take one leap to the desirable lands" (*L6* 478). Yet along with the arguments made by the women's movement of her time, Woolf included in her writings many of its specific goals. Some were discussed in detail, some only mentioned. Together they provide an agenda not yet completed.

It is an astonishing list. Most conspicuously in *A Room of One's Own*, Woolf asked on behalf of women for economic independence and privacy (together, these two items mean autonomy for women then dependent on male relatives), as well as for egalitarian, nonviolent families (legally and psychologically). Repeatedly, she demanded education that would extend as far and as wide as men's, to include the accumulation of experience through leisure and travel. She endorsed working-class women's specific demands, including reformed divorce laws, minimum wages, and the modernization of household equipment. In *Three Guineas* she added the long-term goals of a women's party in electoral politics, progressive education (nonhierarchical and including what we would call women's studies), and state subsidies for underpaid or unemployed single women as well as for wives and mothers. In the shorter run, she argued in that book for childbirth anesthesia, equal citizenship, and equal access for women to all the institutions that currently serve as a basis of power and influence: the senior professions, the political and educational establishments, and those male-dominated structures such as clubs and associations that control access to power. Women were to reform, where they did not abolish, the hierarchies of masculine power and the apparatus of nationalism, religion, and war. This is a feminism that seeks far more than "earning a living."

The audiences of Virginia Woolf's feminist publications are also worth attention, for they add up to a formidable assembly. Among them are the group of young women in the early text "A Society" (which I discuss in chapter 5). Their enquiries lead them to contest all the values of the male establishment, including the paternal rights Engels found so crucial. The women students who heard the first versions of *A Room of One's Own* were being educated as autonomous women. The working-class wives and mothers in the Women's Co-operative Guild—the audience, inspiration, and subjects of Woolf's "Introductory Letter" to *Life as We Have Known It*—had learned together to become social and peace activists. The young professional women of the Junior Council to whom she gave the lecture that would become *Three Guineas* were "new women" who were carving out their own sphere. The members of these different groups shared with Woolf a vision of a society transformed and made peaceful by the injection of women's values and experience. They were not the "liberal," equality-oriented feminists whom men could more easily accept. Instead, they were radical in their image of what life could be if centered on women and women's values. Virginia Woolf said it would be "the life of natural happiness" (*L6* 380). This, finally, was why she attacked war: it was what patriarchy was bound to become, and it could be abolished only if patriarchy was abolished.

All the same, Woolf's dissociation from feminist activism is real; if more involved with feminism and with women's organizations than is usually realized, she was not a "joiner" like many of the women she associated with. That fact goes a long way toward explaining why so many biographers and critics see her feminism as a minor, even trivial part of her beliefs. She recognized that anything identifiable as "feminist" produced hostile reactions and that the anger behind it was potentially dangerous to those who felt it, feminists and antifeminists alike. The age itself is "stridently sex-conscious," she noted in *A Room of One's Own*. "The Suffrage campaign was no doubt to blame," she wrote, giving a very early diagnosis of backlash. "When one is challenged, even by a few women in black bonnets, one retaliates, if one has never been challenged before, rather excessively."[60] For creative artists in particular, the results of the awareness of inequality—an awareness necessary for activism and increased by it—were likely to be dire. Aggressive masculinity damaged men's work, but women artists were crippled by resentment, bitterness, and self-consciousness. Such feelings must be carefully controlled if they were not to destroy what was Woolf's central activity.

That was where Woolf's feminist activism was—in her writing. As a result, she repeatedly predicted hostility, even ostracism as a result of her sequel to *A Room of One's Own* (and to some extent experienced it). But writing was still how she could best serve. "As I've already said, Societies seem wrong for me, so I do nothing. . . . What can I do but write? Hadn't I better go on writing—even by the light of the last combustion?" she wrote in a letter in 1936.[61] "This idea struck me: the army is the body: I am the brain. Thinking is my fighting," she noted in May 1940, as the long-dreaded war began and she no longer found pacifism possible (*D5* 285). We can agree. And we need not accept Woolf's own more constraining definitions of the term, nor her insistence that she and others were not feminists because they hoped to serve not just women, but all of humanity.

In a brief sketch of a glossary in one of her reading notebooks, probably written in the mid-1930s, Virginia Woolf had supplied a possible new and far more expansive definition of feminist: "one who believes that [women?] though now shreds and patches can be brought to a state of greater completeness."[62] This is more than just the search for the vote, for rights, or even for equality. And it need not be limited to conventional activists, even those in women's organizations.

At the start of 1940, Virginia Woolf was thinking about a book that would be explicitly on the topic of women and peace (*D5* 255). "Can one change sex characteristics?" she asked in a letter later in the year. "How far is the women's movement a remarkable experiment in that transformation?" She ended optimistically: "it looks as if the sexes can adapt themselves: and here (thats our work) we can, or the young women can, bring immense influence to bear" (*L6* 379). It was an ambitious project. And it still is, in the long "postwar" period in which we are still living.

Virginia Woolf's arguments in *Three Guineas* were dismissed as irrelevant and misguided by antifascist activists, including close friends and relatives. But the approach was neither new nor superficial in terms of her beliefs and, particularly, her feminist writings. We now turn to those texts.

3 | *The* *Evolution* *of* Three Guineas

The actual, well-documented composition of *Three Guineas* is fascinating just as a puzzle to solve. It is fun to trace how Virginia Woolf quilted together the scraps of information that would support her feminist case. But there is more to this process: during the "making up," as she called it, and then the actual writing and rewriting of *Three Guineas*, Woolf found a way to demonstrate that opposition to fascism was a necessary implication of understanding the situation of women. As the manuscript evolved, so too did the argument that linked domestic or private fascism to the public fascism that was expanding so hideously in Europe.

Three Guineas took a long time to emerge in its final form. The evolution of the text can be traced over a formative period of seven years; it shows how context and time shaped the expression of a set of beliefs that remained unchanged. The book started as a lecture given by Virginia Woolf for the Junior Council of the London and National Society for Women's Service on 21 January 1931. Between 1931 and 1937, *Three Guineas* gradually took shape, to be finished in a frantic but ecstatic rush at the end of 1937 and the start of 1938. During these seven years, what started as a talk about women in the professions and then a "little book" about women's lack of autonomy became a complex and challenging exposition of Virginia Woolf's feminism. As well, in a sort of coda to the process, at some time in the 1930s Woolf apparently started to prepare an essay that would be a revised version of the original lecture. After her death, that unfinished piece was published (in 1942) with the same title as the talk, "Professions for Women."[1]

During the years 1931–38, Woolf also had many other writing projects. Central to these, as always, was a novel. In this case, it was *The Years*, published in 1937. *The Years* also grew out of the 1931 lecture to the Junior Council, and it drew on much of the same material as *Three Guineas*. Tracing the development of the didactive, demonstrative book published in 1938 requires untangling it from the closely related novel published a year earlier. *The Years* is far more than and far different from a fictionalized form of *Three Guineas*, though the shared feminism could certainly be demonstrated. To understand *Three Guineas*, however, it is essential to include consideration of the initial draft that it shared with the novel: the "essay-novel" first called *The Pargiters*.

There is a wealth of material available about the evolution of *Three Guineas*. To begin with, there are the sixty-four "reading notebooks" that Virginia Woolf prepared over thirty-six years of her life as a professional writer.[2] In no less than nine of these compilations there are references to material used in *Three Guineas*. With a few exceptions, these are not the purchased notebooks they sound like but more improvised, almost haphazard collections, often on disparate bits and scraps of paper. From time to time Woolf made ad hoc booklets out of related notes, together with indexes, in preparation for a particular project such as a long essay or review. Sometimes selections from these collections were recopied for other use, or the bound collections were taken apart so that material could be moved and sometimes rebound, while other notes remained separate items in stacks of loose sheets.[3] All the same, the so-called notebooks provide at least a partial record of what Woolf was reading, and what she thought worth selecting from that.

For *Three Guineas*, and only for *Three Guineas*, Woolf also kept scrapbooks, three of them, in which she accumulated a motley assortment of evidence relevant to the situation of women in England and Europe. These scrapbooks contain newspaper clippings and passages copied from newspapers and articles, both longhand and typed reading notes (including copies of material originally excerpted for other purposes), letters and copies of letters, and actual pamphlets and manifestos; they provided the concrete sources for both *Three Guineas* and *The Years*. The many newspaper texts and photographs were usually clipped out and then stuck in with gummed labels; Woolf seems to have accumulated newspaper cuttings and inserted them in batches, usually but not always or accurately writing on their dates and sources. The scrapbooks are, as a result, often frustrating, but the notebooks and scrapbooks together give useful indications of the earliest dates when Woolf saw particular material.[4] In addition, although it would be a mistake to read too much into combinations and sequences of items, they certainly suggest some of the connections she identified among topics.

Perhaps because the themes of the book were so important for her, perhaps because she had it in mind for so long before she wrote its final version, Woolf also gave far more attention in her diaries to the future *Three Guineas* than she did to other nonfiction works. Here, as well as in letters, she included references to many of the main stages of the book's development and also comments about the occasions when conversation or books or the media provided fuel for feminist wrath. Such responses, usually angry, are common in her diary, and after 1931 more and more frequently noted by Woolf as relevant to the book that was to become *Three Guineas*. But these references did not always show up in the book. Thus a diary entry dated 3 September 1931 notes: "Waiting for breakfast I read Montaigne this morning & found a passage about the passions of women—their voracity—which I at once opposed to Squire's remarks & so made up a whole chapter of my Tap on the Door or whatever it is" (*D4* 42). Montaigne was not to appear in *Three Guineas*—and if in 1931 Woolf was, as the editors of her diaries speculate, annoyed by J. C. Squire's broadcast "Idle Thoughts" on 13 August, it was a section of Squire's memoirs, published in 1935, that she cited in *Three Guineas*.[5]

Unfortunately, almost no prepublication versions of *Three Guineas* have survived. Woolf's normal procedures for writing and revision would have generated a succession of texts prepared in 1937–38, as well as two or more sets of marked-up proofs. Some sort of manuscript of *Three Guineas* seems to have been sold in 1939 "for the Refugees society" at the instigation of the young American poet May Sarton, but no one has been able to trace it (or, for that matter, the person called "something Jones" who wrote to her that she had purchased it) (*L6* 314, 319).[6] The manuscript fragments held in the Berg Collection of the New York Public Library were part of a miscellaneous purchase from Leonard Woolf in 1958.[7] Like those at the University of Sussex, they consist of bits and pieces of early drafts. However, we do have two versions of the speech that later became *Three Guineas*, and a third embedded in the early manuscript of *The Years* as well as echoed slightly at the beginning of "Professions for Women." These, with diary and letter references, show how the presentation of Woolf's feminism adapted to circumstances, changing from a discussion of women and the professions that was appropriate for the audience of the initial speech, so that it finally became a book that most readers thought was about war. The posthumously published essay "Professions for Women," which apparently returns to the form and content of the original speech, rounds out the story.

I

The first possible reference to what was to become the two books *Three Guineas* and *The Years* is a diary entry by Virginia Woolf dated 20 January 1931: "I have this moment, while having my bath, conceived an entire new book—a sequel to A Room of Ones Own—about the sexual life of women: to be called Professions for Women perhaps—Lord how exciting! This sprang out of my paper to be read on Wednesday to Pippa's society' "(D4 6). Pippa was her old friend Philippa Strachey; the talk was not to be presented to the London and National Society for Women's Service, of which Pippa was secretary, but to its Junior Council. The L&NSWS was a feminist lobbying association that had grown out of the larger, moderate wing of the women's suffrage movement; its Junior Council drew in younger professional women (and some men) and seems to have served for networking and career advancement. In May 1934, Woolf went back to this diary entry and added the note "This is Here & Now I think," referring to the title that *The Years* had acquired temporarily. *Three Guineas* as such was hardly even a gleam in her eye in 1934, but her husband and editor, Leonard Woolf, was accurate when, years later, he identified this same entry as "Eventually *Three Guineas*."[8] It should be noted that in this first reference Virginia Woolf linked women's professions to their sexuality; in *Three Guineas*, attention to women's bodies has virtually disappeared. *Three Guineas* was also to move very far from being a simple sequel to *A Room of One's Own*.

On 21 January 1931, as scheduled, Woolf gave the talk. Afterward, still very excited, she continued "making up The Open Door, or whatever it is to be called" for several days (D4 6), a title that echoes an image at the end of her talk. In her diary, Woolf seems to distinguish between "making up" texts and writing them in a sustained fashion, but she may have written something at this date. From now on, it is possible to trace diary and letter references to the future *Three Guineas* in variants of a "tap" or "knock" on an opening door," also as a "little book" about women and the professions, and, less specifically, about women being despised. The references gradually change into titles that refer to fascism, war, answers to correspondents, and finally to the three guineas, a title that represents donations to worthy groups that might help to make war impossible.[9]

We know a little about Woolf's 1931 speech about women and the professions, for there are four reports from those present at what Woolf expansively described in a letter as "a party, given by the young women of England, to meet Ethel Smyth and Virginia Woolf" (*L4* 281). Feminist peace activist Vera Brittain reported in her column in the *Nation and Athenaeum* a "hilariously serious" happening, "a delicious entertainment" provided by Woolf and Ethel Smyth. She singled out Smyth's "superb humour." Ethel Smyth, a friend and devoted admirer of Woolf, was a flamboyant ex-suffragette and an aggressive champion of equality for women in music. Brittain mentioned from Woolf's speech her remark that a private income enabled her "to flout the displeasure of authors and editors by writing honest reviews." Woolf had said that women succeeded in literature because paper was cheap and writing made no noise.[10] Brittain also noted Woolf's reference in the talk to Brittain's earlier column about the poverty of women's colleges. That column and a book review by John Maynard Keynes, both in the *Nation and Athenaeum* of 17 January 1931, are the two earliest dateable periodical sources of *Three Guineas*.[11]

The other accounts of the talk were even less informative. The Junior Council's 1931 Annual Report had a paragraph that also focused on what they called Smyth's "witty description" of her life. Of Woolf's presentation, the report stated that she had "charmed them by her personality and account of her literary career, concluding with an expression of her admiration for the young women who had been the first to enter the many occupations hitherto confined exclusively to men."[12] An account in the feminist journal the *Woman's Leader* described the contrasting styles of the two speakers, making Woolf seem romantic and distant.[13] It all sounds as if Woolf was somewhat overshadowed by Smyth, and Woolf's own diary suggests as much: "The speech took place; L[eonard] I think slightly exacerbated: an interesting observation if a true one. Two hundred people; well dressed, keen, & often beautiful young women. Ethel in her blue kimono & wig. I by her side. Her speech rollicking & direct: mine too compressed & allusive" (*D4* 7). If Woolf was correct about her husband's reaction, we have here a first hint of how he and, even more, the progressive literary and political community were to react to *Three Guineas*. But she noted that four people present had said the speech should be published.

Three days later Woolf wrote to Smyth that she would not publish the speech as given, in part because it was "clotted up, clogged . . . no time to comb it out," but also because "the very last morning in my bath, I had a sudden influx of ideas, which I want to develop later, perhaps in a small book, about the size of a Room." And she first had to finish the novel she was then working on, *The Waves* (*L4* 280). We are reminded here, first, of the care that Woolf put into even the slightest published text as well as, second, the priority in her professional life of her novels.

What look like two draft versions of the speech itself have survived. An incomplete holograph that Woolf headed "Speech" and dated 21 January 1931 seems to have been written before the speech was given but includes some sketched-in changes that may have been added later. A second longer and very similar text, unlabeled and undated, is typed with longhand alterations.[14] Woolf may have typed up this manuscript soon after the speech was given; she usually wrote a text first in longhand and then, soon after, preferably the same afternoon, redid it on the typewriter. Both manuscript and longhand versions seem oriented toward comments by Ethel Smyth, though possibly in the first case merely anticipating what Smyth might be expected to say. Or perhaps these twenty-five typed pages and their revisions represent what Woolf noted as two or three days of "obsession" with her "Open Door" immediately following the speech (*D4* 7). Both texts include near the end the words "But then, as Dame Ethel asks, what will be the next step?" The subject of these fragments is, as the reports of the talk had suggested, the experience of women writers and the problems they encounter. Woolf does not discuss here the connection between fascism and the oppression of women, but in the holograph, discussing how she would review a "war book," she notes that she would reject both war and the "masculine point of view."[15]

Woolf apparently had before her, as she prepared her talk, the 1930 Annual Report of the Junior Council, where the members and their occupations were recorded, supplying an impressive list of possible professions for women. She comments how dismaying it must be for men to realize that women can have such occupations. At the end of the holograph draft, changing the individual occupations of members into plurals, she lists no less than fifty-one occupations found in the report, including "married women." Some are as specific (and accurate) as "court dressmakers," "directors of H. P. Truefelt Ltd.," and "organizers of Women's Peace Crusades," though she did not include "Author" or "Student" or many other intriguing occupations such as "Secretary, Imperial Bureau of Mycology." The typescript version of occupations is shorter and less detailed, but its items are all still from the Junior Council's list of members, although "married woman" is no longer one of the categories mentioned. By the time, in 1932, when Woolf had come to writing the first part of the manuscript that was growing into *The Years*, the list of professions had been reduced to "the professions that you are practising and I am not practising . . . medicine and law and architecture and engineering and politics and banking and the civil service—to name a few of the professions in which, as I see from your report, you are now engaged."[16] She thus confirms the source of her lists of professions. This time, the occupations are included as part of the argument, found already in the lecture drafts, that Woolf, as a writer, is an "outsider" compared with other professional women. The tally of professions does not reappear in *Three Guineas*, but the sense of the range of women's occupations is retained, with references to the experiences of governess Nelly Weeton, explorer Mary Kingsley, diplomat Gertrude Bell, and medical pioneer Sophia Jex-Blake, along with aviator Amelia Earhart and artists such as Laura Knight.

As reports of the lecture suggest, the shared central point of its drafts is that women writers, the freest of all women professionals, are still constrained by their own attitudes, their limited experience, and, most seriously, the conventional morality controlled by men. Even economic independence in the form of an inherited or earned income will not liberate them entirely. Coventry Patmore's long, popular poem, "The Angel in the House," is used to symbolize the Victorian ideal of desexualized, self-sacrificing womanhood. The "Angel" censors most effectively any material related to the woman writer's physical, including sexual, identity—the elements of her life that are most different from a man's, as *A Room of One's Own* had dramatized in 1929 with the story of Shakespeare's imaginary sister. This inhuman being, this phantom, must therefore be "murdered" if the creative woman is to be able to voice the truth about her own experience. In *Three Guineas*, by contrast, there are dual inhibiting presences: the "lady," who for the upper-middle-class woman represents social constraints on her economic independence, and the "woman," who represents a daughter's obligation "to sacrifice herself to her father" (*3G* 122, 123). Both also must, metaphorically, be "killed" before women can move freely into the public world. These are powerful images, and it is a shock to see them retained, even expanded in a book whose purpose is at least ostensibly to end war and tyranny.

The typed draft ends, optimistically, with a step upon the stairs, and the door opened to the room of one's own for "the most interesting, exciting, and important conversation that has ever been heard." This version of the speech also includes a remarkable passage urging reconciliation with men. "Imagine what it is like to be a man," Woolf says, how difficult it must be for men to discover that women—servants and also the others who act as servants and supporters to men—have become economically self-sufficient to the point of being competitive in all the professions men have previously monopolized.

> Remember what a tremendous tradition of mastery man has behind him—consider what prestige and power he has enjoyed.... Do not therefore be angry.... Be patient; be amused; It is a situation of extraordinary interest and amazing possibilities both for the present and for the future.... Men too can be emancipated.[17]

The knock or tap on the door that Woolf uses for temporary titles for the future *Three Guineas* comes from the emancipated man who may become an ally of the independent professional woman.

Later versions of *Three Guineas* will expand awareness of the complexity and difficulty of navigating the expected male role, and so will *The Years*. A good deal of material from the speech drafts reappears in *Three Guineas* in the accounts of the impact on men of their education and professional training. However, the lecture draft's admonition to empathy, patience, and good humor is absent. In *Three Guineas*, the most we get is a passage saying coolly that a few of the "brothers" were "very kind" to the women who wished to continue into postsecondary education, although others were not, including the great Walter Bagehot (*3G* 28).

II

Soon after the lecture, *Three Guineas* began what we may call its period of postponement, when Woolf fully intended to write it but kept putting it off. She always had an assortment of writing in hand, usually with a novel at the center, and the very intensity of her feeling about *Three Guineas* meant that work on it was likely to be shelved so as not to interfere with other literary productions. As early as 26 January 1931 she thought optimistically that she could perhaps "dash off the rough sketch" of a little book on the professions in something under six weeks by 1 April, after finishing *The Waves* as well as a review essay or article (*D4* 7). Instead, she wrote five articles on "The London Scene" which, with *Flush*, the playful biography of Elizabeth Barrett Browning's dog, got her through the last stages of *The Waves*. Before the fall of 1932 she had completed the second of the essay collections she called *The Common Reader*, as well as the pamphlet "Letter to a Young Poet" and about a dozen periodical and newspaper articles.

All the same, notes in Woolf's diary show that through 1931 and 1932 she had in mind the expansion of the speech—the sequel to *A Room of One's Own*—and even sketched out some portions of it. In addition, at the beginning of the bound notebook in which she finally began to write *The Years*, there is a single blank page dated 20 July 1931 and headed "Notes for the Knock on the Door." The date is significant, for Leonard Woolf had read and approved the final version of *The Waves* the day before, and Virginia could now develop a polemical text without fearing impact on the novel. She apparently destroyed whatever she had written; in the notebook that blank page is followed by the stubs of several cut-out pages. In a diary entry dated 3 September 1931, Woolf noted that she had "made up a whole chapter" instead of working on her second *Common Reader* (D4 42). In November 1931 she clipped from the *Daily Telegraph*, without noting source or date, some irritating comments by Justice McCardie about women's clothing and psychology; these she later used in *Three Guineas*. At the end of December 1931, "the Knock on the Door" was one of the books "gently surging round me, like icebergs" (D4 57).

During 1932 Woolf made seven diary references to what was to become *Three Guineas*. Most important among these were the much-quoted remarks on 16 February, that she was "quivering and itching to write my—whats it to be called?—'Men are like that?'—no thats too patently feminist; the sequel then for which I have collected enough powder to blow up St Pauls. It is to have 4 pictures." *The Common Reader, Second Series* still had to take precedence as work being prepared for publication, she noted, "for one thing, by way of proving my credentials" (D4 77). The feminism of the book was apparently making her uneasy. That May, on a trip to Greece, she jotted some notes on the process of thinking and planning for "my little book": "I'm subterraneously sunk in scenes . . . make up arguments, see pictures, keep dropping something new into the cauldron, which must bubble as richly as possible before its poured & stilled & hardened" (D4 96).

In 1937, when she had finished "what I think is the last page of 3 Gs," Woolf harked back to her ruminations in Greece five years earlier: "I've had it sizzling now since—well I was thinking of it at Delphi I remember" (D5 112). But in 1932 and even later, she does not seem to have consistently distinguished a project for *Three Guineas* as something separate from the novel she was also working on. Reading notes apparently made in the earlier 1930s—about contemporary and older books, especially Victorian memoirs—were equally applicable to both the novel she started at the end of 1932 and the still vaguely defined pamphlet. So were the articles she clipped: material on women in the professions, especially exclusion from various forms of professional training and certification. After collecting about twenty items from the years 1930–32, Woolf seems to have clipped only two articles in 1933 (on young women's not feeling wanted in the church and on the psychology of women) and only one in 1934.[18] In spite of her reference in 1932 to using photos, the five (rather than four) photographs finally used for *Three Guineas* are all from later dates, and none of them appears in the scrapbooks. Certainly the separate project for *Three Guineas* cannot have been very far advanced in 1933; in a letter sent to Winifred Holtby in February 1933, Woolf referred to discussing professions with Holtby (who had written a short book on Woolf) and added that she was thinking of rewriting a paper on professions that she had read a "year or two ago," in which "I want to keep rather more closely to facts than usual."[19]

As late as 1932, then, we can say in respect to the future *Three Guineas* only that Woolf was planning a sequel to *A Room of One's Own*, not a novel, to be documented from a range of older as well as contemporary reading, and to include pictures. She was also quite clear that the result would be feminist and would offend men. At the same time, possibly even before the visit to Delphi, the novel eventually called *The Years* had begun to take shape. The earliest reference to it seems to be in a diary entry dated 16 November 1931. Basking in approval of *The Waves* expressed by E. M. Forster, Woolf felt justified in plans for a new novel, very different from the one she had just published: "another book—about shopkeepers, & publicans, with low life scenes." Later, on 13 July 1932, she recorded that she had been "sleeping over a promising novel." However, in the same diary entry she noted her delight in the life of Joseph Wright, a working-class man who became a successful lexicographer and academic, and whose life and example were influential on both *Three Guineas* and *The Years*. Recording her admiration of Wright's solid factual work as well as her own ambivalence about "facts," she commented: "I sometimes would like to be learned myself. . . . Still what use is it? I mean, if you have that mind why not make something beautiful? Yes, but then the triumph of learning is that it leaves something done solidly for ever" (*D4* 53, 115, 116).

III

Attracted by two related projects, a feminist pamphlet and a realistic novel, in October 1932 Virginia Woolf was finally ready to start sustained work on what she first planned as an essay growing out of the 1931 speech.

Within weeks, however, this essay turned into a hybrid, an "essay-novel," and then, a few months later, became the obsessive project that ended up as *The Years*. *Three Guineas* picked up the major themes of the lecture and book; in "Professions for Women" can be found some of the reflections about women's creativity and sexuality that had been dropped from *Three Guineas*.

The essay-novel has been transcribed and published by Mitchell Leaska under the title Woolf used when she started writing it, *The Pargiters*, after the family whose lives it recounts.[20] It has been suggested that the family's name and the first title of the novel were both based on Joseph Wright's definition of the term *parget* in his *English Dialect Dictionary*. Given Woolf's interest in Wright and the meaning of *pargeting* as plastering over, therefore combining and unifying, this is an attractive derivation. However, Quentin Bell has suggested two additional plausible sources of the name: a signalman and Labour Party candidate called Pargiter whom the Woolfs "knew and liked," and a house, Pargiters, owned by Robert Bridges and rented to the poet Henry Newbolt.[21] The family kept their name through all the many drafts of *The Years;* the book itself changed titles many times.

The Pargiters is closely connected to at least the origins of *Three Guineas*. The first section of Woolf's novel-essay text still has the form of a speech addressed to the Junior Council of the London and National Society for Women's Service. Your secretary invited me to speak on professional women, it begins, and the lecture refers to the House of Commons "over the way," as indeed it was from the L&NSWS's building, which was located on Marsham Street in Westminster. The first portion of the text is recognizably the same as the original lecture, even though it has been quite substantially rewritten. However, within a very short time, as Woolf worked enthusiastically away in the winter of 1931–32, the text as a whole moved far from the speech and in the dual directions of *The Years* and *Three Guineas*. Before she abandoned the essay-novel form, in February 1932, Woolf had produced a draft that interleaved five chapters of a novel with factual, documented discussions of some of the main themes of *Three Guineas:* the impact on women of paternal power, lack of economic independence, limited education, and the threat of aggressive male sexuality ("street love," in Woolf's words). At this point, militarism is not included among the threats to women. In 1932, when Mussolini was already in power but Hitler was not, neither a future war nor fascism was yet a pressing public issue. This was the hopeful year of the great disarmament conference at Geneva, supported by a wide range of women's and other peace groups; Virginia Woolf refers in *Three Guineas* to a 1932 pamphlet on its concluding declaration, written by Edith Zangwill for the Women's International League for Peace and Freedom (*3G* 144).

In *The Pargiters'* version of the speech, the audience sounds rather less elite than the listed members of the Junior Council. A typical listener is described as living away from the center of London, in a "three-roomed flat above the grocer's shop in Clarence Road S.W. 19," a definitely un-exclusive location from which she commutes by bus to work. The work of what are still called professional women is "hard and sometimes harassing," taking place in a "crowded noisy office . . . from half past nine to six, with an hour off for luncheon." Those addressed sound like clerical workers, the ones whom *Three Guineas* learns about from Whitaker's *Almanack;* they are to be found in the lowest levels of the civil service and other white-collar positions. Woolf recognizes her own privileged situation, as she notes that the woman writer's life is much easier than that of any other sort of professional woman.

As Woolf begins to work her way in *The Pargiters* toward *The Years* and *Three Guineas*, there is no mention of the conventional and psychological barriers to creativity originally represented by the Angel in the House. The text continues, not with a hopeful vision of the future (no knock on this door), but with an introduction to the Pargiter family, whose experience in 1880 serves as "historical preface." That is, the tale of the Pargiters justifies the lecturer's statement that "in trying to earn your living professionally, you are doing work of enormous importance." The pretense of an oral presentation stretches thin as the manuscript grows, and in *The Years* itself the introductory remnant of the lecture will be removed.[22]

By her own account, Woolf wrote hard on the manuscript for the next few weeks; she recorded on 17 December 1932 that she had written 234 typed pages, and then, on 19 December, when she stopped, that the text amounted to 60,320 words (*D4* 132). Next, finishing *Flush* was her major writing project, while she longed to get back to *The Pargiters*. By the end of 1932, the little book on professions had changed into what looked to be a hefty novel, a realistic one with a documented and then suppressed factual basis. On 2 November 1932, Woolf described it as a "novel of fact" like her *Night and Day* (*D4* 129). This was the same day that she noted joining "Pippa's Society"; we know that she became a member at this point of the Junior Council, to which she had given the original speech. The text she was then working on took five more years to complete.

With *Flush* completed, in January 1933 she could turn back to *The Par-*

giters. On 2 February she noted that she was removing the interchapters and "compacting them in the text" (*D4* 146). At this point she still intended to include some scholarly apparatus in *The Pargiters*, in the form of an appendix of dates that survived only as the dates heading the different sections of the novel. There is no record of when she decided to provide endnotes for any version of the book. The documentation from the vanished interchapters, much augmented, was to reappear in *Three Guineas*, after a long period when Woolf fully intended to write the "little book" but kept putting it off. But during this period she made a number of notes that indicate in rough outline how her original idea responded to the demands of composition and the politics of the day.

We have no clear evidence about when, the novel once under way, the idea of writing a second, accompanying "little" book first took shape. As *The Years* becomes more obsessively her concern, Woolf's letter or diary references to the future *Three Guineas* decrease. By 1935, nevertheless, it is clear that the little book has already become a separate text. In her customary New Year's survey of writing plans, Woolf notes her hopes that "Ordinary People," as *The Years* was now called, could be finished in July. The essay that she was now calling "On Being Despised"—the future *Three Guineas*—could then be started in August while she was also preparing for her next substantial project, a biography of Roger Fry (*D4* 271).[23]

Occasionally Woolf succumbed to the temptation to start putting the "sequel" down on paper. Eleven pages of very rough longhand notes labeled "Sketch of Professions" are headed with the date "April 14th 1935."[24] In her diary for the same date, she notes that she made a "rash attempt" at a draft of "On Being Despised, or whatever it is to be called" (*D4* 300). It is possible that Woolf's irritation at Forster and the London Library Committee (recorded in her diary the week before) provoked her into writing down these notes, but neither the draft nor the diary makes any such reference. The notes themselves are keyed initially to H. G. Wells's statement that women had failed in the professions, as found in his autobiography, which Woolf had read "with interest and distaste" in November 1934 (*D4* 262).[25] In the middle of discussions of the professions, there is half a page of notes on war: "there is nothing exciting or romantic" about it. Of World War One, Woolf writes that it was "not a war for wh[ich] women were responsible . . . not an undertaking that gives cause for pride," and she also comments on the war's somewhat ambiguous provision of opportunities for women. This draft also includes brief comments on women's civilization: it was largely one of deprivation—"they had to do without"—

and "renunciation," both of which were valuable sources of education. Much of the material of *Three Guineas* is already present in this early draft, such as the frustrations encountered by Mary Astell and Lady Lovelace, Florence Nightingale's liberation by her experiences in the Crimean War, and the importance for women of the professions along with the need to reform them. The class position of the writer is already specified: not middle or upper-middle class, she is one of the uneducated daughters of educated men. There is also discussion of the fact that even well-qualified women earn very little and indication that Whitaker's *Almanack* will be used for documentation.[26] This is the last time that any title will refer to being "despised."

Woolf may have been referring to this "sketch" when, in May 1935, on holiday, she recorded that she had not thought of "my book on Professions" for about a week, which suggests that she had been giving it attention in April. Now she was again considering dashing it off: "This vacillates with my novel—how are they both to come out simultaneously" (*D4* 314). *The Years*, however, was not anywhere near finished in 1935, in spite of her hopes, and *Three Guineas* remained in waiting.

IV

By this time, *Three Guineas* was taking on its final identity as more than just a lament about the problems of professional women. As the 1935 "Sketch" suggests, the links between sexism, war, and fascism seem to have become evident to Woolf. In 1934, she clipped from *Everyman* an article, "By a Man—C. E. M. Joad," writing on "Women of Today and Tomorrow." In *Three Guineas* she refers, without attribution, to Joad's epigraph that cites Marshall Goering about women being the recreation of the warrior (*3G* 102). In this article Joad laid out clearly the misogynist views about women in public life that Woolf was later to cite in *Three Guineas* from two of his autobiographies. He even suggested that Nazi views about women returning to the home might be "a straw to show which way the wind is blowing."

During 1935 Woolf continued to collect material on how women were excluded from the professions, but what she clipped shows that she was now also interested in demonstrating the implications of fascism, especially its treatment of women. The theme of male criticism of women's dress and appearance was joined by examples of the excesses of men's public attire, and here she noted both traditional British ceremonials and the newly created Nazi regalia. The scrapbooks include ten periodical items labeled as from 1935, twenty from 1936, forty-one from 1937. By the end of 1934, when she was asked to serve on the committee for a communist-inspired antifascist exhibition, Virginia Woolf had developed her own perspective on fascism.

Recent research has documented Woolf's involvement with several antifascist groups in the interwar period; her membership was brief, but she signed letters and petitions, appeared in a few sessions on platforms, and wrote to friends and acquaintances to solicit funds (*L5* 367, 368).[27] We know from her diaries and letters that, like those around her, she was increasingly horrified by what was going on in Germany and Spain: 1933 saw Hitler as chancellor and then effectively dictator; it also saw the start of the civil war that was to destroy the Spanish republic and give the Axis powers their first chance to test weapons and tactics. Woolf noted down her reaction to the Blood Purge of the Nazi Party (Night of the Long Knives) of 30 June 1934, when some twelve hundred of Hitler's supporters were slaughtered on his command. "One of the few public acts," she records herself as saying, "that makes one miserable." "Those brutal bullies go about in hoods & masks, like little boys dressed up, acting this idiotic, meaningless, brutal, bloody, pandemonium" (*D4* 223).

On 26 February 1935, Woolf recorded that she was now thinking of writing an antifascist pamphlet herself, and that her husband, deeply and expertly involved in foreign policy analysis, had helpfully explained to her that she would have to take account of "the economic question." This was the standard leftist approach; Leonard Woolf himself relied more on psychologically based arguments in his own books about fascism. Virginia reflected that "his specialised knowledge is of course an immense gain, if I could use it & stand away"; "I mean, in all writing," she concluded, "its the person's own edge that counts" (*D4* 282). She seems not have taken seriously the analysis supplied by her communist-leaning nephew Quentin Bell at about this time; he thought her bemused by his earnest explanation of the reasons for a United Front of the Left.[28]

Some of the 1935 diary entries give the impression that Woolf had, as well as *The Years*, no less than two smaller related projects: the "sequel" to *Three Guineas* and a separate text about fascism. Projects outlined at the beginning of the year for 1935 include "On Being Despised" and "Despised" but no antifascist text. On 17 April she refers separately to "an antifascist pamphlet" and "professions for women." Toward the end of April, however, a discussion with her nephew Julian Bell and Freudian analyst Alix Strachey about substitutes for war turned her attention back to "my

Professions book" (D4 271, 302, 307). The topics, and the books, were apparently now merged, and in June she wrote to the Argentinean Victoria Ocampo, who had just read and liked *A Room of One's Own*, "I want to write a sequel to it, denouncing Fascism" (L5 405). Finally, in October 1935 she explicitly articulated the connection when she and Leonard attended the Labour Party's annual convention in Brighton and heard the pacifists headed by George Lansbury resoundingly defeated. "On Monday one [woman] said, It is time we gave up washing up. A thin frail protest, but genuine. A little reed piping, but what chance against all this weight of roast beef & beer—which she must cook?" In one of the reading notebooks she made some notes on men and women, war and peace, headed "The meeting at Brighton," including the remark that "m[en] think war necessary." On the same sheet of paper she jotted down, "Cheques for one guinea . . . all moonshine" (D4 345; N56 254).[29]

The stimulus had an immediate effect. In her diary, soon after the Labour Party meeting, Woolf wrote that she was feeling "wild excitement over The Next War. . . . the result of the L[abour] P[arty] at Brighton was the breaking of that dam between me & the new book, so I couldn't resist dashing off a chapter." She had interrupted the novel again; on October 27 she recorded that "my Next War . . . at any moment becomes absolutely wild, like being harnessed to a shark." She was dashing off "scene after scene." But at this stage she apparently only wrote fragments; she was soon back to *The Years*, with thoughts of doing the little book immediately after the novel was completed—"in six weeks" (D4 346, 348). It seems likely that some of the material written in October 1935 is to be found in an undated holograph manuscript mislabeled "Women Must Weep." Here Woolf cites a woman saying "we will not wash up any longer." The next sentence reads: "& then I added, but they'll make you, They have the gun." This text includes a lengthy comparison of Hitler and Asquith (in respect to the way in which the English prime minister treated the suffragists): women are living under dictators and "told that we were hysterical fools for making a protest." None of these points appears in *Three Guineas*, although the comparison of Asquith to Hitler is still present in a much later draft.[30] The logic was now clear: sexism at home and fascism abroad were the same thing. At the end of 1935, the future *Three Guineas* had become "my war book."

At this time, more than four years after Woolf first thought of the sequel to *A Room of One's Own*, she began to work out an organizing device: "to pretend its all the articles editors have asked me to write during the past few years. . . . This wd give me the right to wander: also put me in the position of the one asked" (*D4* 361). This was at the end of December 1935; a few days later this idea had changed into a series not of the requested articles on topics such as "Shd. women smoke. Short skirts. War" but of a text organized as letters responding to such invitations. In mid-March 1936, Woolf considered producing a single "Letter to an Englishman . . . because after all separate letters break continuity so" (*D5* 18). Here she was echoing the titles in a Hogarth pamphlet series for which she wrote in 1932 a "Letter to a Young Poet" addressed to John Lehmann. The incorporation into the framing letter of other letters and texts along with draft texts of responses came only later in the process, at some unknown time. In addition, without noting the fact, she finally decided to organize the book's central letter around requests not for writing but for subscriptions and donations. Can we see an echo here of the young Virginia Stephen who, asked by the People's Suffrage Federation to do some research on suffrage, preferred to address envelopes? Or, later, Virginia Woolf writing to solicit donations to the feminist library at Marsham Street?

International politics were on Virginia Woolf's mind as she was finishing *The Years*. Hitler's troops occupied the Rhineland on 7 March 1936 in flagrant and successful defiance of the 1925 Locarno Treaty guaranteeing postwar boundaries. She declared herself a pacifist, like Aldous Huxley, while Leonard Woolf insisted that the League must be supported. "This is the most feverish overworked political week we've yet had," she wrote; "I go on, like a doomed mouse, nibbling at my daily page" of revisions of *The Years* (*D5* 17). On 8 April 1936 the final pages of revised typescript of *The Years* went to the printer; the next day she recorded that she had made up "the first pages of Two Guineas" (*D5* 22). This entry was followed by a period of near-suicidal collapse, related at least in part to difficulties she was experiencing with *The Years*. There were no more diary entries until June and few during the summer.

On 3 November 1936, when Leonard Woolf had finally read and approved *The Years*, Virginia recorded that she was making up what was for the first time called "3 Guineas," as she continued to refer to it from this time (*D5* 29). Three weeks later, 23 November, when she was feeling much recovered and ready to write again, *Three Guineas* moved up in the queue sufficiently to be started seriously, and January 1937 found her "sunk once more in the happy tumultuous dream: that is to say began 3 Guineas this morning, & cant stop thinking it" (*D5* 52). Writing at *Three Guineas* helped to get her through the publication of *The Years* in mid-March, though the huge success of the novel, both critical and financial, derailed her writing in March 1937. Relieved and delighted with *The Years'* reception, Woolf noted that it would mean more attention for *Three Guineas* to "strike very sharp & clear on a hot iron" (*D5* 68).

That summer she made good progress on the book until, on 20 July 1937, the family learned of the death of Julian Bell, her nephew who had been serving as an ambulance driver in Spain. *Three Guineas* was put aside, so that Woolf could help her stricken sister, Vanessa Bell. At the end of July Woolf sketched out a memoir of Julian, asking herself why he had so desperately needed to go to the war. She ended up with a psychological assessment that was to be important in *Three Guineas:* "its a fever in the blood of the younger generation which we can't possibly understand." She recognized that this was a "cause," that liberty was at issue, but her own reaction was nonbelligerent: "fight intellectually: if I were any use, I should write against it: I should evolve some plan for fighting English tyranny."[31] By the next month, she was back to writing *Three Guineas*, though apparently now finding it hard going. In a letter to Vanessa Bell dated 17 August 1937, she mentioned that she was "completely stuck on my war pamphlet . . . always wanting to argue it with Julian." This was the letter in which she said, rather misleadingly, "in fact I wrote it as an argument with him" (*L6* 159).

Finally, between 27 September and 12 October 1937, the last chapter of *Three Guineas* was written with such concentration that Woolf's diary went entirely untouched until she was finished and noted:

> It has pressed & spurted out of me, if thats any proof of virtue, like a physical volcano. . . . And then I forced myself to put it into fiction first. No, the fiction came first. The Years. And how I held myself back, all through the terrible depression [of 1936], & refused, save for some frantic notes, to tap it until The Years—that awful burden—was off me.

She was not sure "whether it is good or bad" and still had to do the bibliography and notes (*D5* 112). She kept on at it through the winter, and Leonard Woolf's ceremonial reading of the text took place at the beginning of February. He did not respond with enthusiasm:

> L. gravely approves 3 Gs. Thinks it an extremely clear analysis. . . . One cant expect emotion, for as he says, its not on a par with the novels. Yet

I think it may have more practical value . . . [and I] feel it a good piece of donkeywork.

"I didnt get so much praise from L. as I hoped," she noted rather sadly in April when she showed him the endnotes (*D5* 127, 133).

Then, with many complaints and in a great rush so that it could be out that year, in February, March, and April 1938 Woolf corrected and rewrote the text, composed and compressed notes. During the same period, without any mention in her diary, she also drastically cut and revised the text for serialization in the *Atlantic Monthly* before the appearance of the first American edition.[32] Vanessa Bell, who as usual had not yet read the book she was illustrating, designed a dust jacket for both first editions, on the basis of a summary of its contents early in January; it showed the three checks by which middle-class women would have made the donations of the title in the days before credit cards. Woolf did not see the cover at this point. In July 1938, she saw the American edition and wrote to Vanessa, "I think it is one of the best you ever did—quite lovely, and also practical, and so you've killed 2 birds with 3 cheques" (*L6* 251).

The first installment of the serial appeared in the United States in the *Atlantic Monthly* in May 1938; the first English edition of the book was published, finally, by the Hogarth Press on 2 June 1938; the remainder of the serial appeared in the June issue of the *Atlantic Monthly*. The first American edition, published by her usual American publisher, Harcourt Brace, appeared on 25 August 1938. It had been a long haul.

Three Guineas sold reasonably well.[33] Many of Woolf's close friends and associates were rather conspicuously silent, and some, like Vita Sackville-West, were critical. Readers who shared Woolf's feminist views responded with enthusiasm; they included prominent activists such as Emmeline Pethick-Lawrence, Helena Swanwick, and Margaret Llewelyn Davies as well as a large number of otherwise anonymous women and men. Along with the many enthusiastic letters came others asking for clarification or voicing criticism; she seems, sometimes grumbling, to have answered them all.[34]

The last period of frantic work on *Three Guineas* was, in international terms, a truly horrible time. Germany took over Austria in March; Woolf incorporated the events into the notes of *Three Guineas*. Advance copies of the book were distributed in May at the first peak of the Sudetenland crisis when, for the last time, the British and French invoked their alliance in defense of Czechoslovakia and, also for the last time, Hitler backed down.

"One more shot at a policeman, & the Germans, Czecks, French will begin the old horror," Woolf wrote in her diary. War might break out at any moment, "& my book may be like a moth dancing over a bonfire—consumed in less than one second." "We must attack Hitler in England," she told E. M. Forster; he said he agreed with her about local action being necessary, asking, "But how?" She replied, "Oh I'm in touch with Pippa & Newnham." "He seemed to sympathise," she noted (*D5* 142). Hostile responses to *Three Guineas* were to focus on the analysis implicit in Woolf's remarks to Forster. What could the support of women's professional jobs and education have to do with the looming threat of war? For Woolf the connection was crucial, and at the heart of both *Three Guineas* and her feminism.

V

The last version of the speech to the Junior Council is the posthumously published essay "Professions for Women"; it includes no references to the oncoming war or indeed to war at all. Here the essay resembles the original lecture, presented years before postwar had become prewar. However, it is important to remember that, although it appears that "Professions for Women" was rewritten substantially by Virginia Woolf at some time in the 1930s, she did not complete final revisions or take the essay through to publication.

Very different from *The Pargiters* and from *Three Guineas* itself, the essay closely resembles the two speech drafts. It is framed once again as a lecture addressed to women professionals, with a footnote added by Leonard Woolf that it was "A Paper read to the Women's Service League." This comment is not completely accurate; he was using an outdated title expanded by the organization even before Virginia Woolf spoke, and she addressed, not the whole group, but its Junior Council. More important, the published text is substantially different from the surviving versions of the lecture itself.

The essay once again addresses the persistent barriers to "professional" women's effectiveness. Praise of Ethel Smyth and of benevolent or tameable men is gone, as had already happened in *The Pargiters*. The Angel in the House returns as a metaphor for the Victorian ideal of the ultrafeminine, self-sacrificing, and idealized domestic goddess. This inhibiting stereotype can be vanquished, Woolf thinks, by economic autonomy. Less tractable is the necessity for "telling the truth about [one's] own experience as a body." Women writers are "impeded by extreme conventionality of the other sex." In *Three Guineas* Woolf had noted that men too were impeded by conventionality, and quoted Thackeray's indignant comments to that effect in his famous introduction to *Pendennis*, a novel cited several times in *Three Guineas*; in "Professions for Women" her subject is the more severe problems of the writer who is embodied as a woman.

A new description of a room of one's own forms the conclusion to "Professions for Women." The passage also revives reference to an income of five hundred a year, which is not to be found in *Three Guineas*:

> You have won rooms of your own in the house hitherto exclusively owned by men. You are able, though not without great labour and effort, to pay the rent. You are earning your five hundred pounds a year. But this freedom is only a beginning; the room is your own but it is still bare.

The room has to be furnished and decorated, and "it has to be shared." The lecturer poses questions to her audience: How are you going to furnish it, how are you going to decorate it? With whom are you going to share it, and upon what terms? "These, I think are questions of the utmost importance and interest," she says. "For the first time in history you are able to ask them; for the first time in history you are able to decide for yourselves what the answers should be." In spite of those brave words, at the end of the last interwar decade Woolf emphasizes that men still own the house, and that someone else is going to participate in decisions about life and work. And she is clear that the road ahead is not easy, even though it is by their own efforts that women have "won" the first stages of economic and psychological freedom:

> Even when the path is nominally open—when there is nothing to prevent a woman from being a doctor, a lawyer, a civil servant—there are many phantoms and obstacles, as I believe, looming in her way. To discuss and define them is I think of great value and importance; for thus only can the labour be shared, the difficulties be solved.

To discuss and define "phantoms and obstacles": this was the mandate of *Three Guineas*. *Three Guineas* has also already responded to an additional final injunction in this essay: "it is necessary also to discuss the ends and the aims for which we are fighting."[35] The reference here is to women's struggle for autonomy, but perhaps we can also hear an echo of other battles. What "Professions for Women" makes most clear is that the situation and the actions of women will have to be central to any important struggle.

And that *Three Guineas* is not a book about war, but about women, and for that reason about feminism.

Both war and politics as such seem to be absent from "Professions for Women," as from the reported and drafted speech and the related early versions of the merged essay-novel. That is, they have nothing to say about fascism or about the explicitly feminist struggles of women either as suffragists or as the outsider activists still required by postsuffrage conditions. But politics and its central questions for the 1930s are the underlying subjects, for questions about women's rooms in what used to be exclusively men's houses are precisely about the nature of society and the ways in which women can influence it. These questions are central to *Three Guineas*—which it is now time to examine directly.

4 The Argument in Three Guineas

The most common view of *Three Guineas* is that it is a non-fictional antiwar pamphlet, a polemic in which Virginia Woolf says that changes in the status of women will produce peace. It is believed to consist of three letters written by Woolf, who is answering a series of requests for funds that she had received; the first and most important of these is from a peace society that also asks how women can prevent war. "Woolf's consideration of what women can do to avoid war—the question posed to her by a correspondent—finally closes when she decides to send a guinea to each of three societies with particular aims," writes the editor of one of the more widely available paperback editions of *Three Guineas*.[1] But in fact the book is quite strikingly different from such descriptions. This long, dense, extensively annotated volume includes not just three but twelve letters and letter drafts. Furthermore, its narrator is not Woolf herself, the addressees of the letters are imagined instead of actual identifiable individuals, and the narrator herself is the only one to ask how women can prevent war. Nor is war by any means the only topic of the book. At the same time, if *Three Guineas* is not "real" letters addressed to "real" questions or "real" people, it is nevertheless the location of something that is real in all senses: Virginia Woolf's feminism, which can best be traced through the book's letters and letter drafts.

I

If it is not a pamphlet, though, what is *Three Guineas*? There has always been uncertainty about how to describe this book, which seems to be something of an anomaly in generic terms. Shortly after *Three Guineas* appeared, Woolf wrote to Ethel Smyth: "my vanity reminds me, that [*Three*

Guineas] is selling very well, tho' none of the shops at first would take it. Not a novel, they said" (*L6* 247). Not a novel, then, but what? And the answer matters, because if *Three Guineas* is perceived as a straightforward polemic by the well-known author (and aesthete?) who was Virginia Woolf, it is likely to be both misunderstood and underestimated.

Most often, *Three Guineas* is linked to *A Room of One's Own* in terms of genre as well as subject matter, with the two books described as something like "feminist tracts."[2] Leonard Woolf wrote that *Three Guineas*, like its predecessor, was a "political pamphlet."[3] Without the connection to its sequel, it seems unlikely that anyone would have called the elegantly written, endearing *A Room of One's Own* a pamphlet, which seems to imply brevity, a focus on action, and a disregard of aesthetic considerations. Such a description sits uncomfortably on *Three Guineas* as well. To begin with, it understates the book's scale, 329 pages in the first English edition, and 285 in the first American edition. Calling the book a pamphlet also diminishes its importance, turning a carefully organized and documented text into an ephemeral booklet. The Hogarth Press took seriously its pamphlet series, but those topical volumes were typically very short and bound in informal soft covers. Woolf herself occasionally referred to *Three Guineas* as a pamphlet, in the same dismissive way as she called it a "little" book. Yet it seems clear that she thought of it as something more substantial. When she was waiting with a certain anxiety for the first reactions to the volume, she wrote in her diary that she might "sum it all up in 6 months in a pamphlet" (*D5* 146). Perhaps she had in mind something like the thirty-two-page "Reviewing" that she was to publish in the Hogarth Press Sixpenny Pamphlet series in November 1939, in which she continued ferociously the attack on reviewing practices that she had sketched in *Three Guineas*.[4]

Not just a pamphlet, not a novel, *Three Guineas* is a mix of fact and fiction. Especially after the best-selling *The Years*, in her lifetime Virginia Woolf was usually thought of as a writer of fiction, but variety and combination of genres were common among her writing. Her essay collections, the two *Common Readers*, were very successful, and her writing included every genre except poetry; she even wrote a short comic play (*Freshwater*). *The Waves*, a poetic novel, could be said to combine prose and poetry; Woolf described it as a "play-poem" when she started making it up in 1927. *Orlando*, a fantasy published in 1928, had encountered problems when booksellers had classified it as a biography (*D3* 139, 198). Furthermore, Woolf regularly mixed fiction, not to say fantasy, as well as biography into more conventional essays. Most relevant, *A Room of One's Own* incorporated fiction and disguised autobiography in what looked like a straightforward didactive statement. The issue is how to disentangle the fiction from the fact, particularly in *Three Guineas*.

Without being entirely fictional, *Three Guineas* draws, of course, on the long tradition of novels written in epistolary form. The literary device of the letter has a number of implications. Most important, it necessarily implies not just a writer but also a reader. It therefore always incorporates a correspondent—an assumption made by the writer about the identity and nature of the person who is being addressed. Otherwise put, a letter is "a transitive form," with "an objectified reader inside."[5] There are many such readers in *Three Guineas*, for there are a surprisingly large number of letters in the text. Three complete letters are sent to organizations that can contribute to assisting women to generate a nonsexist and peaceful world; enclosed with them are the guineas of the title. But the book also includes five letters received by the narrator of *Three Guineas* as well as four draft versions of letters that she does not send off.

The letter remains very much a woman's medium, even though three of the letters in *Three Guineas* are not from women or women's groups, and the book itself is, at least ostensibly, addressed to a man. The editors of the *Oxford Book of Letters* comment that "a great many of the most accomplished letter-writers have been women." They attribute this achievement to the supposed fact that women "have, historically, had less occasion to write merely performative letters, letters which command, promise, or threaten, so that they can afford to be more interested in themselves than in the achievement of any practical purpose unrelated to the pleasure of writing, and the pleasure of giving pleasure."[6] The letters and letter drafts prepared by the narrator of *Three Guineas*, which are intended to accompany donations and influence organizations, are thus atypical of what might be considered the private dimension of women's letters; after all, they do have practical purposes and goals in public life. At the same time, they argue strongly for the domestic values of peace and peaceful transformation—the alleged central topics of women's letters.[7]

Looking at *Three Guineas* as demonstrative, didactic—and political—we can see two possible functions of letters that are relevant here. First of all, the letter does in general provide a way in which to speak bluntly, as one might not face to face, to someone who may be hostile but still possibly persuadable. Because in *Three Guineas* the (fictional) writer of the letters encloses money, the (fictional) recipients would read to the end and perhaps make some gesture of agreement. We may wonder if a check for one guinea is enough to compel attention. But perhaps it is the symbolism of the donation that matters. This is not the only place where Woolf urges women to use what economic leverage they have, although often she does so more explicitly. We could notice also that she seems to recommend the use of donations as a means of influencing not just male peace activists or politicians, but also the women who run colleges for women and associations supporting women in the professions.

At the same time, the intimate and amused tone of *Three Guineas*' letters, along with the startling facts, is appropriate for a quiet personal communication. That voice—a trifle conspiratorial—suits the discourse of women who feel themselves outsiders looking at male society. Here we move to another important characteristic of letters. As historians have come to realize, the letter is a classic way for women to communicate privately among themselves; even without rooms of their own, they can write and read letters with some privacy. *Three Guineas* then seems to represent something of a paradox, for printing 23,750 copies of a published letter is the opposite of private, and certainly Hogarth Press made serious efforts to get booksellers to stock the book.[8] But if we see the intended recipient as plural—all the women who might be supportive of Woolf's version of feminism—then circulation is more to the point than privacy.

And perhaps the readers can after all count on privacy to some degree, because it is not to be expected that men like the fictional correspondent would want to read the book—which in the real world does not hand out guineas to them but instead costs seven shillings and sixpence.[9] That many men would read the book through was unlikely, anyway, given what we know about how men have responded to the subject and to the tone of the book. Take Quentin Bell, Woolf's nephew and future biographer, who found *Three Guineas* so infuriating that he felt obliged to refute it repeatedly, even in a memoir written in his patriarchal eighties.[10] He would probably not have read it when he was a young socialist hoping for a United Front of the Left if it had not been written by his aunt. For men who were not relatives, the prestige of the actual writer of the letters might prove to be an attraction. This is the point at which the letters of *Three Guineas* cease to be just the communications from some deferential and anonymous woman that they claim to be.

II

We should not think of *Three Guineas* as a series of letters either to or from Virginia Woolf, even though the book drew attention because she was its author. Today the common reader as well as the scholar have available in print almost all of Virginia Woolf's own marvelous personal letters. Perhaps this encourages us to assume that the three principal letters of *Three Guineas* are addressed to specific correspondents of the real-life Virginia Woolf and that they are answers to real-life requests. But that *Three Guineas* is fiction as well as fact is evident when we try to identify the writers and readers implied in the letters in *Three Guineas*.

Thus, the distinguished peace activist Robert, Viscount Cecil of Chelwood, president of the League of Nations Union and a Nobel Peace Prize laureate in 1937, has been nominated as the target of the main letter of the book. His name was on a leaflet from the International Peace Campaign found in Woolf's scrapbooks; the International Peace Campaign would then be the organization that is asking the narrator to join an association, sign a manifesto, and make a donation (*N*59 284). Viscount Cecil and his wife, Nelly, however, were longtime friends of Leonard and Virginia Woolf, so she hardly had to imagine him as some unknown barrister. In addition, Lord Robert would not have been as ignorant of women's organizations as the addressee of *Three Guineas* is assumed to be, for he had been one of those instrumental in causing provisions supporting women to be inserted into the League of Nations' Covenant. He was also the honorary president of the London and National Society for Women's Service in the 1930s.[11] When Nelly Cecil read *Three Guineas*, she wrote enthusiastically to Virginia Woolf in tones far from those of the implied inactive wife of the interlocutor of *Three Guineas*: "I have enjoyed it enormously & maliciously. The best of it is that when *you* write something it won't be out of date like a pamphlet but will be there for use whenever the occasion comes."[12] At least one person thought *Three Guineas* more than a "pamphlet." And if George Duckworth's and Maynard Keynes's interest in pig breeding seems to have supplied one feature of the imaginary correspondent's character, they had no other resemblances to the rather stereotyped, unknown lawyer sketched out at the opening of *Three Guineas*; Duckworth was Woolf's half brother, while the famous economist was a close friend.[13]

Is the representative of the peace society perhaps one of those few emancipated men with whom a woman can feel safe, whom Woolf had noted in her first speech draft in 1931? It is with ironic pleasure that the narrator of *Three Guineas* notes that her fictional addressee is now "fighting with us, not against us" in the struggle for human freedom (*3G* 94). But, in truth, we know virtually nothing about the recipient of *Three Guineas*, beyond his age ("the middle years of life"), and that he has graying and thinning hair, wife and children, and land in Norfolk with pigs and pear trees. He is a barrister and has signed a letter on behalf of a peace society. He is not a personal acquaintance of the narrator of *Three Guineas*, who is an even more shadowy figure (*3G* 3–4).

The writer of the letter to the peace society describes herself as from the same elite background as her addressee—the movers and shakers who progressed from public schools to the ancient universities to the professions. She presents herself as a representative of women like herself, who are described relationally, as daughters, sisters, and wives of "educated men." Although the letter that frames the book begins as a personal statement, its writer immediately and consistently speaks in the plural, on behalf of the larger group of women like herself. "I had hoped that [your letter] would answer itself, or that other people would answer it for me," the narrator says on the first page of the book, but in the next paragraph she is saying, the first of many times, that it will be difficult for "us" to explain our views. A single impersonal "one," followed by a reference to "a woman" being asked her opinion, then becomes, "let us make the attempt" to respond. Only occasionally does the narrator reappear as an individual, most conspicuously in the last paragraph of the letter, saying "let me make an end" (*3G* 3, 131).

Under these circumstances, it is difficult to say much about the narrator herself. The way in which she speaks of the women's colleges implies that she has not, herself, attended them. In *Three Guineas*, professionals are nearly always men, which is accurate enough, but suggests that the narrator is not one of the few women among them. Though some of her remarks seem to imply that she is a writer, she does not say so, and she is apparently not to be found among the small imagined group of women writers who read and write for their own pleasure and not for the market and critics. Rejoicing in women's formal access to professions, she is insistent about how little financial and career success they have had. All the same, she herself is sufficiently autonomous and prosperous that she is solicited for contributions to good causes and can choose freely among them. She assumes that nearly all women marry and have children, so it would not be unreasonable to assume that she too is a wife and mother; after all, the "profession" of marriage, which requires learning about human nature in order to select a husband, is described as the main educator of women, and the basic source of the insights offered in *Three Guineas*. She apparently reads widely, and sympathizes with women's service organizations and their leaders, but she knows little about what they actually do. She definitely does not consider herself a feminist.

Obviously not all of the characteristics of the narrator of *Three Guineas* describe Virginia Woolf herself, the married but childless daughter of a particularly well-known, well-connected educated man, who herself was by 1938 a significant public figure and on occasion saw herself as a feminist. In the lengthy discussions of the beginnings of the women's colleges at Cambridge and of the university's strife-ridden resistance to them, we may feel that we can hear the personal voice of Virginia Woolf. We know that she resented not having attended university, and that her friends and relatives were Cambridge men (and, in the postwar period, some of the few women). In addition, the narrator (also imaginary) of *A Room of One's Own* reports that she experienced at Cambridge a more than symbolic exclusion from the grassed courts and a library.[14] But we should note that, along with Cambridge's colleges for women, Somerville College at Oxford is mentioned in *Three Guineas*. More generally, the narrator includes Oxford in her condemnation of the older universities' response to women, even though Cambridge was in reality the footdragger, and there were no misogynist riots at Oxford. Nor do we have evidence other than *A Room of One's Own* that Virginia Woolf herself was personally barred from anything at Cambridge, where she often visited and was invited to speak. She felt herself significantly honored by Trinity College, Cambridge, in 1932 when she was invited to present the prestigious Clark Lectures initiated by her father (she refused, reluctantly).[15] In addition, as we have seen, her knowledge of women's organizations was extensive, and her contacts with them were substantial.

Even in *A Room of One's Own* the distinction between fact and fiction is far from clear, and many readers think that it is about Virginia Woolf herself, although the imaginary narrator is individualized to the point of an imaginary name, an imaginary aunt (killed by a fall off a horse in Bombay), and imaginary employment as a governess and a maker of artificial flowers. In *Three Guineas* the fictionalized narrator is far less clearly delineated, but she is still not Virginia Woolf. The most important part of the difference lies in the reasons for Woolf's relative independence from economic pressures at the time when she was writing *Three Guineas*. Her career was far different from that of the "professional" women central to *Three Guineas*. In the long years before the financial success of *The Years*, Woolf had a small inheritance and the support of her husband to supplement a gradually increasing income as an independent writer and journalist. After 1917 the Woolfs' own Hogarth Press removed the usual middlemen of editing and publishing for all of her major work. For future Outsiders, *Three Guineas* could go no further than recommending self-publishing for self-expression through use of the typewriter and mimeograph machine; for them, economic security would have to precede autonomous literary activities rather than growing out of them.

Virginia Woolf, the author, resembled the narrator in one important respect, however. She was not in any way a recognized expert on public affairs. Here the contrast is with her husband, who had helped develop the plan for the League of Nations, advised the Labour Party on colonial and foreign policy issues, and published widely on issues of international politics. It has been suggested that the opening query of *Three Guineas* that is supposedly cited from the peace activist's letter—"How in your opinion are we to prevent war?"—might possibly echo a question posed in a letter from Albert Einstein, then famous as a pacifist as well as a physicist, to Sigmund Freud. "Is there any way of delivering mankind from the menace of war?" is the beginning of their public exchange that was published in 1933 as a League of Nations pamphlet titled "Why War?" and later reprinted by Hogarth Press. Freud's response begins disingenuously with an avowal of surprise and incompetence that somewhat resembles the phrases at the start of *Three Guineas*.[16] But the novelist Virginia Woolf was not asked that question by Einstein, who addressed instead a more obvious source of relevant wisdom, the internationally recognized expert on human psychology. About war and more generally about human nature, Woolf was indeed an amateur, though she was hardly such about feminism.

At the same time, it hardly makes sense to think of Virginia Woolf as relying, like the narrator of *Three Guineas*, on feminine intuition, developed through the "unpaid education" of domestic life. In fact, Woolf's own experience of domestic responsibility was unlike what she assigns to women as a group and the narrator as their example. Q. D. Leavis, reviewing *Three Guineas* in 1938, was unkind when she accused Woolf of not knowing which end of the cradle to stir; she was correct in sensing that conventional domestic occupations were far from central to the well-known author's consciousness.[17] Woolf enjoyed making bread and the occasional meal, but, as she was well aware, servants did all the basic household work for her as for other women of her class and time. The long drawn-out difficulties of attempts to deal fairly with her own cook-housekeepers, a recurrent theme in Woolf's diaries and letters, seem to have had only an indirect and limited impact on her sympathetic account of the travails of the maidservants who attended protected daughters of the middle class. Nor was the search for a husband ever a central preoccupation or educational force for Woolf, as she alleged it was for most women. Her own yearnings and uncertainties about children did not find their way into the portrait of the narrator. Furthermore, she had a remarkable education, even if not in school and university. It hardly needs adding that she was a highly cerebral, self-aware, and professional reader and writer, very different from the *fausse-naïve* narrator (who nevertheless, of course, cites a very wide range of material identifiably drawn from the eclectic reading of Virginia Woolf).

In addition, the account given in *Three Guineas* of public appeals and public responses does not correspond to what Virginia Woolf, as opposed to the narrator of *Three Guineas*, actually experienced. The peace society letter that she filed in her scrapbook had not asked her for advice about how war might be prevented—a question seldom posed to those approached for support—but instead for support of a particular policy. Woolf received many such letters asking her to lend her name to a preferred response to the rise of fascism in the 1930s, such as supporting international organizations or making a pledge of war resistance. The political positions she actually supported were not limited to the pacifist and gender-oriented ones described in *Three Guineas*. In a letter dated 7 March 1937, she laments, "Why does everyone bother me about politics? Six letters to sign daily—or nearly so." Among these was a request—to which she agreed—to put her name on a public petition by well-known authors in favor of setting up expert international commissions to enquire into the economic and structural causes of war (*L6* 112). Only Princess Bibesco's letter about the antifascist exhibition in 1935 seems to have provoked a recognizably feminist response echoing *Three Guineas*, when Woolf wrote back to ask whether the display would include something about Hitler's reactionary policies toward women.

When Woolf was asked—also frequently—to further feminist endeavors related to education, to professional activity, or to other projects related to the status of women, she did not respond with the occasional frivolity that lightens the tone of *Three Guineas*. We have actual examples of her correspondence with feminist activists, and in them her anger is real and unmediated. "Yes my blood boils," she wrote to Pippa Strachey in 1937 about press silence concerning the Contributory Pensions Bill that proposed to disadvantage women (*L6* 145; *3G* 290).

The letter writer of *Three Guineas* is, in short, a symbolic figure significant for the negative characteristics of the group she represents, in that she did not share the formal, institutional education, the professional activity, or the power of her father and brothers. The designated recipients of the letters are equally generic, both the addressee of *Three Guineas*, the middle-class man of power who is finally recognizing women's possible usefulness in sustaining a free society, and the leaders of women's groups supporting women's education and professional activity. These are all fictional characters, even though the book is very definitely not a novel.

In fact, as might be expected, Woolf reworked rather than simply reproduced the appeals that she used as an organizing device for *Three Guineas*. For example, the letter from the International Peace Campaign (which Woolf labeled "War and Writers" when she stuck it into her scrapbook) is in fact signed by Dame Adelaide Livingstone as vice chairman, although the letterhead lists the Viscount Cecil and Pierre Cot as joint presidents.[18] So much for *Three Guineas*' repeated comments about how unusual it is for men to ask women what to do about war. Nor does the writers' group For International Liberty (FIL) entirely fit as the original of the peace society. FIL's manifesto is close to that of *Three Guineas*' peace group, but Leonard Woolf was one of the founders of this group and supplied its name, while Virginia Woolf herself attended its first meetings; she would hardly imagine any representative of this group writing to ask her for a donation or about the causes of war.

Woolf's presentations of the other groups' requests in *Three Guineas* should also be taken with a few grains of salt. A letter from the Newnham Fund was pasted into one of Woolf's scrapbooks, and it is often assumed to be the second letter answered in *Three Guineas*. But it entirely lacks the anonymity implied in *Three Guineas*' impersonal response. Pernel Strachey, the principal of Newnham from 1923 to 1941, and signatory of the letter sent on behalf of the college's building appeal, was Pippa's sister; she did not need to be imagined or to be pressured by any condition joined to donations. The appeal itself does not use the wording "rebuilding"; instead, it speaks in more measured tones of "the need of raising funds to reconstruct out-of-date buildings and to provide additional accommodation."[19] It was Newnham's first campaign for capital funding, to which a guinea would be a ridiculously low subscription. Woolf had in fact been asked not for a donation but to join a list of legitimating patrons who would, among other tasks, attend a launching featuring Prime Minister Stanley Baldwin. What Woolf did was to transmute the letter into a direct request for money and the occasion to dictate how best to restructure not classrooms and dormitories, but the education provided by the college.

The third of the central letters of *Three Guineas* is addressed to the honorary treasurer of "a society to help the daughters of educated men to obtain employment in the professions." An endnote keyed to this part of the text is dated 1938, suggesting that the letter would have arrived when Woolf was completing *Three Guineas;* it includes a rather surprising request for donations of clothes for resale to professional women, and it is described as received from the London and National Society for Women's Service (*3 G* 40, 144). As result, most commentators have assumed that the recipient of Woolf's third guinea was the L&NSWS. The source of this citation and of the phrases pulled out for attention in the text is not to be found in Woolf's *Three Guineas* scrapbooks, or in the surviving records of the L&NSWS, its Junior Council, or its offshoot, the Women's Employment Federation. Closer examination makes the reader wonder if the phrases that the narrator presents in quotation marks in the text of *Three Guineas* are actual quotations at all. It seems unlikely that any treasurer, honorary or not, would have written asking for a subscription "in order to help us earn our living." Translated into more conventional language, the appeal sounds more likely to have come from the WEF than the London and National itself, whose goals in the 1930s were more overtly political. However, the L&NSWS and its Junior Council held a number of fund-raising events in the 1930s, including Christmas fairs with stalls and sideshows, a "Bierhalle Tanzconcert" in 1937, and a "Bavarian Evening" in 1938; activities such as these could have provided material for *Three Guineas'* famous fantasies about requests for fruit and old clothes.

The Women's Employment Federation itself, whose honorary treasurer was Pippa Strachey, was a federation of national women's groups interested in women's employment, and its fund-raising seems to have consisted of formal appeals to trusts, organizations, and relatively wealthy individuals. The federation did, however, hold fund-raising dinners in 1934 and 1935. According to Kalyani Menon, the last director of the WEF, at one of these there was a sale or raffle of donated items; was this what Woolf transmuted into a bazaar? An undated list of authors, titles, and subjects for *Three Guineas* includes the words "The Bazaar. Pippa," and in a letter to Pippa Strachey dated 25 October 1935, Woolf wrote, presumably enclosing a check: "With Mrs Woolf's compliments, in order that Miss Strachey may buy something at the bazaar" (*N7* 62; *L5* 437). Menon recalls that this very letter was sold by the WEF after the war at Sotheby's for about £500: "I suppose you could say that VW made her biggest donation unwittingly more than 30 years after her death." The boundaries between the L&NSWS and its offspring were probably a bit unclear, given the role in both of the Strachey sisters-in-law.[20]

It is perhaps unnecessary to note that the appeals referred to, when real, did not remain unanswered. To her friend, the principal of Newnham College, Virginia Woolf wrote both informally and formally to accept the invitation to become a patron of the building fund, and although she did not attend the meeting at Downing Street mentioned in the invitation, she noted in her diary that she wished she had; in *Three Guineas* she quotes from Baldwin's remarks on that occasion (*L6* 15; *D5* 21).[21] Woolf supported the London and National Society for Women's Service, particularly its library, over the years. And we may recall that Woolf joined both the L&NSWS and the WEF, paying in guineas.

At the same time, the imaginary women's groups addressed in *Three Guineas* resemble those that Woolf knew; she shared their concerns and goals. In addition, those women represented in the text of *Three Guineas* by fictional honorary treasurers of women's organizations are part of the intended actual audience of the real book. Woolf was much relieved by Pippa Strachey's enthusiastic response to *Three Guineas:* "It is what we have panted for for years and years."[22] Seasoned feminist activists such as Strachey would not be surprised by anything in the book as it stood, but they could still find satisfaction in how it was expressed. Woolf repeatedly tells such women, apologetically, that she has presented a very simple version of what they know far better. "I was writing for the very common, very reluctant, very easily bored reader—not for you," she wrote to Margaret Llewelyn Davies (*L6* 251). In addition, the book was something that activists could use. They responded with ironic hopes that men would read it. "Gentlemen of our acquaintance will be forced to take it up on account of its author & will be unable to put it down on account of its amusingness until they have reached the bitter end," according to Pippa Strachey. This "strong pepper & curry mustard" should be stuffed down the throats of "the leading gentlemens," wrote Nelly Cecil, using the words of a Norwegian activist.[23] Ray Strachey, who had been Lady Astor's parliamentary secretary when Astor was the first woman MP, wrote to say that she had told Astor that "she must send a copy to all the male devils she knows"; her letter to Astor said that she found the predictable discomfiture of the men "thoroughly gratifying."[24] These are not comments that expect conversion. It seems likely that the book would be more useful as something to supply to the women who had not yet become the knowledgeable feminists they could be: "ignorant gentlewomens," to adapt the phrase supplied by Lady Cecil.

The occasionally comic man of goodwill who is the ostensible recipient of the letter does not appear among the activists' descriptions of who should read *Three Guineas*. The appropriate readers of the book would be quite another group—those women, not yet converted to feminism, who might be persuaded by the documentation provided. Such women might also respond positively to the tone of the book, which the feminists had so delighted in. Not likely to join even the Outsiders, they are nevertheless the necessary support for activism. Today they would be among the majority of the female population who approve of the achievements of the women's movement, without intending to become activists themselves.[25]

Let us now look directly at the argument of the book that these women might be expected to read.

III

The first point made is with the title: *Three Guineas*. The title, as indeed the whole book, is about status and power, and gendered power at that. By the time of the writing of *Three Guineas*, the guinea was a notional unit of money, for historical reasons worth a pound plus a shilling, with no material equivalent in coinage or bills. Instead, it figured in invoices and payments, made by checks like the three on the cover of the book, laid out for a professional fee, for a subscription to a society or institution, or for the prices obtained for works of art, racehorses, and sometimes landed property.[26] In the 1930s, three guineas was the standard fee for a session with a prominent doctor. By then, the value was what would be the equivalent to about $150 (U.S.) today.[27] For a middle-class man at this time, the sum comprised a reasonable total for three not-particularly-generous charitable donations. So it did also for those few professional women as successful as Woolf herself. But Woolf was not typical; *Three Guineas* makes it clear that most women have far less money—and less power—at their disposal than their men do.

The title page of the book is followed by a list of illustrations, identifying five photographic portraits: "A General," "Heralds," "A University Procession," "A Judge," "An Archbishop" (see illustrations following page 166). These illustrations are important for the book's argument, for they represent the male establishment. We know at this point that *Three Guineas* will pay significant attention to the military, to trappings of social position, to the institutions of postsecondary education, to the law, and to religion. The major bases of hierarchy in English society, and indeed worldwide, are present in pictorial form, as they will be in written.

Beginning with the phrase "Three years is a long time to leave a letter unanswered" (a figure that fits nothing in the genesis or possible sources of *Three Guineas*, or even Virginia Woolf's usual practices), the book is set up as the response to a representative of a peace society, a correspondent whom the letter writer does not know personally but who shares her social position. As she will repeatedly note, he has access to class privilege in ways not possible for her as a woman. In the interest of preventing war, he asks her to sign a manifesto supporting intellectual liberty, to give money to his society, and to join it. She reinterprets his letter, saying that it means he is asking for her opinion—as a woman—about how war can be prevented. By the end of the book, the letter writer has agreed to sign the manifesto and to make the moderate donation of one of the three guineas of the title.

The correspondent-narrator will not, however, join the proffered society, proposing instead to found one of her own. She also sends two other guineas, with brief cover letters, to rather different good causes that have asked her for money: a women's college and a women's group supporting women in professions. In these last two cases, the donation of a guinea is so small as to be simply symbolic. It can nevertheless represent the right to influence the goals and activities of the groups that have been singled out. These women's organizations will contribute to ending war by enabling women to enter public life as equals and then to transform current society.

Once readers have recognized that *Three Guineas* is made up of more than one letter, and not a real one at that, they tend to think of its three chapters as corresponding to three letters, each to be sent with an enclosed check for a guinea. Each of the first two chapters does focus on a single request for funds, but the response to the peace society's request organizes the whole argument and rounds out the conclusion. Furthermore, no fewer than twelve letters are mentioned or quoted from in the text of *Three Guineas*, five of them presented as letters that the author has received and seven as letters or draft letters that she writes. Tracing these letters and the material supporting them makes it possible to map a path through this dense and sometimes confusing book.[28]

First, there is the imaginary letter that is the frame of the book—a very odd letter, with no indication of date or place, no salutation or closing statement or signature. Instead, in the Hogarth Press edition, this letter is 322 pages long, including 66 pages of endnotes, two footnotes, and five satirical photographs. The voice in the framing letter, as in the other drafted or dispatched response letters, is hardly that of a correspondent. There are frequent interpolations of "Sir" and "Madam" that strike the ear oddly today.

But neither does *Three Guineas* read like the lecture it once was. That speech in all its metamorphoses was specifically presented to women, described as young professional women.[29] In every version we have of the book as speech, Woolf addresses the audience informally and colloquially. *Three Guineas*, by contrast, sounds more like an intervention in a parliamentary debate than anything else. In terms of written forms, it is most like an extended essay—perhaps an unimaginably expanded op-ed piece for a fairly highbrow newspaper.

This first or encompassing letter presents the stated purpose of *Three Guineas:* to examine how women can best contribute to ending war. The peace society's letter to the author is the second letter to be found in the book, but we are told little of that letter's content apart from its advocacy of the support of intellectual freedom and the requests it makes. The narrator describes the peace society's letter as "perhaps unique in the history of human correspondence, since when before has an educated man asked a woman how in her opinion war can be prevented?" (*3G* 3). Fictional or real, however, the letter would not have been addressed to a woman as such. Virginia Woolf herself might have received such an appeal as part of a relatively anonymous mass mailing or, more specifically, as a relatively well-known author whose signature on a petition could add weight to an argument focused on cultural activities as preventive of war. In either case, the representative of the peace society would not have been asking for her support as a woman. All the same, the narrator proceeds to use the letter to invoke outsider status and women's perspective. Her initial presentation of them leads into discussions of the nature of patriotism (different in men) and of the range of views about war (even the Church is divided about whether it is ever acceptable).

The next letter discussed is used rather differently, to focus on the consequences of armed combat, in this case one of the civil wars that Hobbes thought represented the vilest expression of the war of all against all. This letter, number three, is represented in *Three Guineas* only by a description of its enclosed photographs of dead children and devastated buildings from the Spanish Civil War that had started in 1933. Men and women react with the same horror when faced with such a "crude statement of fact addressed to the eye," says the narrator of *Three Guineas* rather disingenuously (*3G* 10). Such images of desolation generate opposition to war in both sexes, in spite of differences in education and tradition. The reader is told in a footnote that the package of material was sent by the Spanish government in the winter of 1936–37; we know that on 14 November 1936, Virginia Woolf wrote to her nephew, Julian Bell, "This morning I got a packet of photographs from Spain all of dead children, killed by bombs—a cheerful present" (*L6* 85). Given its source and timing, this letter would most probably have used photographs of the devastation occurring during the siege of Madrid, and it would have sought the end of the weapons embargo imposed on both sides of the war in Spain by a group of nations under British leadership. The embargo was blatantly ignored by the fascists led by Generalissimo Franco, who, with the support of weapons and troops from Italy and Germany, were destroying the leftist, democratically elected Spanish republic.

The third letter is thus different in intention from the peace society's, for it seeks to support the righteous side of a civil war. Virginia along with Leonard Woolf was among a group of intellectuals signing a public letter to that effect on 20 August 1936.[30] The reported photographic images echo Goya's series on the disasters of war; they are repeatedly cited in *Three Guineas* to reinforce the argument that women must seek some new way to prevent wars and what causes them. As the title of the second installment of the serial puts it, "Women Must Weep—Or Unite to End War." The more so because, according to the next few pages of *Three Guineas*, there is little that middle-class women can now do, conventionally, to prevent war. "Daughters of educated men," they are unable to wage war or to be politically powerful as men are (the vote has done a little, not much). Lacking the economic leverage of working-class women, barred from the overrated feminine indirect influence available to titled or wealthy women, those like the narrator have only one possible way of influencing war. This is "an influence that is disinterested," based on the ability to earn one's own living, that is, economic autonomy.

The stodgy-sounding and somewhat limited Sex Disqualification (Removal) Act of 1919 thus becomes an icon, the means to enable women like the narrator to have an impact on preventing war. But they must do it differently, because women are different. Women's specific education, memory, and tradition generate a different view of the world of the powerful. Next come the well-known passages ridiculing "the clothes worn by the educated man in his public capacity." "How many, how splendid, how extremely ornate they are," the narrator exclaims (*3G* 17). The first of the five illustrations underlines the point, presenting a general in his plumed and braid-adorned and be-medalled splendor, followed two pages later by the mislabeled heralds, who are actually the equally splendid state trumpeters of the Household Cavalry on display at a royal event. Later in the book, a judge in a legal procession, a prime minister/chancellor in a university procession, and a triumphal archbishop complete the images of the glories of the professions in full fig.

The fourth letter mentioned in *Three Guineas* is the "manifesto" of the peace society, intended for newspaper publication when legitimated by signatures of well-known people. Its purpose, "to protect culture and intellectual liberty," referred to repeatedly in *Three Guineas*, though not cited as such until page 79, is close to the slogan of the group For Intellectual Liberty, which was founded in February 1936 to support French intellectuals against the rightist pressures in that country.[31] For such groups, the immediate problem of protecting writers and another artists at risk in Europe segued into the larger question of how fascism could best be combated; writers and artists, threatened with repression by totalitarian regimes, were also best placed to combat them on an intellectual level. "Let us consider how we can help you to prevent war by protecting culture and intellectual liberty" is how the narrator of *Three Guineas* puts it (*3G* 79). As referred to in *Three Guineas*, the manifesto therefore resembles many public statements made in the 1930s by British and European intellectuals who hoped to prevent war by stopping fascism without supporting rearmament. Thus, the International Peace Campaign manifesto that Virginia Woolf put in her scrapbook called for writers "to establish in every country a resolute and truly cosmopolitan nucleus which will stand for the integrity of the mind, for freedom of expression, for education untainted by militarism or racial myths and hatred," certainly causes both Virginia Woolf and the letter writer of *Three Guineas* could support.[32]

Three Guineas is often thought of as Virginia Woolf's own manifesto about how to prevent war. However, the book-length "letter" makes a larger and more transformative argument than its real-world models ever did, because it makes the connection among all forms of oppression, beginning with gender-based ones:

You are feeling in your own persons what your mothers felt when they were shut out, when they were shut up, because they were women. Now you are being shut out, you are being shut up, because you are Jews, because you are democrats, because of race, because of religion. . . . The whole iniquity of dictatorship, whether in Oxford or Cambridge, in Whitehall or Downing Street, against Jews or against women, in England, or in Germany, in Italy or in Spain is now apparent to you. (*3G* 94)

As both critics and enthusiasts have noted, such an analysis portends a complete restructuring of society.

Thus far, the letters to the narrator that are quoted or described in *Three Guineas* are directly related to war, whether their goal is peace or victory. With the exception of the framing letter, they have been prepared by societies or groups made up of both women and men though headed by men. The remaining letters consist of two requests for donations from women's groups and six versions of the narrator's possible responses to them (two of them actually sent off). The nature of these appeals and responses is what moves *Three Guineas* out of the antiwar context and makes clear how feminism is fundamental to an argument that, as a consequence, is pacifist.

Three Guineas makes it sound almost accidental that the narrator has in hand two other letters appealing for money. Woolf herself received many such requests. The two letters that the narrator selects for discussion are, in context, surprising, even startling, though readers of *Three Guineas* now take them in their stride. The argument, remember, is supposed to be about war. The relevance of the peace committee's appeals, and the Spanish government's, is obvious, even if the narrator's responses are somewhat unusual. But *Three Guineas* next turns to what is described as an honorary treasurer's letter asking for money to rebuild a women's college at Cambridge, and after the narrator presents a number of draft responses to that letter, most of the rest of the book is organized around a letter asking for money and other support for professional women. What, asked Quentin Bell, and many others, does this have to do with the doomed Spanish Republic and the rise of aggressive fascism that its defeat represents? Everything, the narrator says: "the public and the private worlds are inseparably connected . . . the tyrannies and servilities of the one are the tyrannies and servilities of the other" (*3G* 130).

Woolf has now reached the core of her argument: that the educational and professional structures of public life, which exclude women, are intrinsically hierarchical and oppressive, and therefore the basic causes of war. In fact, hierarchy, oppression, and exclusion are worse than war, for they are all pervasive. The patriarchal family is not a refuge from aggression and conflict but a source and justification of them.

The argument develops as *Three Guineas* supplies three possible responses to the appeal for support of the women's college. A first draft letter outlines what a women's college ought to be like in order to teach its students how to oppose war; it has been preceded by a slightly fictionalized account of the resistance by Cambridge to equal treatment of women and a completely factual description of the (related) poverty of the women's colleges. The violence of the rejection of possible intrusions by women suggests that the old models for university structure and curriculum actually generate aggression, even militarism. Therefore, in order to teach students to oppose war, a new college must be developed. It will have to abjure ceremony, tradition, and any structures of evaluation and certification. Unfortunately, however, as now at the Cambridge colleges for women, the graduating students, lacking degrees, would be unable to get work. Therefore, a second draft letter, despairing of possible reforms, tells the honorary treasurer to spend a donated guinea for rags, petrol, and matches to burn down the existing woman's college. Finally, a much shorter letter gives money to the college with no conditions. Women must be educated so that they can earn their own living; otherwise they will be at home facilitating war and also imperialism by their ignorance and dependency.

Although it is not made a condition of the donation, the narrator points out that the women's colleges can, if they wish, make certain changes in established procedures. They can refuse to teach "any art or science that encourages war" (she does not say what these would be, though she suggests that science and the classics both have had a baleful influence). The colleges will, unfortunately, have to keep chapels, degrees, and examinations—but they can "pour mild scorn" upon them. Though students cannot be expected to do without awards and degrees, women such as the narrator can refuse them for themselves and also refuse to lecture (a form of education the narrator labels "vain and vicious" and attacks in an endnote, as Woolf had earlier in the essay "Why?" that she wrote for *Lysistrata*, the journal of Somerville College, one of the two first women's colleges at Oxford).[33] This eighth letter thus focuses on the crucial role of education in changing the situation of both women and, therefore, society. The discussion reflects the tension between educational qualifications as a means to economic autonomy—an extension of the theme of *A Room of One's Own*—and the impact on students of the sexist, racist, and militarist content of elite education as it currently exists. The compromise solution may remind us of the situation of women's studies programs in the universities of our time, where advocacy of alternate modes of research, pedagogy, and institutional structure accompanies a reluctant acceptance of the traditional structure of departments and degrees.

Letter nine, described and quoted in the text, is from another honorary treasurer, this time asking for help for needy professional women, including items such as fruit or used clothing to sell at a bazaar. A related example of an appeal from a society to support professional women is given in an endnote; it asks for money but also for donations of reusable worn evening dresses and stockings that seem to be destined for some sort of thrift shop for professional women. Here are some of the book's most effective dramatizations of the plight of even middle-class women in the labor force.[34] The appeal first draws from the narrator the satirical draft response (letter ten) that surely professional women are rich and powerful, so why haven't they ended war? Joad and H. G. Wells are cited attacking women for not having united for peace, as they did for the vote. As this draft letter puts it, apparently "what was called 'the woman's movement' has proved itself a failure" (3G 42). Take this guinea, buy what is needed to burn down the association's building; then go back to the kitchen where you belong. This is the second draft suggesting that women turn to self-punishing arson. Such incendiary images in this polemic against violence are startling; they are among the many indications of Woolf's underlying anger and of her ambivalence toward violence.

Next comes a lengthy demonstration of women's poverty, or, rather, middle-class women's poverty. A close reading of relevant sections of Whitaker's *Almanack* for 1936, one of the major sources of information for *Three Guineas*, demonstrates how women are doing in the civil service—which is not well at all, quite apart from the marriage bar that eliminates married women entirely. Opinion decrying the employment of women is cited, and the English letter writers sound a lot like Nazis. Women whose only profession is marriage have even less money under their control. The professions, where money is to be made, entail a horrible life, which women should not want to enter—but from which men have barred them, even with violence (Sophia Jex-Blake's attempts first to earn money and then to become a doctor are retold at some length).

Letter eleven, reflecting on the competitive and exclusionary nature of professional life, ends with stipulations about how women can join professions and remain uncontaminated, this last being the condition of an enclosed guinea. Once again, in the interest of being able to change it, women must be enabled to take part in a corrupt system. The narrator hopes that it will be possible to take into public life the admirable virtues that women have perforce developed in their segregated private realm—along with obvious defects—as shown in the biographies not of the few great but of the many obscure women. She sums it up fancifully: professional women must "refuse to be separated from poverty, chastity, derision and freedom from unreal loyalties." By poverty is meant the insistence that they must earn only enough money "to be independent of any other human being and to buy that modicum of health, leisure, knowledge and so on that is needed for the full development of body and mind." Not a penny more; when they have earned enough to live on, they must work for disinterested motives, such as research, experiment, the arts, or in the unpaid service of others. "Chastity and derision" means abjuring and casting scorn on fame and praise, medals, badges, order, and degrees. Finally, they must get rid of pride in nationality, religion, college, sex "and those unreal loyalties that spring from them." They will then "possess an independent and disinterested influence with which to help . . . to prevent war" (3G 74, 75, 78). The letter writer notes, ironically, that all her requirements are easy to satisfy, apart perhaps from earning an adequate living, since the laws and practices in England still exclude women from wealth, great possessions, and professional opportunity along with independent nationality. Once in the senior professions, she insists, women must encourage to join them "all properly qualified people, of whatever sex, class or colour" (3G 74).

The last letter (number twelve) is the start of an appeal addressed initially to the "daughters of educated men," urging them to sign the manifesto of the peace organization to which the framing letter of *Three Guineas* is written. This comes at the start of chapter 3, which again attacks the ancient universities for their failure to teach how to prevent war. At this point *Three Guineas* picks up the question of women's culture that had drawn Woolf's attention in her response in 1935 to exclusion from governance of the London Library. She notes that the peace society manifesto states that "by protecting intellectual liberty and our inheritance of culture," women can help prevent war. But this is not our culture, says the letter writer; we have been barred from it (though we have contributed materially to making it possible). We are not welcome to teach boys in adolescence, and our place as both students and teachers in postsecondary education is still small. Women's share in "culture" is, in short, still basically limited to whatever they can get outside its official locations, for example, in libraries. In 1938, she specifies, it "largely consists in reading and writing our own tongue." Therefore she will ask the daughters of educated men to help prevent war "not by advising their brothers how they shall protect culture and intellectual liberty, but simply by reading and writing their own tongue in such a way as to protect those rather abstract goddesses themselves" (*3G* 82, 83). This is the only appearance of the word *goddess* in *Three Guineas*, which has long passages of attack on God the Father and His earthly representatives. The audience of this last letter is next, appropriately enough given the redefinition of culture, narrowed to those few women who earn their living by reading and writing. Writing is one of the few professions from which women have not been barred, the narrator notes. However, let us consider Mrs. Oliphant, a successful popular writer of novels, biography, and journalism who "sold her brain, her very admirable brain, prostituted her culture and enslaved her intellectual liberty in order that she might earn her living and educate her children." We must "applaud her choice and admire her courage," but her example shows that those dependent on writing to earn a living are necessarily unable to act disinterestedly. The target of this appeal therefore has to be narrowed yet again, to those women writers who can be disinterested because they have enough to live upon and "read and write for [their] own pleasure" (*3G* 85). The narrator does point out that independence can come from publishing and distributing one's own writing (as, although she does not say so, the Woolfs did with their Hogarth Press).

The relative powerlessness of most of the women even among the elite is highlighted in this section of *Three Guineas*: the appeal to support "culture" may be destined for as few as 250 self-sufficient English women, given the limited opportunities and inferior pay available to women and their disadvantages in respect to ownership and inheritance of property. But these women, the narrator suggests, might be extraordinarily influential if they could avoid "adultery of the brain." Here she plays with the definition of *adulterate* as meaning to "falsify by admixture of baser ingredients"; she might more correctly have written "adulteration of the brain." But perhaps there is a link here with the use of sexually loaded images in this part of the discussion: "brain prostitution" encouraged by the "pimps and panders of the brain-selling trades" as well as "prostituted culture and intellectual slavery" (*3G* 87). What is meant by these derogatory terms emerges when the narrator lists what must be done to protect culture and intellectual liberty: condemn writing for money and oppose mixing charm, advertising, or publicity into art. In addition, writers should, as earlier recommended, refuse any offer of honors or status. They could then "speak the truth," which means to "speak your own mind, in your own words, at your own time, at your own length, at your own bidding" about war, about politics, and about art. That is what "intellectual liberty" means to writers (*3G* 90). In addition, in their capacity as readers, they should boycott publications and lectures that degrade culture.

Demanding conditions are necessary, it seems, if those few women capable of it are to attempt to put into practice the promise made by signing the manifesto. The narrator recognizes that her recommendations entail loss of money and fame, as well as censure and ridicule. But such culturally related activities promise a transformation of society. She is not yet discussing, it should be noted, the famous Outsiders' Society but a series of measures targeted on the small group of economically independent women writers and readers able to protect culture and intellectual liberty. They are measures that Virginia Woolf increasingly adopted herself.

As for the narrator, she will sign the manifesto if she can keep to the terms she has just specified. She has, she considers, been trying to help prevent war by "attempting to define what is meant by protecting culture and intellectual liberty." Now she has to consider whether she will donate a guinea to the peace society. This is the point at which she proposes to burn the word *feminist* with hopes of, in the future, burning also the words "Tyrant, Dictator." Feminists will be replaced by members of the Outsiders' Society, "the kind of society which the daughters of educated men might found and join outside [the peace society] but in co-operation with its ends" (*3G* 97). Like recent feminist theorizers of coalition, *Three Guineas* advocates alliances and separate organizations; women and men may support the same causes, but "since we are different, our help must be different . . . by remaining outside your society but in co-operation with its aim" (*3G* 130–31). And perhaps "your society" has more than one meaning here, including those hinted at in Woolf's remarks about "your civilisation" made in response to Forster's teasing about the London Library committee in 1935.

Refusing such structures as officers, meetings, and funds, the Outsiders' Society is a virtual organization that will merely pledge its members to do a number of things. In general, they will begin by rejecting those few activities by which they might possibly support war directly. They will not bear arms (easy to do, she notes, because women are not going to be drafted). Unlike during the First World War, their activities this time will not include making munitions or nursing the wounded. Along with these obvious measures comes a more obscure and difficult one: maintenance of complete "indifference" toward war and fighting. Indifference here means neutrality in action, avoidance of both support and opposition. Perhaps feeling uncertain about the plausibility of this injunction, the narrator tells her readers that it can be justified to them by "fact," which will make clear that patriotism is appropriate for women. Therefore a daughter of an educated man should learn, first, about women's status in the country she is supposed to identify with, and then about the relative merits of that country: she must learn about the views of "subject peoples" as well as the history and culture of other countries. Her conclusion, says the letter writer in a famous passage, will have to be that "as a woman, I have no country. As a woman I want no country. As a woman my country is the whole world" (*3G* 99).

This is not as vague a recommendation as it may seem. The narrator is specific about the geographic location of her Society. It is England, for the Irish and the Indians are the subject peoples whose opinions matter, subject peoples who in the 1930s were in the throes of active battles for independence from the British Empire. French and German versions of history are to be compared to English ones, she says. Any remaining emotional attachment can legitimately direct the woman to whom she is speaking "to give to England first what she desires of peace and freedom for the whole world" (*3G* 99–100).

In addition, the Outsiders' Society requires its members, in practical terms, to do a number of specific things, beginning with abstention from patriotic demonstrations and any form of "national self-praise" as well as from attendance at ceremonies that encourage dominion or imposition of culture on others (military tattoos, prize-givings) (*3G* 100). More generally, these women must earn their own livings, but do it in a way to discourage hierarchy and militarism. They must work for a living wage for all professional women, they must try to create new professions where women can acquire economic autonomy (and this includes a wage for married women and for mothers), they must become so expert as to be indispensable, and they must watch for and denounce abusive conditions in their own professions. The narrator repeats her insistence that professionals should not seek riches, but earn only enough to live on (that is, they must not work excessively like the successful men whose lives have been pilloried earlier in *Three Guineas*). As we already know, they must not accept honors or office from any group that, claiming to respect liberty, restricts it; here Oxford and Cambridge are explicitly cited. In general, they must scrutinize tax-supported public institutions as well as private charitable ones, including schools and universities and religion.

With the exception of the self-imposed limit on personal enrichment and glory, the measures to be taken by the Outsiders can be found in one form or another in the programs of women's organizations in the interwar period. Surprisingly, the narrator insists that they can be pursued only secretly. She refers to the precarious situation of women who have to earn their own living, which she has earlier documented at length. But her reasons are also of a psychological nature, and she now makes arguments she has not made before. Here, toward the end of the book, she inserts a lengthy examination of the profession of religion. This discussion is based on material from the Archbishops' Commission on the Ministry of Women, which, reporting in 1935, in effect concluded that the likely hostile male responses—and only that—justified continuing the exclusion of women from the priesthood. This section of text is supported by the last photograph, of an archbishop. The content of the discussion makes it clear that the letter writer (and/or Virginia Woolf) would not be surprised to hear that the ordination of women was not approved by the Anglican Church until 1992.

From clerical patriarchy, *Three Guineas* then moves to private patriarchy and the psychological attitudes that underlie both, which are labeled with the Freudian term *infantile fixation*. Here we find extended discussions of the tyranny exercised by the fathers of Sophia Jex-Blake, Elizabeth Browning, and Charlotte Brontë, along with the contrasting and unusual experience of Barbara Leigh Smith. The narrator is once again underlining the links between the private and public forms of male domination: "the fear which forbids freedom in the private house . . . is connected with the other fear, the public fear . . . the fear which has led you to ask us to help you to prevent war" (*3G* 129).

The book and the letter end with the statement that the causes of intellectual liberty and peace are ones that both women and men can and should support. However, women will oppose fascism by means of opposition to the patriarchy that produces it. Although Outsiders will become participants in public life, they will abjure hierarchy and domination. Perhaps their principled noninvolvement will discourage men's inclinations to be competitive and warlike. Women will thus do their own particular best to prevent war by countering the conditions that produce it.

Clearly, this is not an argument about war as such but about the larger structuring of human society. The refusal to participate in the use of force had already in the 1930s been developed into a theoretical range of modes of active noncooperation. But in Woolf's feminism, violence itself, even its most extreme form, international war, is only a symptom or dimension of the hierarchy, the domination that distorts all social relationships. Woolf called it fascism but extended this concept to include domestic tyranny at one extreme and imperialism at the other. And the situation of women is both the most accurate indicator of fascism and violence and the source for remedies. These are not arguments about war as such. In *Three Guineas*, Hitler and Mussolini represented the extreme of that sexism and hierarchy that Woolf thought was characteristic of men's civilization. For her, the evils of the modern day were direct results of the prevalent structures of power, with patriarchy central in both private and public life.

The arguments expressed in *Three Guineas*, and a continual accumulation of supporting material, can be found in Woolf's feminist writings from the very earliest date, and we now turn to those.

5 Other Feminist Publications by Virginia Woolf

Three Guineas is the fullest statement of Virginia Woolf's conviction that fascism in the public world was no less—and no more—than a dimension of patriarchy in the private one. In 1938, experience and context combined to made possible an explicit analysis of the interlocked systems of dominance rooted in sexism. However, Woolf also published a number of other nonfiction feminist texts, identifiable as such by their locations or their topics. All are concerned with related themes that link women's autonomy and values to a transformation of society and, in the process, to the achievement of a peaceful world. They foreshadow (and, in one case, echo) *Three Guineas*. In these texts, we can trace the emerging contours of Virginia Woolf's feminism.

I

I do not want to exaggerate how much identifiably feminist material Virginia Woolf wrote or published outside her major works of fiction, or how large it looms among her writing. This is a writer who completed eight substantial novels. Her nonfiction works include a full-length biography as well as hundreds of essays and reviews, without counting hybrid texts such as *Flush*, *Orlando*, and *Three Guineas*. Yet Woolf's feminist publications are not insignificant, given the short period within which they appeared in print. We tend to forget how little time separated the two so-called world wars—just over twenty years. During that period, Virginia Woolf published several public letters and essays that, whether or not they appeared in feminist publications, were explicitly feminist in theme and topics. So too was an important piece published in 1921. In 1926 and 1934 she published short but interesting sketches in feminist locations. Most important, in 1929, 1930, 1931, and 1938 she published different versions of three substantial items that would be recognized and valued by the revived feminism of the next postwar period. In 1940, finally, she published an essay looking forward to peace—and a nonsexist world.

In this chapter, I restrict my attention to work completed and published in the author's lifetime, without consideration of material Woolf was working on at the time of her death in 1941. Conspicuously absent, therefore, is the essay "Professions for Women," which I have already discussed in an earlier chapter in relation to the evolution of *Three Guineas* itself. Here, by contrast, we turn to a different lineage of the book in specifically feminist writing.

The locales of Woolf's feminist writing differed substantially. She published in only one of the many suffragette or suffragist journals, the *Woman's Leader*. Originally published by the National Union of Women's Suffrage Societies as the *Common Cause*, the journal was produced from 1920 by the London and National Society for Women's Service under its new name.[1] In the early 1920s, four signed items by Woolf appeared in this publication.[2] Two other feminist publications successfully solicited contributions from Woolf: in 1926, *Atalanta's Garland*, a fund-raising volume for the Edinburgh University Women's Union and in 1934 *Lysistrata*, the student journal of Somerville, one of the two women's college at Oxford. And that is the limit of feminist pieces in clearly feminist locations. Although Woolf published in *Vogue*, which at a stretch has feminist relevance, and *Time and Tide*, an explicitly feminist and activist journal founded and edited by ex-suffragette Lady Rhondda, nothing that Woolf wrote specifically for these periodicals has any feminist interest. That is, nothing that Woolf wrote for these journals can be thought of as feminist in topic, nor do they in any other way resemble *Three Guineas*.

Virginia Woolf's earliest feminist publication in a nonfeminist location is a 1920 exchange of public letters with Desmond MacCarthy in the *New Statesman* about "The Intellectual Status of Women"; this includes two letters by Woolf. I stress that this was an exchange, for the public letters that responded to Woolf (including a letter to the *Woman's Leader* complaining about her first article there) express criticisms that were to be made of *Three Guineas*, while Woolf's own public responses to these critics are also illuminating. Next, chronologically, comes the sketch "A Society," published by Hogarth Press as part of Virginia Woolf's early collection of short pieces, *Monday or Tuesday* (1921); it importantly anticipates both content and style of *Three Guineas* a decade before the lecture in 1931. The essay "Women and Fiction," published in the *Forum* in March 1929, presents a first written version of the 1928 lectures that became *A Room of One's Own* later that year. Then comes the "Memories of a Working Women's Guild," the first, 1930 *Yale Review* version of the "Introductory Letter" to *Life as We Have Known It*, which in turn was in press in 1931 when Woolf spoke about the professional life of women before the Junior Council of the London and National Society for Women's Service. *Three Guineas* itself followed seven years later, in very similar hardbound first editions in England and the United States, along with a severely compressed, somewhat altered serial version in two installments (in the *Atlantic Monthly*). Finally, in October 1940, an essay titled "Thoughts on Peace in an Air Raid" appeared in the *New Republic*.

A Room of One's Own, the "Introductory Letter" to *Life as We Have Known It*, and the English version of *Three Guineas* were all published by Hogarth Press, which was founded, owned, and controlled by Virginia and Leonard Woolf. The press was a congenial environment for women's and feminist writing, publishing a substantial number of such items, some of them solicited.[3] It also published all of Woolf's books except for her first two novels. These facts do not make the Hogarth Press a feminist site of publication, for it never had any particular emphasis on feminist or women's books, nor were any among its various series dedicated to such causes. Perhaps it is best described as feminist-friendly.

The publications discussed in this chapter focus on women and the situation of women. Although mostly insignificant in themselves, they nevertheless provide the outlines of a position that can be seen fully developed in *Three Guineas*.

II

Virginia Woolf's feminist publications in the 1920s remind us of her Bloomsbury connections. Ray Strachey, sister-in-law of the more famous Lytton, was editor of the *Woman's Leader* from 1920 to 1930; is it possible that her suffragist chronicle, *The Cause*, echoes the earlier title of the journal? It was Desmond MacCarthy, a central member of the Bloomsbury Group and a close friend of the Woolfs, who in his capacity as literary editor of the *New Statesman* set off an exchange of letters there about women's achievements and potential. Both Strachey and MacCarthy appear in Woolf's only surviving comment on her first publication in the *Woman's Leader*, an article ostensibly about the trade in ornamental feathers: "Now for oh Reviewing!—Three weeks I think have passed without a word added to [*Jacob's Room*]. . . . Yet its all my fault—why should I do the Cherry Orchard & Tolstoy for Desmond, why take up the Plumage Bill for Ray?" (*D2* 53).

At this time Woolf was doing a good many reviews for the *New Statesman*.[4] Her friendly, close relationship with MacCarthy is suggested by her agreement, however much regretted, to take on reviewing when deep in a novel. But her public disagreement with him is not surprising. "Progressive" men, even close friends, are often noted by Virginia Woolf as voicing or demonstrating an unconscious sense of self-importance and superiority to women. It is about a visit from MacCarthy himself that she comments in her diary in 1925:

> The egotism of men surprises & shocks me even now. Is there a woman of my acquaintance who could sit in my arm chair from 3 to 6:30 without the semblance of a suspicion that I may be busy, or tired, or bored; & so sitting could talk, grumbling & grudging of his difficulties, worries; then eat chocolates, then read a book, & go at last, apparently self-complacent & wrapped in a sort of blubber of misty self satisfaction?

"Not the girls at Newnham or Girton," she concludes. "They are far too spry; far too self-disciplined. None of that self-confidence is their lot" (*D3* 204).

There is both affection and irritation here; her closest friends, successful products of the existing social systems, were also on occasion examples of just how chauvinist the systems were. Sexism was, for her, not personal but structural. In 1922, reflecting on a "general account of my friends," she noted that MacCarthy had become relatively distant: "I blame myself a little for writing sharply in the N[ew] S[tatesman] (but I was right) about women" (*D2* 157).[5]

Before examining the dispute that temporarily distanced MacCarthy, let us look at "The Plumage Bill," which preceded it in July 1920. This short article is a comment on an earlier column in the *Nation* by H. W. Massingham, its editor, writing under his customary pseudonym "Wayfarer." Using material from the article she is criticizing, Woolf evokes graphically the brutalities of egret hunting, which involve torture of decoy birds, murder of others, and the death by starvation of the abandoned nestlings. However, it is not the plumage trade that she is angry about, but the way in which Wayfarer blamed the continuation of that trade, as well as the failure of the Plumage Bill that would have stopped it, on "child-bearing women" who wear exotic feathers in their hair and hats. In reply,

Woolf points out that it is men who hunt and sell plumage, and men also who have failed, as members of Parliament, to support the Plumage Bill. She concludes:

> So far as I know, the above, though much embittered by sex antago-
> nism, is a perfectly true statement. But the interesting point is that . . . I
> have said more about [Wayfarer's] injustice to women than about the
> sufferings of birds. Can it be that it is a graver sin to be unjust to women
> than to torture birds?[6]

It is an analysis that puts women and their wrongs center stage. Woolf's argument is that if women contribute to the sufferings of birds, it is not because of hard-heartedness or a taste for luxury, but ignorance and dependency. In 1920 she does not comment on why the "disinterested" members of Parliament do not make the effort even to go to committee meetings about the Plumage Bill; later she will realize that they too are the products of their education and of the social and political system they inhabit. But she sees already that what we now call sexism or heterosexism is responsible for a good many unpleasant by-products and that it is wrong to blame for it the women who may be its agents but are more often its victims. The purchaser of ornamental feathers is not admirable—but she is not nearly as bad as the hunter and the seller. Later, *Three Guineas* will outline the whole system, the one that produces dead birds and also dead children.

Woolf's Plumage Bill article provoked a response from Massingham in which he accuses her of sectarianism because she has put the interests of women before those of ending the slaughter, and he adds that she is reading morals into facts when she should be concerned instead with "truth." Such comments are very close to criticisms later to be made of *Three Guineas*, when it is read as an incompetent analysis not of the situation of women but of war. There is the same disagreement about what are to be considered facts or, more to the point, relevant facts. Because she discusses women as a group and as a topic, Woolf is accused of interfering with acceptance of standard gender-free solutions to the problems of, in the one case, the trade in exotic plumage and, in the other, fascism and militarism.

Woolf replies, to explain that she had been writing, not about the plumage trade (of which she entirely disapproves), but about the view of women expressed in Wayfarer's article. Annoyingly no doubt, she continues the whimsy that irritated Massingham: "I am not writing as a bird, or even a champion of birds; but as a woman." She makes her priorities clear: "it seems to me more necessary to resent such an insult to women as Wayfarer casually lets fall than to protect egrets from extinction." She had contributed to Massingham's anger by starting her article with the ironic proposal to break a long-standing objection to exotic plumage by buying an egret feather; she now promises instead to give any fee she receives for the article to the Plumage Bill group.[7] Irony, comedy, and exaggeration have, as they will so often in the future, both leavened her prose and confused, then angered a "progressive" audience. And, as years later in *Three Guineas*, she offers to put some of her much-valued income where her mouth is, as a donation to a male-dominated but nevertheless worthy cause.

Not long after, on 2 October 1920, Desmond MacCarthy, in his regular literary column, signed "Affable Hawk," provoked Woolf's second angry feminist outbreak of the year. MacCarthy had endorsed the views about women expressed in *Our Women*, a slight publication by the highly successful realistic novelist Arnold Bennett. When she read Affable Hawk's column, Woolf had already recorded in her diary her annoyance about press reports of Bennett's short, unmemorable book (*D2* 69).[8] Reviewing the book, Affable Hawk agreed with Bennett that "no amount of education and liberty of action will sensibly alter" the fact that women are inferior to men in intellectual power.

Woolf's letter of response, printed with a riposte from MacCarthy, begins by saying that she has not read Bennett—but what do he and MacCarthy mean by saying that it stares them in the face that women are inferior and not improving: surely every modern century has produced more remarkable women than the previous one. "Pessimism about the other sex is always delightful and invigorating," but "though women have every reason to hope that the intellect of the male sex is steadily diminishing, it would be unwise, until they have more evidence than the great war and the great peace supply, to announce it as a fact." That is, war and peace alike are men's work, and work badly done. If you are looking for a great "poetess," what about Sappho, well thought of in her day, and "I have often been told that Sappho was a woman." Affable Hawk wasn't persuaded: many men have overcome unfavorable conditions, and even in the easier arts women have not reached the top level. "In spite of education, in pursuits requiring pure intellect, they have not rivalled men." He is willing to concede that a very few women are as clever as clever men, but he insists that "they fall short of the few men who are best of all."

Next issue: Virginia Woolf strikes back. Sappho, she notes, whom Affable Hawk has dismissed as perhaps a pretty good regional poet whom we know only from fragments, is praised by those contemporaries who knew all her works. More importantly, putting geniuses to one side, Woolf asks why there were no mediocre women poets or novelists until the eighteenth century. "To account for the complete lack not only of good women writers but also of bad women writers I can conceive no reason unless it be that there was some external restraint upon their powers." This is a forerunner of arguments that will be presented *A Room of One's Own*. *Three Guineas'* style and argument appear in a citation of J. A. Symonds about the status of women in Lesbos and the education and freedom available to women in classical Greece. For *Three Guineas*, Woolf was to document the difficulties that women such as her musician friend Ethel Smyth had in getting a proper education; here there is room only for quick references to Smyth, along with provocative questions and assertions. Arthur's Education Fund, later to loom so large as diverting family resources from women's education, appears, still unnamed: painting is now within women's reach "if that is to say that there is sufficient money after the sons have been educated to permit of paints and studios for the daughters and no family reason requiring their presence at home." Women, she concludes, "have brought forth the entire population of the universe. This occupation has taken much time and strength. It has also brought them into subjection to men, and incidentally—if that were to the point—bred in them some of the most lovable and admirable qualities of the race." Women need more than simply education; they need "liberty of experience," a central topic of *A Room of One's Own*, where Woolf will examine the material conditions for such possibilities. Importantly, she insists, "I do not agree with 'Affable Hawk' that men and women are alike."

Woolf's second letter concludes with the comment that opinions such as Bennett's and MacCarthy's make it more likely that "we shall remain in a condition of half-civilised barbarism . . . an eternity of dominion on the one hand and of servility on the other. For the degradation of being a slave is only equalled by the degradation of being a master." MacCarthy, who can hardly have liked being told that he was a barbarian and a slave-master, in effect threw up his hands with the response, "If the freedom and education of women is impeded by the expression of my views, I shall argue no more."[9] We should note, however, that women were also described by Woolf as barbarians, and as slaves, even if their subjection was given credit for reproduction and for various, unspecified loveable and admirable qualities. "Thoughts on Peace in an Air Raid" was to reprise the theme of the mutual and continuing degradation of both of the sexes under conditions of male domination.

If Woolf had actually read *Our Women*, she would surely have been even angrier, for, like its title, the book has a fatuous, patronizing tone of superiority only feebly represented by excerpts provided by Affable Hawk. Yet, interestingly enough, Bennett, once past his insistence on intellectual and creative superiority, makes a number of points that Woolf would have accepted: that the domestic mission reserved for women is both important and generative of significant skills and values, that men and women are different yet equally entitled to opportunity in public and creative life, that economic independence is the main motive and main result of women's movement into the paid labor force, and that (heterosexual) love will improve when women are no longer dependent on men's approval for the occupation called marriage and, more generally, a role in life. Perhaps Woolf would also have shared our amusement at Bennett's sententious pronouncement that "one may be enthusiastic for Jane Austen without putting *Pride and Prejudice* in the same category with *Anna Karenina* or [Hardy's] *The Woodlanders*."[10]

Two other sets of public letters relating to the theme of privacy of public figures look as if they might have some connection with *Three Guineas*, for they indicate clearly Woolf's abhorrence of any sort of personal promotion or advertisement by artists. Unlike even the 1920 quarrel with Desmond MacCarthy, however, these are straightforward statements addressed to an undifferentiated literate public by Virginia Woolf as a novelist and essayist; there is no semi-fictionalized, ironically distanced narrator. These letters are thus very different from the imaginary letters of *Three Guineas* and also from the letters in which Woolf defended recognizably feminist positions. This is the more remarkable in that privacy and anonymity are among the concerns of *Three Guineas*. There, egotism and co-option are seen as characteristics of the male-dominated hierarchies of public life, and to be avoided particularly by women seeking to change the system. By contrast, two sets of public letters by the real Virginia Woolf seem to express little more than irritation and alienation. Letters exchanged in the *Nation and Athenaeum* with the society artist and photographer Cecil Beaton in 1930 do seem to be related to Woolf's general commitment to anonymity and refusal of honors. In this case, she was angry that Beaton had included drawings of her in a *Book of Beauty* without her permission.[11] But though the nature of Beaton's project might well have provoked feminist responses with its objectification of public figures who were women, it did not. In 1926 Woolf and Roger Fry had correctly identified "famous men and fair women" as the subjects of her photographer aunt Julia Margaret Cameron. In her correspondence with Beaton, Woolf was not responding to the different roles assigned to men and women, but writing, indignantly, as one of the famous men, now treated like a beautiful woman.[12]

A more substantial October 1933 letter to the editor of the *New Statesman* may perhaps be related to *Three Guineas*, which Woolf was "making up" at the time. But for all that it can hardly be seen as feminist. The letter's topic is again artists' collusion with or encouragement of publicity. The last paragraph proposes a Society for the Protection of Privacy, whose members' pledge does resemble what will later be asked of the members of the Outsiders' Society: not to allow pictorial representations of themselves, to give no interviews or autographs, not to attend public dinners or appear at public events, or to see unknown admirers. This early society is not restricted to women members, however, and it is conventional in nature. It would have funds, an office, and a badge, and its members would swear an oath—formalities *Three Guineas* will explicitly abjure. The letter concludes with the offer to subscribe "not less than five guineas annually" to the society (*L5* 237–38). This odd letter may reflect Woolf's unease with her growing fame; it seems to be seeking to justify what may have seemed curmudgeonly about her attitude toward public attention, as when she refused to allow her portrait to be painted for the National Portrait Gallery (*L5* 277).[13] But for all its foreshadowing of some aspects of *Three Guineas*, the piece lacks any focus on women or attention to sexism.

III

The remaining publications in the *Woman's Leader*, none of them as important in themselves as the writing already examined, all show some features later to be found in *Three Guineas*. Woolf's February 1921 review of *Art and Design*, by her friend Roger Fry, is straightforward and very favorable, as might be expected. It includes an example of Virginia Woolf pleading ignorance (of art, this time), and some typical whimsicality, in this case about eyes described as "oval balls of jelly-like matter."[14] These are common stylistic stances for her, and in *Three Guineas* they charm some readers and annoy many others. But here she does not make any argument that women or those who are formally unlearned have particular claims to perceptiveness.

The final *Woman's Leader* sketch, "A Letter to a Lady in Paraguay," published in July 1922, is more interesting both for its form and for its mixture of fact and fiction.[15] The article is presented as the reply to another letter, which is described and apparently cited—a strategy that Woolf will use again. In this case the addressee is presented in more detail than, for example, the recipients of the three guineas. The "lady" has written about the heat and that she sits upon "seven and sixty committees." And she has complained " 'that there are no books to read. The ants destroy them. . . . somehow one can't read a pocket Shakespeare in one's bed-room.' " These last phrases are supplied in quotes by Woolf and used as a take-off point for the article. The writer of the response that is the article is also described, and she sounds more like Virginia Woolf than even the narrator of the "Introductory Letter" for *Life as We Have Known It*. She will talk about books she is reading herself while she suffers in gray, cold London from an attack of flu: "Mrs Barclay and Boswell and Princess Bibesco."[16] But though Woolf did indeed in 1922 have a bout of flu, complicated by heart murmurs, lasting from January into March, the narrator of the piece is not quite Virginia Woolf. There is no trace in Woolf's diary or published letters up to 1922 of any Latin American correspondent, and she could not have read then all the books she refers to in the essay.[17]

Nor is the essay exactly as outlined at the start. Boswell is barely mentioned—was he included simply for alliteration? There is only one paragraph about stories by Princess Elizabeth Bibesco, Prime Minister Asquith's daughter. Woolf does not seem to have much liked what she read, not to mention their author; as we have noted, an acid exchange with Bibesco about fascism and its treatment of women was to occur thirteen years later. The main part of this "Letter" is a discussion of the prolific, best-selling novelist, Florence Louise Barclay (1862–1921), the author of the immensely popular novel *The Oracle*. In 1922, Virginia Woolf is already addicted to biographies or memoirs of the Victorians and, more specifically, to the lives of those who will not appear in the *Dictionary of National Biography*. In a comic description of this biography, she is accurate enough in detail if not in tone. She also goes into one of her familiar flights of fantasy apropos Barclay's many successful books: they are like purple pumpkins that multiply prodigiously and soon rot, after having been inedible (Barclay's signature color was purple).

Woolf is not, at this point, sympathetic to the economic situation of the woman writer supporting herself or a family. She had mentioned Barclay along with Marie Corelli, in her dispute with Affable Hawk, as part of the argument that because second-rate women novelists now flourish, their absence in earlier centuries must be the result of the constraints on women in those times. In this "Letter," Barclay is grouped not just with Corelli, Ethel M. Dell, and Ella Wheeler Wilcox but also with the popular second-rate male novelists Charles Garvice and Hall Caine.[18] In *Three Guineas*, women writers are considered as a category in themselves, not grouped or compared with men.

IV

So far, these are slight items, each only a few pages long. "A Society" is more substantial and points far more directly and clearly to *Three Guineas*. The irritation with Bennett that fueled Woolf's earlier dispute with Affable Hawk may, it seems, also have helped to generate "A Society," and certainly we can see in this fantasy the reappearance of themes present in "The Intellectual Status of Women."[19] By Virginia Woolf's own wish the sketch was not reprinted in her lifetime.[20] Could this be because so much of its content was to reappear elsewhere, particularly in *Three Guineas*? Did it strike its author as too youthful, too jokey? Or was she perhaps uncomfortable with the attention given in "A Society" to women's reproductive role? Children appear in *A Room of One's Own*, the "Introductory Letter," and *Three Guineas* mainly as burdens, the source of responsibilities that interfere with women's potential freedom and creativity (though they are also a social good that society ought to subsidize). In "A Society," by contrast, a girl child represents the hope for the future for an insouciant single mother and her female friends.

The story looks like a very preliminary version of *Three Guineas*. Central is the notion of the "society" itself, most likely a mocking spin-off from the Cambridge Apostles Society to whom so many male members of the Bloomsbury Group belonged (can we speculate here at another motive for avoiding reprinting?). In the context of Woolf's feminism, this informal association of young women can also be seen as the forerunner of the Outsiders' Society so important in *Three Guineas*. Its members decide that "before we bring another child into the world we must swear that we will find out what the world is like." They examine the senior professions and the academy and are not much impressed. The results of their research include a farcical version of the armed services' responses to any threat to their "honour," as well as a verdict that judges show "no signs of humanity," and hysteria in response to pictures on display at the Royal Academy. A member's investigation of Oxbridge generates for the group some ribald speculation about research on Sappho (again) and revulsion at the dreariness of the professors. For the young woman who visited the universities, it also produces a daughter named Ann, courtesy of someone who is described as "only twenty-one and divinely beautiful." This paragon is presumably not a professor; professors had reminded Ann's mother of the cactuses kept by an aunt in Dulwich: "dozens of them, ugly, squat, bristly." Among the repulsive succulents in pots is an aloe that blooms only once in a hundred years.[21] The aloe will reappear in *A Room of One's Own* to represent how long it would take to read all the books men write about women; in the later book, professors will be caricatured as giant crustaceans moving with difficulty on the floor of an aquarium.[22] Studying the universities also sets off two pages of uproar in the society about chastity.

Apart from the baby, this material will be found in *Three Guineas*, as will a continuation of the young women's half-amused, half-appalled discussion of men's use of the regalia of power. In addition, prefiguring Woolf's research for *Three Guineas*, the members of the society study "a vast tangle of statistics," including the "percentage of women [who] die from maladies incident to childbirth" (an example used in *Three Guineas*). They also discuss the British colonial empire and "our rule in India, Africa and Ireland." War, which they do not examine in detail, is nevertheless central to their experience, for their deliberations are disturbed by the outbreak of war in 1914 and then by celebrations of the peace treaty. Why, they ask, "do men go to war?" The answer to what will be a central question for *Three Guineas* is at this point merely, "Sometimes for one reason, sometimes for another."[23]

"A Society" concludes with the thought that there is only one thing to teach a little girl: to believe in herself. *A Room of One's Own* will observe how difficult life is for both sexes, an "arduous, difficult, a perpetual struggle" that most of all requires "confidence in oneself."[24] Here, the problems are handed over to the next generation of women. Happily playing with her doll, Ann is told that she is to be "President of the Society of the future," and she starts to cry. The last words of the story are "poor little girl."[25] The weeping woman of the serialization of *Three Guineas*, whom that book urges women not to emulate, is still an infant in "A Society"— with perhaps a chance of growing up different and stronger.

In 1928 the young women of Girton's ODTAA society referred to "A Society" in a letter inviting Virginia Woolf to give the lecture that became one of the sources of *A Room of One's Own*; she replied that she certainly hoped their society would be better than hers.[26] By the time she came to write *Three Guineas*, she no longer believed in officers or meetings. But she recommended to women, both young and old, the same purposes and values as those that animated Ann's mother and foster mothers.

v

Continuing in chronological sequence, we have next the sketch "A Women's College from the Outside," which was drafted as a chapter in *Jacob's Room* but instead revised and published in November 1926 for the Edinburgh University Women's Union.[27] The Women's Union, then celebrating its twenty-first anniversary, had successfully appealed to a wide range of literary figures in England and on the Continent to donate writing and pictures for a publication "to aid the fund for [the Union's] extension and endowment."[28] Women were not segregated in their own colleges at Edinburgh, where, as the editors of the volume note, they were admitted to the Faculty of Arts in 1892 and were matriculating by 1905; Woolf was to write at length in *Three Guineas* about the struggles of Sophia Jex-Blake and her associates as medical students at Edinburgh beginning in 1869. A building project for what seems to have been a sort of early Women's Place would have appealed to Woolf and foreshadows the significant role she was to allocate to a fund supporting a women's college in the more hostile environment of Oxbridge.

Set at Newnham College, here not disguised or combined with Girton as in *A Room of One's Own*, this brief, dreamy, atmospheric piece presents a blissful image of life at the new women's colleges at Oxbridge: the girls all together in beautiful surroundings, playing cards and laughing. Woolf romanticizes the setting as "a place of seclusion or discipline, where the bowl of milk stands cool and pure and there's a great washing of linen." *Three Guineas* recounts with angry emphasis the way in which Bishop Burnet had blocked Mary Astell's desire to found a college for women; this description of Newnham, however inaccurate, sounds very like the Protestant nunnery the bishop feared a women's college might be. *A Room of One's Own* will be more critical of the lack of amenities at "Fernham."

This sketch epitomizes Woolf's admiration of the women's colleges, as well as her understanding of the economic reasons that brought the students there and later led to their campaigns for full degree certification. A woman student—Angela—had come to Newnham for the purpose of "earning her living," a central phrase and concept in *Three Guineas*. She is supported by "the cheques of her father" at Swansea; her (uneducated?) "mother washing in the scullery." But Angela herself is hopeful of better; she cannot sleep for thinking of "this good world, this new world, this world at the end of the tunnel."[29] There is mockery in the story, but there also seems to be yearning on the part of the woman who resented her own failure to attend university. The spectator from the outside, however, has a neutral voice, without any fictional persona or even gender. The narrator of *Three Guineas* will also examine the women's colleges from the outside, but she will make a larger argument about how all women remain outsiders in the academic world.

Three years later, returning to the women's colleges, Virginia Woolf was to publish in *A Room of One's Own* an explicit statement of her feminist views. It comprises, with the "Introductory Letter" to *Life as We Have Known It*, the bridge to *Three Guineas*.

VI

There is a misleading resemblance between the origins of Woolf's two "little" feminist books. *A Room of One's Own* also started in spoken form, based not on one lecture but on two that Woolf gave in 1928, going at a week's interval to talk at each of Cambridge's women's colleges. As in the case of the book that started as a lecture to the Junior Council of the London and National Society for Women's Service, the origins of *A Room of One's Own* remind us that Woolf changes and fictionalizes what she presents so disingenuously in written form. "'I' is only a convenient term for somebody who has no real being," she writes in *A Room of One's Own*, after insisting that "Oxbridge is an invention; so is Fernham."[30] Unlike *Three Guineas*, *A Room of One's Own* retains the form of a lecture. But it is no more a lecture than *Three Guineas* is a series of real letters. At 172 pages (the first edition), this "lecture" would have taken some eight hours to read aloud. In addition, the two lectures from which it grew took place under very different conditions and can be assumed to have been correspondingly different themselves. Most importantly, Woolf's actual experiences in presenting the lectures, transmuted, became part of the framing of her ideas in the book that grew out of them. All the same, those ideas, judging by their printed versions, seem to have been entirely consistent with earlier and later feminist presentations.

We do not have any text that even looks as if it corresponds to what Woolf said to the two groups of women undergraduates in October 1928, nothing like the two early drafts that may mislead us into thinking that we know exactly what Virginia Woolf said to an audience of professional women in January 1931. The nearest we have to the Cambridge lectures is a brief article titled "Women and Fiction" that Woolf published in the

Forum in March 1929. In the context of Woolf's feminism, rather than the literary context in which it is more likely to be discussed, this article is interesting for a distinction between two sorts of writers, the "butterfly" or creative artist and the writer who is a "gadfly to the state." The latter is a reformer whose "novels will deal with social evils and remedies."[31] Such fiction has been "a male prerogative" but will in the future be produced also by women. *The Years* may perhaps be seen as such a reformer's novel. Or perhaps not, for Woolf makes it clear that she prefers the artist, the butterfly. One implication might be that gadfly activities belong more properly in nonfiction.

Certainly laws and customs related to the status of women must continue to improve, and "material things" are crucial. The essay ends with the demand for women to have "leisure, and money, and a room to themselves." Here is the first appearance of the famous "five hundred a year and a room of one's own." In general, however, the message seems to be that, although social and political campaigns and topics are important, they are merely instrumental in value. That will also be the case in *A Room of One's Own*, for which this article is a very limited sketch. Progress for creative women writers will mean greater impersonality, greater ability to move beyond the details of life and "personal and political relationships." Then they will be able to look at wider questions and generate, not the feminist or activist stance we might expect, but "the poetic attitude." This is an argument that is not about daily life as such but instead about how it must change for the purposes of women's creativity.[32]

Previous themes reappear, as they will in later writings: the suppression of women's literary activity (although there is no mention here of the absence until recent times of the mediocre woman writer), the incompatibility of domesticity and especially children with literary greatness, the "necessarily narrow range" of women's experience, the detrimental impact on women of men's denigration of their work. But there is no personal or seemingly personal experience presented, no fictionalization, no charm to speak of. The contrast between men's and women's colleges is absent, along with other important aspects of *A Room of One's Own* such as the concept of androgyny, the cautionary tale of Shakespeare's imaginary sister, and the hints at lesbianism.

Which brings us to *A Room of One's Own* itself. Repeatedly reprinted and translated, and widely influential, the book has had extensive commentary already. Most discussions are favorable, and most focus on Woolf's analysis of creativity and especially of the elusive concept of androgyny. It is worth noting, now that the book has been so happily assimilated into the mainstream, that Woolf herself expected reactions to it much like what she later predicted, more accurately, for *Three Guineas:*

> [I suspect] that there is a shrill feminine tone in it which my intimate friends will dislike. I forecast, then, that I shall get no criticism, except of the evasive, jocular kind, from Lytton [Strachey], Roger [Fry] & Morgan [Forster]; that the press will be kind & talk of its charm, & sprightliness.

"Also I shall be attacked for a feminist & hinted at for a sapphist," she thought (*D3* 262). In fact, *A Room of One's Own* was a critical success and also a popular one, selling ten thousand copies within four months.

Virginia Woolf's letters to MacCarthy in 1920 had already sketched out how difficult it is for women to acquire a full professional education and lead a productive, creative life. In *A Room of One's Own* she quotes him again, anonymously, as a 1928 example of a condescending, discouraging male critic.[33] Focusing on the nature of women's creativity, she now gives fuller consideration to the need for a community and predecessors, the improvements in women's achievement over the centuries, and the tradition of ridiculing and belittling women's abilities, as well as a discussion of the nature of "real" education, which includes freedom to experience life and the world as widely as possible. Women's education even in the women's colleges is seen as inferior in resources to what is available for men students, but in *A Room of One's Own* Woolf does not include *Three Guineas'* critique of all existing systems of education and professional training.

In *A Room of One's Own*, the material dimensions of independence are spelled out: the "room of one's own" is a symbol of privacy and of income at a level that *Three Guineas* will show to be rarely attainable by self-supporting women. "My room is secure," Woolf wrote in her diary in December 1928, when she was working at what she still referred to as "Fiction," the future *A Room of One's Own;* she was reflecting on her acquisition of her own bank account and her pleasure that it had now reached a level when she could "spend freely, without fuss or anxiety." Bourgeois though she was, and never lacking in necessities, she still understood "the perpetual limitation of everything" that came from being short of money: "no chairs, or beds, no comfort, no beauty; & no freedom to move" (*D3* 212). It is all there: the practical and the psychological impact of women's lack of economic autonomy.[34]

Finally, *A Room of One's Own* develops Woolf's conviction that women are different than men. Female and male qualities exist potentially in both men and women, and must somehow be combined in a way that preserves the value of both. To identify the result she adopts Coleridge's term *androgyny:* a writer must not be simply a man or a woman, but "woman-manly or man-womanly." However, Woolf's particular version of androgyny is one that focuses on bringing to bear on men's minds the "womanly" part that has not had impact until now. For women, what is needed is not really a manly mind or mind-segment. What their writing lacks is freedom and experience along with detachment from their grievances against men—something that will be easier when they are less deprived and dominated. Men's literature in turn will presumably improve as it becomes less strongly influenced by egotism and gonads, and by the anger they currently feel about women's assertion of equality. Woolf also argues, however inconsistently, that women's own developing literary tradition will remain distinct and ought to produce a new sort of novel, written differently and based on everyday experience. The concept of androgyny is not to be found in *Three Guineas*, which instead concentrates on raising women's awareness of their specific wrongs and achievements. The later book shares, however, the other expectation of *A Room of One's Own:* that women, once liberated from social, economic, and psychological constraints, will be able to generate new forms of art and of life.

In spite of Woolf's anticipatory anxieties, a charming and lucid persuasiveness endears *A Room of One's Own* even to those readers who might have trouble with some of its practical implications. There are no facts or figures, no sarcastic endnotes or photographs that might disturb the male reader. In *A Room of One's Own*, the indictment of Oxbridge is less hard-hitting than in *Three Guineas*, which includes much of its predecessor's description of women's education. In *A Room of One's Own*, the indictment is more seductive, as it takes the form of fables, including a comically gruesome dinner of boiled beef and greens at an Oxbridge women's college, contrasted with an impossibly sumptuous repast at a place that sounds like King's College. And the ordeal of the creative woman becomes a new myth about "Judith Shakespeare," who ran away to London to become a poet but killed herself when she became pregnant; even if she had shared her brother's genius she would not have been able to share his achievements and success. Some, though not all, of the colorful details in *A Room of One's Own* will reappear in *Three Guineas*, such as the "tufts of fur" on shoulders (in this case, of professors) that indicate worldly status.[35]

In *A Room of One's Own*, women do not seem likely to do anything about their own subjugation; the women's movement is only briefly referred to, and there is no sign of the more diffuse covert resistance that Woolf is later to praise. Activism is marginal to the argument, discussed only as a source of sex antagonism and, for women, of self-consciousness and bitterness that could interfere with creativity. Nor does this earlier book discuss other forms of domination than sexism. In *Three Guineas*, consideration of the relationship between women and men will generate a larger condemnation of all forms of domination, including that based on race, religion, or national or imperial power. Women's activism becomes the instrument of enormous change, as women apply their own experiences to the removal of all forms of domination. In *A Room of One's Own*, the focus is narrower: the issues surrounding women's literary creativity and the related practical and psychological constraints.

Quentin Bell was one of many to interpret Woolf's best-known feminist work as relating entirely to private life. In his *Bloomsbury*, first published in 1968 and reissued after the success of his biography of his aunt, he singled out *A Room of One's Own*, along with *Orlando*, as representative of Virginia Woolf's "solution of human affairs." It would, he suggested, be based on "androgynous affection." Here he overlooked the conclusion to *A Room of One's Own*, which has a young man and a young woman meeting and going off together in a cab. Furthermore, in *Bloomsbury* as elsewhere, his final reflection was dismissive of any relevance of Woolf's feminism to the larger world: "Needless to say these meditations upon aggression and affection had no effect on the world of practical politics. That world was soon to be left to the management of Mussolini, his pupils and his opposite numbers."[36]

And yet, and yet—as the narrator of *A Room of One's Own* returns to the hotel where she is staying on her visit to Oxbridge, she reflects on "how unpleasant it is to be locked out," as she was when she attempted to visit a college library, and "how it is worse perhaps to be locked in." She is thinking, she says, "of the safety and prosperity of the one sex and of the poverty and insecurity of the other."[37] The argument could be expanded to include all forms of creativity and, eventually, all dimensions of life. As it will be in *Three Guineas*, where the narrator perhaps has in mind silencing as well as imprisonment, when she refers to women of an earlier generation who were "shut out" and "shut up" (*3G* 94).

VII

Virginia Woolf on occasion described *Three Guineas* as the sequel to *A Room of One's Own*. Between the two books, however, came Woolf's "Introductory Letter" to *Life as We Have Known It*, written in 1930 at Margaret Llewelyn Davies' request to accompany a collection of memoirs by members of the Women's Co-operative Guild. Twenty-four pages long, this relatively unknown literary letter by Virginia Woolf is importantly related to *Three Guineas*. Thanks to Woolf's letters and diary entries, we have information about the preparation of the text of the "Introductory Letter" that is missing for, in the most conspicuous example, the serial version of *Three Guineas*. We know that it was in May 1930 that Virginia Woolf received from Davies a bundle of letters from guildswomen and that she completed her first version of the text that summer, with some consultation with Davies (*L4* 65; *D3* 306). The "Introductory Letter" was then first published in the *Yale Review* in September 1930 with the title "Memories of a Working Women's Guild." An apologetic letter to Davies explains that Woolf has sent a version of the introduction to the *Yale Review*, to which she had promised an article; she defends herself with what would also be her own basic criticism of the piece: "It would be read as literature simply" (*L4* 191). The process of completing the piece, first affected by this preliminary American publication, was then complicated by consultation with the Women' Co-operative Guild. As a result, the second, final published version is not identical with the first one, though many people assume it is; Leonard Woolf compounded the confusion by selecting the *Yale Review* version for posthumous reprinting.

In both versions, in conspicuous contrast to *A Room of One's Own*, this essay focuses on a segment of the women's movement, the very real Women's Co-operative Guild. It identifies and centers on an account of the national meeting of the guild that both Leonard and Virginia Woolf attended in 1913. In it, Woolf reports some of the proceedings and, more importantly, what she says she felt at the time (she is writing almost twenty years later). In other ways, also, the piece is closer to the autobiographical than *Three Guineas*, though it is never safe to assume that the narrative "I" is Virginia Woolf herself. The final, Hogarth Press version states explicitly that this "Introductory Letter" was written by Virginia Woolf to Margaret Llewelyn Davies; even in the *Yale Review*, with its masking names, there is no anonymous, semi-fictional narrator or recipient of letters such as those in *Three Guineas*.[38] However, the author's connection with the guild's general secretary was not as distant as the text implies, given that it was an old friend and not some sort of casual acquaintance who had initiated the project of writing an introduction to letters and other material by guildswomen. Furthermore, this real appeal for an introductory essay did not go to some invented daughter of an educated man, as in the case of *Three Guineas*, but specifically to the famous writer Virginia Woolf, the gatekeeper for her Hogarth Press. In addition, the resulting public letter is very different from the many private letters that Woolf exchanged with Margaret Llewelyn Davies, including ones about the project itself, and they should not be confused with them. Thus Woolf complained to Davies in a private, personal letter in 1930, while she was revising the essay for the book, that the working class, as represented by the Women's Co-operative Guild, is unimaginative: "Why, with such a chance to get rid of conventionalities, do they cling to them?" (*L4* 229). In the "Introductory Letter" itself, by contrast, she is careful not to cast such aspersions.

In the "Introductory Letter," Woolf reflects explicitly on the limits to how far middle-class sympathizers could understand the lives of members of the working class. We have money and servants, "we do not know the liver from the lights," and our sympathy is therefore fictitious, unreal, "because it is not based upon sharing the same important emotions unconsciously." The "Introductory Letter" does not resolve the problem, described there as "the somewhat contradictory and complex feelings that beset the middle-class visitor when forced to sit out a Congress of working women in silence."[39] In *Three Guineas* the solution will be spelled out: it is necessary to work inside one's own class as well as one's own gender, in both respects, in cooperation with those from the other. In the real world, Woolf had experience in working with the working-class guildswomen in the years that came between attending the 1913 Congress and writing about it. She was also hardly the novice in Co-operative matters that the "Introductory Letter" makes its author seem. But the dilemma presented by her class position was a real one for her.

The "Introductory Letter" is written in a casual and conversational tone, without even the few footnote references provided for *A Room of One's Own*, but its sources are rather more complex than appears. Leonard Woolf, who regularly attended the guild's congresses in the early years of the Woolfs' marriage, published articles about several of them, including two about the 1913 Congress. Some material about the guild seems to have been drawn by Virginia Woolf from those accounts, a well as from a history of the guild written by Margaret Llewelyn Davies.[40] In particular, she employs a phrase her husband also features in one of the articles about the 1913 Congress and was to repeat in his autobiography: "we can wait." Characteristically, Virginia Woolf attributes the words to a "Mrs. Winthrop of Spenny Moor," and in the *Yale Review* she adds, "what demand she had been making I do not know." Possibly responding to guild comments on her draft—she had, after all, rather trivialized the topic of Mrs. Winthrop's remarks—Woolf provides for the Hogarth Press version a far more evocative phrase, writing that Mrs. Winthrop spoke "as if she had waited so long that the last lap of the immense vigil meant nothing for the end was in sight."[41]

Leonard Woolf for his part attributes the phrase about waiting merely to "one of the Northern delegates," but he does identify the topic: the proposed "fusion of labour forces" that would combine the Co-operative movement, trade unionism, and the Labour Party. He also gives a longer version of the remarks: " 'We can wait,' she said, 'we can wait. We women have waited years, thousands of years, even to be able to discuss things like this. We can wait.' " "Things like this": the woman who is speaking means those elements of public life, such as leftist politics, that women were traditionally excluded from.[42]

We do not know exactly the impact of the American publication on Woolf's text. Woolf seems to have taken the initiative to move the congress to Manchester and to change the names of people associated with the guild (L4 192). At this stage, "Miss Janet Erskine," actually Davies' companion and assistant Lilian Harris, kept her real-life pipe and detective story. Later, these disguises were removed, and the congress returned to where it had actually occurred. The essay's title, "Memories of a Working Women's Guild," was suggested by the editor of the journal (L4 193); the author herself did not use that title again.[43] Editing by the *Yale Review* seems to have produced some changes, but the only identifiable one was changed again in the final "Introductory Letter," an inserted sentence commenting on a letter by "Miss Wick" about being made pregnant by her employer. In a letter to Helen McAfee of the *Yale Review*, Woolf agrees to suggested alterations and says specifically that she will rewrite slightly to emphasize for readers "the very stiff words the woman uses," which she agrees have "something rather fine in them" (L4 201). In both versions, Woolf quotes a letter that Miss Kidd, the guild's secretary, long dead, had sent when first being considered for employment by the WCG. In "Memories of a Working Women's Guild," the following sentence reads: "The stiff words, which conceal all emotion conventionally enough, are yet illuminating." In the "Introductory Letter," the comment on the letter becomes, "Whether that is literature or not literature I do not presume to say, but that it explains much and reveals much is certain."[44] We have no way of knowing if we are now back to Woolf's original sentence; both versions are pretty gnomic, though the second (original?) one is certainly more literary.

The two versions are different in more than trivial ways, and we can guess that they reflect changes made after preparation of the text for the *Yale Review*. Rewriting for successive states of publication was unremarkable for Woolf, and the use of periodical and book sources, such as those concerning the guild, was common in her writing, even before *Three Guineas*. But there was a unique additional influence on the "Introductory Letter," in the shape of the opinions of the guild itself.

The brief literary collaboration between Virginia Woolf and the leaders of the guild was not an entirely easy one. When Davies and Lilian Harris sent their responses to the first post–*Yale Review* draft, which had already reinstated the correct names and made other changes, including some of what they had earlier suggested (though "by no means all"), Woolf almost withdrew her text. Sending Davies a further revised account, struggling with (as she wrote Ethel Smyth) "circumventing those intolerable hedgings that the Cooperative movement dictates," she suggested that it might be better to hand the project over to a different writer (*L4* 205, 213).[45] Possibly in response to this veiled threat, Davies took the new text to the current general secretary of the guild, her successor, Mrs. Eleanor Barton. We do not know who else Mrs. Barton may have consulted; we do know that members of the guild apart from Davies and Harris expressed their views with some degree of vigor. In Woolf's next surviving letter on the subject, she comments that it's a shame that working women "cant be told that they weigh on an average 12 stone—which is largely because they scrub so hard and have so many children" (*L4* 228). But in respect to the guildswomen's physique, the Hogarth Press text has the same wording as the *Yale Review*, an admiring reference to "the sculpturesque quality that these working women have."[46] Had the guildswomen become more specifically weighty in an intermediary version, one wonders?

Reflecting on the changes requested by the guildswomen, Woolf wrote to Davies, "I never know what 'reality' means; but Lilian smoking a pipe to me is real, and Lilian merely coffee coloured and discreet is not nearly so real. . . . the workers seem to have taken on all the middle class respectabilities [which artists] have faced and thrown out. . . . we have to be polite, insincere, uneasy" (*L4* 228–29). In this exchange we are reminded that Woolf does indeed believe in referentiality, that she is convinced that there is a real world out there however much she may choose to alter it in her writing. But she also believes in art: although Harris becomes "coffee coloured" and loses her detective story, her pipe is replaced in proof by a cigarette because "a blue cloud of smoke seemed . . . aesthetically desirable" (*L4* 287). Working-class women would not have smoked, nor liked references to smoking; Woolf herself smoked, and in drafts for *Three Guineas*, though not in the text itself, cigarette smoking appears as one of the acquired freedoms of modern women.[47]

Over all, Woolf seems to have changed the piece considerably in response to the guild's complaints. Most important are the differences in the passages about how the guild meetings moved from something like a reading group to an active involvement in public policy. In the two versions of the text, Woolf's account has a similar beginning. It centers, once again, upon a space for women—a room. The guild, she writes in both versions, "must have given to the older women . . . a room where they could sit down and think remote from boiling saucepans and crying children." The room where the guild started meeting in 1883 was more than a place of independence or refuge. As Woolf puts in the "Introductory Essay," "that room became not merely a sitting-room and a meeting place, but a workshop where, laying their heads together, they could remodel their houses, could remodel their lives, could beat out this reform and that." They "learnt to speak out, boldly and authoritatively, about every question of civic life," to ask "not only for baths and wages and electric lights, but also for adult suffrage and the taxation of land values and divorce law reform." In the *Yale Review* text, the passage concludes: "It was thus that they were to ask, as the years went by, for peace and disarmament and the sisterhood of nations." In the "Introductory Letter," by contrast, the last sentence reads: "Thus in a year or two they were to demand peace and disarmament and the spread of Co-operative principles, not only among the working people of Great Britain but among the nations of the world."[48]

To the feminist reader of the next millennium, the new wording is less appealing, and we miss the lovely phrase "sisterhood of nations." Yet the substituted wording is more specific and concrete. Grounded in the Co-operative movement, it refers to a program for achieving peace and disarmament through international consumer co-operation and through women's activism. The WCG itself used the term *co-operation* in two different senses. Co-operation, usually but not always capitalized, most often meant their own specific sort of "consumer" co-operation (different from either industrial or agricultural co-operative societies in its focus on shops and retail purchases). The concept of co-operation also referred more broadly to working together as in some sort of idealized, conflict-free family. From these combined beliefs the guild developed its own opposition to international violence, including the organization in 1921 of an International Women's Co-operative Guild.

The "Introductory Letter" is also important as the only feminist writing of Woolf's besides *Three Guineas* that touches at any length on the issue of class. The account of the WCG foreshadows *Three Guineas'* Outsiders' Society, but in this case the members are married working-class women with children and also with a specific commitment to Consumer Co-operation. Their accounts in *Life as We Have Known It* are mainly of their experience, before marriage, in the paid labor force, but not at the professional level characteristic of the women to whom Woolf's 1931 lecture was addressed. These women recounted their experiences as mothers' helpers and maids, factory workers and hat-makers and agricultural laborers, and as wives of poorly paid workers; they wrote about what the guild meant to them, and some supplied, as requested, lists of their reading. Woolf noted their specific class position, noted her differences from it, and presented their views with sympathy.

In both versions, the article presents Woolf's general feminist arguments about the value of anonymity, autonomy, self-help, challenges to hierarchy, and the development of transformational goals based on women's experience and co-operative efforts (as well as, in this case, Co-operative movement efforts). It is in the "Introductory Letter" that Virginia Woolf makes most explicit the need for women to gain resources and also to transcend accepted values without losing sight of those values' potential for good. Class and educational advantages are not to be despised. Ladies have "mincing speech" and ignorance of "reality," but, as the first version puts it, they "desire Mozart and Cézanne and Shakespeare; and not merely money and hot water laid on." In the second version, the point is made more precisely and less demeaningly: "ladies desire Mozart and Einstein— that is, they desire things that are ends, not things that are means."[49] Class prejudice is still there, but it has diminished with the rewriting: how could Virginia Woolf have belittled in the *Yale Review* the desire for hot water and money, in a piece that outlined how the desire for just such things could become a powerful reforming influence?

Even with the shift in appropriate ideals, what matters is that the "Introductory Letter" manages to state explicitly that the final goal of social change should be something good in itself. This idea was necessarily central to the argument of *A Room of One's Own:* rooms and money are important instrumentally, because they make creativity possible. In *Three Guineas* Woolf was to be very clear about how useful money and power were, even if entailing the risk of co-optation. The distinction between means and ends comes straight from the works of G. E. Moore, who so influenced both the student Apostles who became the Bloomsbury Group and Virginia Woolf herself.[50] In the final version of the "Letter," the proposed ends of life include the work of the world-changing physicist/pacifist as well as the heavenly composer; this surely more than compensates for the loss of the bard and the transformational painter.[51]

The Hogarth Press "Introductory Letter" preserves and presents the general argument and approach of its first published version and of Woolf's feminism in general. And we can perhaps argue for some distinctively feminist aspects of the conditions under which it was (re)written and (re)published. Woolf's Co-operative article, in both versions, retains the writer's personal, gender, and class perspective even as it responds (though not entirely) to the comments of the subjects of the piece. The latter seem to have liked it: letters to Woolf from the writers of the collected letters were mostly generous and friendly about the "Introductory Letter." Feminist epistemology and methodology require the interaction reflected by such responses, and welcome such approval. Many other readers wrote to Virginia Woolf praising the collected letters, including, she reported, "very unlikely people—young intellectuals who had never heard of working women or guilds or co-operation. They thought the letters amazing" (*L*4 341). It seems unlikely that such people would have looked at the book without its prestigious introduction, so Woolf had performed a double feminist service, first by enabling Hogarth Press to publish the collected letters and then by providing the preface that was bound to draw attention to the organization and to the documents.[52]

Another, nonfeminist, lecture, delivered to the Workers' Educational Association in Brighton in 1940 and published as "The Leaning Tower," reiterates the fact that class entered into Woolf's condemnation of hierarchy, while also reiterating *Three Guineas'* arguments about the necessity for the widest sort of education. This text includes a crucial statement of intentions: "In the future we are not going to leave writing to be done for us by a small class of well-to-do young men who have only a pinch, a thimbleful of experience to give us." The rhetorical emphasis on the word "men" can hardly be accidental; the next sentence adds, very much in the tradition of *A Room of One's Own* and even more so of *Three Guineas*, "We are going to add our own experience, to make our own contribution."[53]

Nor can we consider feminist the pamphlet *Reviewing*, published by Hogarth Press in 1939 with a deprecating note added by Leonard Woolf. Here Virginia Woolf expands the invective against reviewers started in *Three Guineas*, and the sum of three guineas does reappear as the suggested fee—correctly identified as the standard sum for consulting a physician—for the professional critic's private consultation that is to replace the current system of journalistic reviews of published writing. But the argument takes the reader away from the central themes of Woolf's feminism, away from the particular situation of women, and back to her personal sensitivity to reviews.

VIII

Two more feminist publications by Woolf remain to be examined. The last of them to precede *Three Guineas*, the essay "Why?" is slight, though characteristic; 1940's "Thoughts on Peace in an Air Raid" is more significant.

"Why?" first appeared in 1934, in a publication of Oxford's first college for women. Basically, it is a spin-off from *Three Guineas*, in which a particularly exasperating endnote had attacked the teaching of English literature at university and specifically the use of lectures. There, possibly remembering her own experiences lecturing to working women at Morley College, Woolf grudgingly allowed that lectures might be appropriate for those whose homes lacked books. The essay is a useful reminder that Woolf was liable to mock both feminism and the potential for a feminist education and scholarship, although she took them very seriously indeed. Slight and light-hearted, "Why?" nevertheless touches on many of the central themes of *Three Guineas*: women's education and the women's colleges, women's poverty and lack of power, the transformational potential of feminism. It is particularly interesting to see Woolf apparently labeling as feminist the innovative roles possible for the new, young women's colleges, if a bit disheartening to learn in it that the editors of the boldly named *Lysistrata* apparently told Virginia Woolf to avoid feminism. Or was she merely being wicked in that statement? Certainly some of the most enterprising among the early women students at Oxbridge were hostile to feminism; Queenie Roth, who was present at Woolf's October 1928 lecture at Girton, was later to attack *Three Guineas* ferociously under her married name of Leavis. Three short drafts for "Why?" have survived, and none mentions feminism, although the first two link *Lysistrata* itself to "the Woman Movement" and the desirability of not imitating men.[54] The essay is, at most, a confirmation of feminist views more fully expressed elsewhere.

The same is not true of "Thoughts on Peace in an Air Raid," published in the *New Republic* in October 1940. This short but important wartime essay gives a last look at Woolf's feminist views, along with a foretaste of the future feminist writing she might have produced if she had lived: the sequel to *Three Guineas* perhaps? We know that Woolf had been thinking about the situation of women in an imagined postwar world. At the beginning of 1940 she outlined for Shena Simon some hopeful "views on peace." Among the topics she tried out on Simon, an admired and admiring feminist activist, was "sharing life after the war: about pooling men's and women's work." "Mustn't our next task be the emancipation of men?" Woolf asked, and she described what she hoped for: "whats now so stunted—I mean the life of natural happiness" (*L6* 379). That phrase—"the life of natural happiness"—comes as close as any single form of words can to expressing the goal of Woolf's feminism.

On 12 June 1940 Woolf noted in her diary an invitation "to contribute to some Womens Symposium in the USA"; by 2 September what she is writing has become "that infernal bomb article for USA" (*D5* 295, 314). The progress of the article, from an initial focus on women to an argument related to war, thus resembles on a much smaller scale the evolution of *Three Guineas* itself. In both cases, consideration of the situation of women moves to consideration of how we can end war by means of a feminist transformation of the world. In the *New Republic*, Woolf's essay appeared among "General Articles," preceded by a piece about the recent U.S. elections and followed by one about the war.[55]

"Thoughts on Peace" represents Virginia Woolf's last considered word on how to end war, to "make happiness."[56] London was being bombed when she was writing, and so too was the area of Sussex where she lived. She pictures herself, the archetypal Englishwoman, lying imprisoned by fear as, overhead, young men fight, equally imprisoned in their planes and their military roles and attitudes. It is a new version of being shut in and shut out. Writing of the voteless, marginalized women of the 1913 Women's Co-operative Guild, she had used a strikingly martial image: "Let them fire off their rifles if they liked, but they would hit no target; there were only blank cartridges inside."[57] Now she writes of how women, literally, lack weapons to face the fascists. And the former pacifist says that if this is a fight to protect freedom, she must do her part to support it. But how?

It is possible for women to make arms, or clothes, or food, the activities Woolf had previously urged Outsiders to eschew. Or, as she had consistently said in reflection on her own proper role, "we can fight with the mind. We can make ideas that will help the young Englishman who is fighting up in the sky to defeat the enemy." As in *Three Guineas*, she now quotes periodicals and books. The *Times* has reported Lady Astor, the first woman to serve in Parliament as an MP, saying that women have no voice in the politics that shape the war. But Woolf notes that women are complicit with the attitudes that sustain "the desire for aggression; the desire to dominate and enslave. . . . We can see shop windows blazing; and women gazing; painted women; dressed-up women; women with crimson lips and crimson fingernails. They are slaves who are trying to enslave." "If we could free ourselves from slavery," she says, "we should free men from tyranny. Hitlers are bred by slaves." Twenty years earlier she had told Affable Hawk that the servilities and tyrannies of the private and the public were connected; now their most brutal fruits are visible. The enemy is now called "Hitler" but he is more: "aggressiveness, tyranny, the insane love of power made manifest."[58]

She quotes Blake on mental fight, and she quotes an Englishman who had fought in the First World War (Frank Lushington). In his memoirs, he said that it was to war and its decorations and medals that his whole life had been dedicated, his education, his training. Disarmament, which the peace is supposedly to bring (this is 1940), will not be enough unless men "try to conquer in themselves their fighting instinct, their subconscious Hitlerism." Kinder to men than she was in *Three Guineas*, back to the tone of her 1931 lecture notes, she writes, "We must compensate the man for the loss of his gun," the young Englishman but also the young German and Italian. She suggests that this will be possible, because creative feelings exist in young men. The piece ends hopefully. The antiaircraft guns fall silent and the narrator imagines that a raider has been shot down behind the hill. The German pilot knows enough English to say "How glad I am that the fight is over!" He is given cigarettes by an English man, tea by an English woman. And Woolf comments, "if you can free the man from the machine, the seed does not fall upon altogether stony ground. The seed may be fertile." Country sounds resume, apples falling, an owl hooting. She speaks to the Americans, not yet involved in war:

Let us send these fragmentary notes . . . to the men and women [in America] in the belief that they will rethink them generously and charitably, perhaps shape them into something serviceable.[59]

"The seed may be fertile," and perhaps, rethinking generously and charitably, we too can make "something serviceable." It is a good final comment on the feminist writings of Virginia Woolf as we turn back to her most fully developed feminist text, *Three Guineas.*

6 Versioning Feminism

       In the summer and fall of 1938, Virginia Woolf's most explicit statement of her feminism—*Three Guineas*—appeared in print in three different forms, apparently related to their different conditions of publication. Although very similar, the two first editions were not identical, and the serial is rather more distinctive than has usually been recognized. Modifying earlier images, we can say that the skeleton is the same but there are some interesting differences in the flesh that clothes the bones, or at least in the skin. It seems reasonable to compare the versions, to see if their message is significantly different, and to ask if the different versions seem more or less feminist. Certainly, without understanding these varying texts, we cannot fully understand either *Three Guineas* or Woolf's feminism.

We have already looked in some detail at both the evolution and the contents of *Three Guineas*, as well as situating it in Virginia Woolf's other feminist writing. In the process, it has been obvious that Woolf's feminism is expressed differently or directed differently at different times, even though it remains basically the same. Naturally enough, this variety can make the reader wonder both why the versions differ and which of the texts are the more feminist. Such speculations fuel the feminist discussions (and criticisms) of Woolf for muting anger as she prepares a text for publication, and they are also implied in many comparisons of *A Room of One's Own* with *Three Guineas*. The answer to variation seems to depend on context, in the widest meanings of the term, along with more complex aesthetic considerations. Judging the resultant different versions is another problem.

Part of the context for published texts is, simply, how and where the different articulations appeared in print. Thus, as we have seen, the two different texts concerning the Women's Co-operative Guild reflect their preparation for, respectively, the *Yale Review* and a Hogarth Press book edited by the general secretary of the guild. But *Three Guineas* is, among Woolf's nonfiction feminist writing, perhaps the least dependent on context. This sounds odd: we know how it was written, we can trace its development from lecture to essay-novel to its final form, and we know the relevance of changes in the situation of women and of the world. All the same, *Three Guineas* stands out among Woolf's feminist writing because it has a sort of autonomy that the others lack. Among the publications growing out of the 1931 lecture to the Junior Council, there is no obvious reason for *Three Guineas* as such, as a separate item. *The Years* incorporated most of what Woolf wanted to say about women in the nineteenth and early twentieth centuries, and made it clear that opposition to war was central to Woolf's vision of the future. So why add another book, and a substantial one at that, carrying the same message? Yet even as *The Years* painfully developed, responding in part to Woolf's desire to write another novel of "fact," *Three Guineas* persisted as a separate, if related project. To a certain extent *Three Guineas* did function as a more factual and also more polemical annex to *The Years*; we know Woolf believed that a novel must avoid preaching or propaganda. It seems, though, that *Three Guineas* was more than some sort of nonfiction gloss on the related novel. Instead, it represented the desire to make a separate, clear, and explicit statement of deeply held beliefs—the feminism implicit in *The Years* and in Woolf's other writing. But Woolf then gave us three different presentations—and what are we to understand from their differences?

I

As I have already recounted, we know a considerable amount about the evolution of *Three Guineas*. But we do not know how Virginia Woolf prepared the texts for the two first editions of the book, not to mention the much-compressed serial published in the *Atlantic Monthly* between the appearance of the English and American editions. We cannot even be certain of the sequence in which the author prepared the three texts for final publication. Nothing remotely like a complete manuscript of *Three Guineas* has survived, either in holograph or typed form. No sets of proofs of *Three Guineas* are to be found; this matters because Woolf always made substantial and often significant changes in proof. It is reasonable to assume that the serial was prepared after the date, in the middle of proofing the book, when the Woolfs learned that it had been accepted for publication in two issues of the *Atlantic Monthly;* the author did not record anything about the process of rewriting, any more than she had about the process of proofing the various texts (*D5* 130).[1]

Let us begin with the two first editions of *Three Guineas.* They are very similar, and there is no evidence to argue convincingly that one or the other represents the author's more considered choice. The American text, though published later, does not look like an authorial improvement over the English one. Some errors are shared, and, over all, the mistakes found only in the later, American edition actually seem slightly worse than those found in the first English.[2] Nor, by and large, do the differences between the two first editions have any substantive meaning. Almost all of them relate to punctuation, and most of these are related to the complicated patterns of double and single quotes in the main text of the book, which Harcourt Brace, the American publisher, handled more consistently than Hogarth did.[3] However, four passages are to be found only in the first American edition, in each case at the end of an endnote; they are thus also absent from the serial, which does not include any material from the endnotes. Three of these are relatively brief additions, which could even be passages deleted in proof from the first English edition and overlooked in proofing the first American.[4] By contrast, one of the "American" passages, also located in an endnote, is interesting and potentially significant.

At issue is who is to care for children in those years when they require full attention. The first English edition has the following wording:

> The bold suggestion has been made that the occupation is not exclusively maternal, but could be shared by both parents to the common good.

In the first American edition, the passage reads:

> The bold suggestion has been made that the occupation is not necessarily maternal, but should be shared by both parents. And actually an English Member of Parliament has resigned in order to be with his children.[5]

This MP may have been Captain Michael Wentworth Beaumont, who on 19 April 1938 resigned from the Aylesbury Division of Buckinghamshire, which he had held for the Conservative Party for nine years.[6] Beaumont gave two reasons for his resignation, of which the first was that "my private affairs have come to require my spending a greater portion of my time at Wotton than is consistent with regular attendance at the House of Commons"; the second related to policy differences with the National Government.[7] Beaumont had married in 1924, and his wife had died in 1935, leaving him with one son, presumably less than eleven years old; he remarried in 1938. In *Who's Who* he listed his recreations as "hunting & shooting." If Beaumont is indeed the reference for this example, then even a man who has been a Master of Foxhounds can put forth domestic arguments for public actions and perhaps show himself to be the sort of person with whom a woman can live in equality.[8]

Is the American version more feminist because of the longer fragment of an endnote? Yes: by adding the example, it gives more emphasis to the possibility of altering male roles as well as female, by sharing maternal responsibilities usually linked to childbearing. More interesting is the presence, in both editions, of the invitation to men to share domestic roles and specifically the care of young children. Q. D. Leavis's review had zoomed in on just such an implication, but Woolf herself does not refer to it anywhere else. Accordingly, we can estimate the impact of the added passage in two different ways. On the one hand, the absence of such arguments elsewhere means that the impact of even the expanded passage is minimized, because it stands alone. On the other hand, the unexpectedness of the added example might make it, as a result, more significant.

Woolf's account of Beaumont's resignation (if it is indeed his) simplifies and dramatizes the situation in a typical fashion, when she suggests that he resigned in order to care for his children. In fact, a widower acquiring a wife would seem likely to need to do less rather than more for his offspring. Was the new wife perhaps the attraction? Or had she refused to be a parliamentarian's grass widow? In any case, the restatement of the matter obscures the fact that family responsibilities would not be regarded as sufficient reason why a politician, particularly a male one, should resign from a public position. Aesthetic and polemical considerations may in part explain the simplification, for it would have been far less effective to report the real situation, that an opponent of government policy cited as an additional reason for his resignation his wish to spend more time at home. In *Three Guineas*, Woolf makes clear that rhetoric is indeed allowed a major role in the use of examples, as when she writes about "decorated ink-pots" that, like medals and other symbols, serve in Nazi Germany to encourage support of hierarchy and militarism. "To speak accurately," she writes in an endnote, the recognition of civilian service to the German state took the form of "a large silver plaque in the form of a Reich eagle" to be displayed on a desk (*3G* 104, 161). Accuracy is available to anyone who reads the endnote, but effectiveness takes priority in the main text. And the child-caring ex-MP is certainly an effective example.

II

We should not, however, overstate the distinctive features of the first editions of *Three Guineas*, which are after all very close to each other. The serial version of *Three Guineas* is another, more interesting story. Never reprinted, it has had little attention. B. J. Kirkpatrick's magisterial bibliography of Virginia Woolf first dismissed the serial as "a summary." The amended description as "an abridgement . . . with some additional passages," substituted in 1997, is still somewhat of an understatement about what happened to *Three Guineas* on the way to the *Atlantic Monthly*.[9] In fact, "Women Must Weep" has to be taken seriously as a version of the book. Virginia Woolf had full editorial control over the first English edition, published like all but her first two books by her own press, and the Harcourt Brace edition was virtually identical to the Hogarth edition. By contrast, the serialization might possibly represent her response to actual or anticipated dimensions of the magazine's nationality and audience. We may then ask how the changes, made for this or other reasons, affected the underlying feminism.

"Women Must Weep," the over-all title of the two installments, seems, in the twenty-first century, far more appealing than the rather obscure *Three Guineas*. In addition, Woolf expanded the title for the second installment, adding four words to produce "Women Must Weep—Or Unite against War." Here she echoed standard and recognizable feminist rhetoric, familiar in both England and the United States. She also added to the serial a passage making a feminist argument not to be found in any of the other texts related to *Three Guineas* or, indeed, anywhere in her writings. Yet, at the same time, the text of "Women Must Weep" concludes more tentatively than *Three Guineas*, and for that and other reasons it seems possible that its final impact might be different than the book's.

The life of *Three Guineas* as a serial can be dated back to 1931. Three weeks after Virginia Woolf delivered her speech about professions for women to the Junior Council of the L&NSWS, she wrote to the literary agent Nancy Pearn about *Good Housekeeping* magazine, which apparently had expressed interest in "more than one" article. The book she had "to some extent finished" was not appropriate, but "I have some vague idea that I shall turn a speech I made the other night into a sequel to *A Room of Ones Own*."[10] So perhaps she already saw what she was then calling "A

Knock on the Door" as something that might be suitable for periodical as well as book publication. An unpublished letter from the *Atlantic Monthly*'s archives indicates that on 6 September 1933, Woolf told its editor, who seems to have asked for another serial, that "the next book will be long, and not ready for some time."[11] There is no record of when or why the decision was finally made to offer *Three Guineas* for American serialization; at this point in Woolf's career, most of her American publications seem by contrast to respond to requests from publishers. After at least three refusals, it was once more the *Atlantic Monthly* that accepted—but they wanted only 12,000 words of text (*D5* 130).[12] Assuming that the magazine did not want the not-yet-completed endnotes, that still left more than 60,000 words that Woolf was expected to cut by some four-fifths. The figures imply massive compressions or omissions, and indeed both occurred.[13]

There is no reference at all in Woolf's diaries or letters to preparing the serial text, although it must have been a tedious enough task, and she grumbles in her diary about how boring the completion of the book became: "too much drudgery donkey work" (*D5* 132).[14] But we do have some evidence about the actual way in which she composed the serial. The Massachusetts Historical Society owns what appear to be two pages of instructions to a typesetter for the *Atlantic Monthly*. Woolf seems to have marked up galley proofs to produce the required shorter text. The first page makes it clear that it was Woolf herself who made the revisions, including cuts, insertions, and rewriting.[15] Over all, specific allusions are changed to more general ones, so that, for example, "Grenfell" and "Knebworth" points of view becomes "the solder's and airman's point of view."[16] Sometimes such changes are necessary simply because lengthy specific examples have been removed and there must be a summary as replacement. In this way, a new inserted passage about the contradictory guidance received from "the clergy" takes the place of a *Three Guineas* passage referring explicitly to the Church of England and quoting disagreements between the Anglican bishops of London and Birmingham. Often such an insertion bridges a substantial deletion, as of a discussion of the informal, necessarily limited influence exercised by great ladies and how even such influence was not available to women like Virginia Woolf.

At first sight, it seems as if Woolf was responding to her American audience, for the deleted references and examples are very English, but after all, most of the examples in *Three Guineas* are English, so any shrinkage or omission of detail was bound to cut down on the book's Englishness. Unlike the first American edition, which made no such concessions to its audience, "Women Must Weep" uses American spelling and makes a very few trivial changes that could represent adaptations to an American periodical audience.[17] But no other allowances are made for possible American ignorance. For example, the serial lacks eight pages about the two women's colleges at Cambridge but includes the statement that headmistresses' preferences for a "belettered staff" disadvantage students at "Newnham and Girton" ("WMW" 590). We have to wonder if American readers would recognize the names of the colleges, let alone know that in 1938 their graduates were not granted more than nominal university degrees even when they had completed all the normal requirements.

Adaptation to American publication does not obviously explain the different title. The only other work of Woolf's to appear in serial form was also published in the *Atlantic Monthly;* in 1933 the parody biography of Elizabeth Barrett Browning's dog retained the uninformative title of *Flush*, so presumably Woolf could have kept the title *Three Guineas* if she had wished.[18] By 1938 the best-selling *The Years* had made her so well known in the United States that even an obscure title would have drawn readers. The donations remain guineas in the text, and their meaning, if not their exact value, is clear. Instead, the serial used the phrase "women must weep," which sums up the conventional view of female responses to catastrophe and the loss of life.

More specifically, the periodical title most likely echoes Charles Kingsley's phrase in his poem "The Three Fishers": "men must work and women must weep." Kingsley's words were conspicuous in nineteenth-and early-twentieth-century feminist rhetoric. Thus, Josephine Butler, one of Virginia Woolf's heroes in *Three Guineas*, wrote that she had "rejected the old ideal of division of labour 'that men must work and women must weep.'" She was reporting a prayer meeting held in 1883 toward the end of the successful attempts to obtain repeal of the Contagious Diseases Acts.[19] As Butler came into the room, many women were weeping, but "a venerable lady from America rose and said: 'Tears are good, prayers are better, but we should get on better if behind every tear there was a vote at the ballot box.'" We can assume that Woolf read this passage. To begin with, she cites Butler's memoirs twice in *Three Guineas* (3G 147, 149). In addition, Butler's anecdote about the weeping women is included, in full, in a 1927 pamphlet honoring her life and work—and *Three Guineas* quotes in two places a footnote on the page in the booklet where the story ends (3G 135, 153).[20]

The title's reference to the Kingsley poem, which is not identified by Butler or in the *Atlantic Monthly*, also links the serialization to the National Union of Women's Suffrage Societies. In a relevant example of feminist discourse, when the secretary of the NUWSS explicitly referred to "The Three Fishers" in September 1914, she added, "as long as men think that women must only weep for the errors of men, they will not trouble much."[21] That is, historically, there has been nothing for women to do but wait and lament while the men go off to sea. They weep because some of the men will not survive; they do the same in response to war and its losses. Such stereotypes of female passivity and domesticity were rejected by the women activists who, from early days, opposed traditional gender roles and claimed for women an entitlement to resist the brutalities of the public sphere.

It is not obvious, however, that the serial's title is more feminist than the title of the book, even though it echoes the feminists of Woolf's generation and earlier. Today, at the beginning of the twenty-first century, the reference to guineas in the original title is likely to seem antiquated, almost meaningless, so that almost any alternative is likely to seem preferable to the contemporary feminist reader. If the guinea has any meaning at all, it has to be in reference to the depressing fact that, even now, men continue to have larger disposable incomes available for the luxury goods and charities usually paid for in guineas. Yet the original title of *Three Guineas* should be recognized as having a set of feminist references, and any evaluation of the change of title must take account of that fact. The meaning of donating guineas shifts subtly, if it is a woman making the payment. The ability casually to hand out guineas identifies the narrator of *Three Guineas* as a successful woman and as a possible role model. In addition, the references to charitable donations, guineas or not, can be thought of as feminist simply because of the narrator-donor's unusual decision to support women's organizations not usually seen as relevant to issues of war and peace.

The target of the third guinea, and the whole framing letter, is less obviously feminist, for the peace society is headed by a man. But this is no more than reality: such societies are run and supported by women but usually have men in charge. It is still to influential men that women must look for significant changes in social policy. Requests for influential participation and cash donations are unlikely to be made to women and even less likely to produce a response. As a result, the narrator's insistence that she will not join the organization, but will instead support it by a donation, delineates a role that asserts women's autonomy.

Whatever the implications of the title, in "Women Must Weep" the general argument remains what it is in *Three Guineas*. However, the emphasis on preventing war becomes stronger for the negative reason that so much of the material about the women's movement and individual women is removed, either as part of the missing endnotes or, in more active intervention, with the shrinkage of the text. For example, in "Women Must Weep" there is no more than a reference to Elizabeth Barrett Browning's struggles for independence, to the diplomat Gertrude Bell, to Josephine Butler, or to the first heads of the women's colleges at Cambridge. Sophia Jex-Blake's unsuccessful attempt to get her Victorian father's permission to work for pay is retained but nothing about her role as leader of the "battle of Harley Street" that got women the right to become doctors. Missing also is nearly all of the indictment of the Church and the civil service for sexism. It is true that, in the serialization, some points were sharpened by rewriting and by the need to state briefly the points the book could make at leisure. "What reason is there to think that a university education makes the educated against war?" Woolf asks crisply ("WMW" 589). But the copious and leisurely documentation in the book is sorely missed in the serial.

The text most conspicuous by its absence in the serial is, of course, the endnotes. Woolf might well have felt that it did not matter if she omitted formal documentation for her argument; the first English edition of the book was due out just after the first installment of the serialization, and the first American edition was to appear not long after the second. The adaptation in "Women Must Weep" is very skillful, as we might expect. Only in one case would endnote material seem likely to be needed for the reader, who will look in vain for a definition of the central, crucially important term "educated man's daughter." But apparently in 1938 the term was easily comprehensible, as can be seen in the *Atlantic Monthly* itself. A "Contributors' Column" that appears before the second installment, which refers the reader to *Three Guineas* for a fuller statement of the arguments presented, sums up serialization and book as urging " 'the daughters of educated men' to unite in concerted opposition to man-made war."[22]

There are eighty-one notes in *Three Guineas*, however, that are not merely citations of sources. Without these endnotes, although the book is comprehensible, it is incomplete. The endnotes do more than provide sources and examples. Their absence demonstrates the extent to which they are less explanatory than expansive. In particular, there can be no doubt that in "Women Must Weep" Woolf's feminism seems less complex without the additional comments, often lengthy and substantial enough to be considered short essays, that are to be found in the endnotes. One of the most important absences from "Women Must Weep" is a long note about Sergeant Amalia Bonilla, a Loyalist "militia woman" in the Spanish Civil War who is presented very sympathetically; Woolf excerpted it from a French journalist's reports. Here we lose a clear indication that Woolf is no essentialist about women and war. It is not biology but circumstances that make women into pacifists, and some females may choose to become fighters: "if sanctioned the fighting instinct easily develops" in women (*3G* 160).

Without the endnotes, the book also becomes far more conventional in both form and tone. In this respect it is less feminist. Nor is the omission of the illustrative photographs trivial, for they too provide ironic and comic comments on the male elite and its trappings. The subversive and highly significant nature of these notes and illustrations is the topic of the next chapter.

III

Virginia Woolf did not just cut *Three Guineas* to make it into "Women Must Weep," however. She also rewrote, and in several cases the changed wording is worth attention. It is not easy to illustrate these changes, for there is necessarily a fair amount of rearrangement of passages as a result of revision and compression.[23] There are a number of places where the texts are both parallel and importantly different. Among these, the most interesting are those related to the burning of words and to the lighting of candles.

As will be recalled, the first conflagration in *Three Guineas* is the symbolic destruction of the word *feminist,* in a ceremony celebrating a new, postfeminist era. Write the obsolete word on a piece of paper and burn it, says the narrator; it will clear the air. In *Three Guineas,* a lengthy passage about Josephine Butler follows. Woolf rejoices that the representative of the peace society is now an ally of those like Butler, miscalled feminist, who had larger goals than simply women's rights. The resulting coalition should be celebrated by a second bonfire, burning the words *Tyrant* and *Dictator* (except that, unfortunately, those words are not yet obsolete) (*3G* 93, 94).

Of this long section of the book, "Women Must Weep" retains only the sad conclusion that the words designating the oppressors are still valid. Further, in "Women Must Weep," feminism is quietly laid to rest in one phrase. The relevant passage begins, "a celebration seems called for," and continues as follows: "What could be more fitting, now that we can bury the old word 'feminist,' than to write more dead words, corrupt words, upon sheets of paper and burn them—the words 'tyrant,' 'dictator,' for example? Alas, these words are not yet obsolete" ("WMW" 752). Thus, although in *Three Guineas* the destruction of the names of evil will comprise a second celebration postponed to some time in the future, in "Women Must Weep" it is the single, but still future one. The two passages then continue with the same wording in both book and serial, except that what in *Three Guineas* is identified as merely "a peculiar and unmistakable" odor to be smelt in the neighborhood of Whitehall and Westminster is named in "Women Must Weep" as "the odor of masculine tyranny" (a phrase not to be found in *Three Guineas*). The reader of the serial could be excused for wondering who buried feminism and why. Narrower and wider definitions of feminism are at issue here, as in the parent text. In the absence of the fuller discussion found in *Three Guineas*, in "Women Must Weep" all we have is a passing dismissal of an ambiguous label that, the narrator says, used to be attributed, perhaps unfairly, to women's activism. It is the easier to infer (incorrectly) that Virginia Woolf was no feminist.

Both texts also consider, but only in drafts for letters that are not finally sent, some more substantial incitements to arson, including burning down the existing women's college that has asked for funds. In addition, in *Three Guineas* but not in "Women Must Weep," the letter writer also considers burning down the house rented by the society for supporting women in the professions. There are issues of light and of celebration as well as of destruction here, as in some related images of candles. And these differ somewhat between the book and serial versions.

The impact of what might be called the heat-and-light variations is difficult to assess, given the complexity of the rearrangement. Perhaps the easiest way is to start with *Three Guineas* at the point when, pretty far into the book, after dealing with the women's groups, the letter writer in *Three Guineas* finally decides to give a guinea, her third donation, to the peace society. By now that group is described as working against tyranny alongside women who are no longer to be called feminists. The letter writer of *Three Guineas* says to her main correspondent: "Put this penny candle in the window of your new society, and may we live to see the day when in the blaze of our common freedom the words tyrant and dictator shall be burnt to ashes, because the words tyrant and dictator shall be obsolete" (*3G* 95). The serial does not include this passage, where freedom will be the destroyer of the names as well as the reality of fascism. Nor does it endow the peace society with a physical location, which in any case is mentioned nowhere else in the book.[24] Instead, in "Women Must Weep," the donation once made to the peace society, the writer moves directly to consideration of whether or not to join it.

A slightly different version of the passage about a penny candle is to be found in the serial, but it occurs much earlier, at the end of the donation letter to the society to assist women in the professions. As a result, the candle plays a different role. In the serial, the letter writer concludes her letter to the honorary treasurer of the association supporting professional women with words like, but not identical to, those addressed to the head of the peace society in *Three Guineas:* "It is a penny candle, no more, but may it help to set light to those photographs of dead bodies and ruined houses and ensure that no other generation shall be forced to see what we have seen" ("WMW" 594). The narrator has dropped the playful image of registering change by burning words written on pieces of paper. Now the pictures of a real-world disaster are to be burned, as perhaps the recipient might have wished to treat photographs of actual dead children and ruined houses. The serial thus destroys, not just words, but also visual images of horror. The Spanish Civil War photographs have been given a larger role than in the book, and the result is a far less abstract gesture of hopes for change. It also links the work of the women's groups more directly to the prevention of war.

In *Three Guineas,* the letter to the association aiding professional women ends differently, with a piece of whimsy about arranging a bazaar's hares and coffee-pot for sale and awaiting the benevolent condescension of "Sir Sampson Legend, O.M., K.C.B., LL.D., D.C.L., P.C., etc." (*3G* 78).[25] This is the sort of flippancy that annoyed so many readers. It seems to have delighted women already committed to feminist activism. Pippa Strachey, writing to praise *Three Guineas,* echoed this and other passages that seemed to refer to her role as fund-raiser for the London and National Society for Women's Service and the Women's Employment Federation, saying she was sending blessings "unmitigated by hares and stockings."[26] But Sir Sampson Legend of the many honorific titles does not appear in "Women Must Weep." The absence of *Three Guineas'* fantasy about the bazaar in fact serves to emphasize the seriousness of the mandate of groups that attempted to assist beleaguered professional women during the inter-war years. No photographs, however horrific, are burned in *Three Guineas.*

Another fiery example, again with differences in the versions, appears in relation to unsent draft letters that, in the book, fantasize about burning down buildings. When the narrator of "Women Must Weep," like the narrator of *Three Guineas*, finally says to the honorary treasurer of the association for professional women, "take this guinea then and use it, not to burn the house down, but to make its windows blaze," we can see one of Woolf's few slips in revision for the serial, for "Women Must Weep" does not include any earlier dispirited suggestion of burning down what roughly corresponds to the London and National Society for Women's Service. The building housing the society supporting wage-earning women is in fact more clearly identified in the serial, where an additional phrase about "voices of ships" coming in from the river seems to be a reference to the Thames Embankment near the Marsham Street building belonging to the L&NSWS and also housing the Women's Employment Federation ("WMW" 594).[27] In both texts, it is the uneducated mothers who laugh from their graves in approval of the blazing—shining, not burning—windows that stand for the continuation of support for self-sufficient women.

IV

"Women Must Weep" does include one new idea, one that is not to be found in any other of Woolf's published writings. In both the book and the serial, the author explains how Outsiders are to avoid encouraging militarism and chauvinism. She then shifts to considering possible economic actions that might, more proactively, help them to prevent or end wars; most importantly, they must be economically self-sufficient. In "Women Must Weep," a new section of the text now begins.[28] After stating, as in *Three Guineas*, that Outsiders must earn their own living, Woolf inserts a unique passage:

> But there is another way in which the Outsiders can bind themselves to carry out this duty—a more positive, if a still more difficult way. And that is by earning their own livings: by continuing to earn those livings while the war is in progress. History is at hand to assure us that this method has a psychological influence, a strong dissuasive force upon war-makers. In the last war the daughters of workingmen proved it by showing that they could do their brother's work in his absence. They thus roused his jealousy and his anxiety lest his place should have been filled in his absence, and provided him with a strong incentive to end the war. ("WMW" 753)

Woolf seems to mean that if middle-class women go on working during the war, then middle-class men, fearing women's takeover of their workplace, will hasten to make peace.

This is a very odd passage, and unlike Woolf's other discussions of the role of middle-class women in wartime. The context suggests that, clumsily, she is seeking some sort of economic-based leverage. By contrast, the Crimean and World War One examples in *Three Guineas* are of women who gained personal freedom by means of war service—Florence Nightingale finding a cause and liberation, society women escaping the private home to go overseas as nurses. During the Second World War, women of all classes would become essential for the war effort; in Woolf's lifetime, in England, it did not seem that middle-class women could play any significant role either to help or to hinder. At most, like the mayoress of Woolwich cited in *Three Guineas*, who said she would not mend socks for the war effort, they could make symbolic statements of their unwillingness to provide civilian support to war. Middle-class women also had a reproductive role, of course; the mayoress had contributed a son to the war effort, though Woolf does not mention it in her reference to that lady (*3G* 106).[29]

In both book and serial, Woolf had suggested earlier that, in specific contrast to middle-class women, working-class women could in principle have a direct impact on war-making by withholding or threatening to withhold their labor from the industries necessary for war. She does not, however, consider the consequences to women or their families of such actions, particularly at a time when the usual breadwinners were serving in the military. The admonition to middle-class women to continue working professionally in wartime presents similar problems. The reader may well wonder what alternative they have. Surely Woolf is not arguing against some possibility that unpaid war service might replace jobs for women, hardly an option for those who were supporting themselves or dependents.

There is some submerged argument here about the middle-class women who might move into the jobs of men who were off to war. In this case, is Woolf assuming that women would replace men on a temporary basis, in order to encourage men to feel the need to reclaim their prewar occupations? This is a strange argument at a time when, as *Three Guineas* fully recognizes, women were desperately seeking entry into the more lucrative male-dominated occupations, professional as well as service and industrial. The argument appears in an early fragment of draft, so it is no last-minute addition. There Woolf specified that she had professional occupations in mind: lawyers, doctors, civil servants.[30]

Woolf may have been influenced in this argument, as in so many others, by Ray Strachey's account in *The Cause* of women's movement into industry during the First World War. Strachey describes resistance by male workers to the "dilution" of their trades by women as follows: "it filled them with fears for the future. . . . if [women] were brought in, and especially if, when they were brought in, they did well, where would the men's position be in their 'own' trades after the war?"[31]

The problem of job access, put this way, sounds psychological, but it was more. At the 1916 Congress of the Women's Co-operative Guild, the second of those that both Woolfs attended, one of the topics discussed was "the replacement of men by women in industry." In a report on the previous year's congress, Leonard Woolf had described the guild's views on women in men's jobs: women must be neither temporary nor cost-cutting alternatives. Instead, trained, experienced women should be taken on at men's rates, while partially trained and inexperienced women would advance to men's rates as they acquired the necessary training. A December 1916 article titled "Women's Wages" by Leonard Woolf outlines the problems. Even in the same or equivalent jobs, women traditionally received lower pay than men before the war; the guild's earlier campaign had not achieved equal pay for women employees of the Co-operative Union but instead a minimum wage considerably below that received by men. Therefore, for employers, not just labor shortages but also motives both of profit and of opposition to unionism suggested taking women on at these lower wages, which could then be used as a norm for the male workers who would return from war to replace them. If the women were kept on after the war, it would be specifically because they were undercutting the male workers whom they had ousted.[32] The central issue was therefore wage parity. For women, the additional possibility of continuing employment in secure, unionized jobs was potentially transformative both for themselves and for the structure of work more widely. But Virginia Woolf registers no awareness of any of the issues involved.

It is worth noting that there is no evidence that men of any class wanted or needed to end the First World War in order to retrieve their jobs from women. After the war ended, women were systematically turfed out of their wartime positions in deference to returning veterans, a process documented by Strachey in *The Cause* immediately after her discussion of men's hostile reactions to women's wartime work. British trade unions were able to ensure that women had no permanent claim on positions in which they replaced men. Resisting government and industry attempts to undercut prewar union agreements, they also managed to avoid adverse impact on pay or working conditions for unionized jobs that women held on a temporary, wartime basis. As a result, during the war women usually received the same salaries as men had received, an enormous increase for them and possibly, though improbably, an incentive for working women to favor the continuation of the war.

We have to conclude, however reluctantly, that this particular addition to the text of *Three Guineas*—Woolf's fantasy about the impact of middle-class women's work during wartime—was hardly an improvement; its absence from *Three Guineas* seems like a good thing. And the same can be said of some other changes, where more than once we find what looks like an unexamined idea absent from the book. For example, there is the passage that includes the famous phrase "to fight has always been the man's habit, not the woman's." In *Three Guineas*, the short second sentence then reads, "Law and practice have developed that difference, whether innate or accidental"; this discreet statement would arouse no argument even today (*3G* 6). However, in "Women Must Weep" we find instead the following: "Education and practice have developed what may be a psychological difference into what may be a physical difference—a difference in glands, in hormones" ("WMW" 586). The changed wording produces in this case a change in meaning: law has been replaced by education as an enhancer of what have become different biological tendencies toward bellicosity. Then a new idea is inserted, as with middle-class women's war work. It is interesting, though a bit unnerving, to see Woolf apparently taking a Lamarckian view of sexual dimorphism. But her views of biology tend to the unreliable: fertile eggs are preferable for breakfast, she thinks, and mules are castrated horses (*3G* 128, 154). What she probably has at the back of her mind—the social shaping of physical tendencies—is sensible enough, whatever we may think of the revised expansion. And as so often in the serial, Woolf protects herself by a qualifier not found in the book—"however that may be"—as well as a reference to allegedly "indisputable" fact.

The most significant example of reworking in "Women Must Weep" is the conclusion. Woolf seems to have had some difficulty with the last part of the book; at the late date of 22 March 1938, well into her revision of proofs, she wrote in her diary that she had "once more tried to recast the last page" (*D5* 131). But we have no way of telling if the "Women Must Weep" version was written before or after she settled on the conclusion that was used in both of the first editions. All we know is that the endings of *Three Guineas* and "Women Must Weep" are substantially different, and that the periodical version is both less assertive and strikingly less feminist.

At the end of "Women Must Weep," the Outsiders' Society, the organization without officers or official identity that will replace for women the existing peace societies, is presented with a rather surprising tentativeness. The narrator says that its name is too pompous, and it is "pedantic" to refer to the group's "rules" as she does in both book and serialization ("WMW" 759). This though we know that the author and her feminist readers were all deeply committed to the concept of outsider activity. Most notably, in its last pages the serial emphasizes disagreements about the possible value of warriors, war, and authoritarian society, again issues about which Woolf's—and *Three Guineas'*—views were hardly ambivalent.

In both *Three Guineas* and "Women Must Weep," the narrator states that she and her peace society correspondent agree that the figure of the virile, militaristic fascist Man in Uniform is abhorrent: "it is evil." In both cases, like a good liberal, she then notes that others may disagree. But the emphasis is very different. "Opinions differ," is all that she says in *Three Guineas* (*3G* 130). In "Women Must Weep," she writes instead, "And we may both be wrong, not only in the methods by which we attempt to destroy that evil, but in our judgment." Two substantial inserted paragraphs then review the arguments for and against war, obedience, and the supremacy of the state, and a third says, rather desolately, "What judge is there to decide which opinion is right, which wrong? There is no judge; there is no certainty in heaven above or on earth below" ("WMW" 759). These are sentiments Woolf expressed elsewhere in *Three Guineas* in much the same words, but she did not include them in the conclusion of the book.

The end of "Women Must Weep" also omits the crucially important linkages between domestic and public tyranny. Of the title's three donations, at this final moment only the guinea to the mixed-sex peace society is mentioned. The serial's conclusion also lacks *Three Guineas'* important statement that the three donations, "though given to three different treasurers are all given to the same cause, for the causes are the same and inseparable." Finally, Woolf chooses to end "Women Must Weep" by quoting Josephine Butler, though without attribution. The guinea given to the peace society, she says, is to help it "assert 'the rights of all—all men and women—to the respect in their persons of the great principles of Justice and Equality and Liberty'" ("WMW" 759). *Three Guineas* had quoted this noble passage earlier, though the serial had not, and Woolf includes it in middle of the third paragraph before the end of the book (*3G* 95, 131). As the finale to "Women Must Weep," it presents the most gender-neutral possible version of social activism.

We should note that for all the cutting and pasting, the serial's basic argument is still clearly recognizable, just as radical, and certainly as feminist as the book's. The three donations are still distributed as before, while the discussion still gives substantial attention to the role of women and women's organizations and outlines women's disabilities as well as the role of hierarchy in producing fascism and war. But the presentation is less confrontational. Those critics who faulted *Three Guineas* for linking the status of women with war, who found it too insistent and too linked to gender, would surely have felt more comfortable with the conclusion of "Women Must Weep" than with that of *Three Guineas*. The title "Women Must Weep—Or Unite against War" might strike us today as more overtly feminist than *Three Guineas*. Perhaps it was in fact milder and more acceptable because of its reference to conventional sex-role expectations. Women "uniting" against war is an unthreatening enough prospect, particularly at a time long before the antiwar militancy of the 1960s. The serial also lacks those annoying endnotes and photographs that can leave male readers feeling so uneasy, as if the joke is on them in some way they do not quite understand.

It seems likely, in short, that at the time of publication, "Women Must Weep" would have provoked less of the irritation that responded to Woolf's feminism and the dense, whimsical, and semi-academic style in which she expressed it in *Three Guineas*. We should not, I think, interpret this to mean that "Women Must Weep" is less feminist, any more than we should see the slight differences in the first editions of *Three Guineas* as significantly changing their argument. The serial addressed what was potentially a substantial and possibly receptive audience, however forgotten its text has since become.

We should be aware of the differences in the versions of *Three Guineas*. These texts are not written in stone, nor need they be; what matters most is what they say. "Women Must Weep" is finally most distinctive because it lacks the photographs and the scholarly apparatus that make *Three Guineas*, the book, so very feminist and both so attractive and so off-putting. We turn now to the reactions to the main text, and in particular to the reactions to its distinctive—distinctively feminist—form.

7 | *Scholarship and Subversion*

       The day after her husband's lukewarm reaction to the endnotes for *Three Guineas*, Woolf pronounced her own measured judgment on the whole book: "Am I right though in thinking it has some importance—3 Gs—as a point of view: shows industry; fertility; & is, here and there as 'well written' (considering the technical problems—quotations arguments &c) as any of my rather skimble skamble works? I think there's more to it than to A Room" (*D5* 134). Most readers have disagreed with her, being either more or less enthusiastic than she was able to be in this moment of anticlimax. Over time, the book's reception, particularly from members of the literary establishment, has tended to be unfriendly. Woolf would not have been surprised. "Sneer enthusiasm, enthusiasm sneer": so she anticipated responses to *Three Guineas* at the end of May 1938, a week before it was to be published in England (*D5* 146). When sales seemed stalled six weeks later, she speculated that "3 Gs has struck the rock of rage" (*D5* 155). The angry or uncomprehending questioned the links that Woolf postulated between patriarchy and war. In addition, there was irritation about the style and format of the book. Underlying all of these responses were, once again, attitudes to Woolf's feminism.

       We can get an interesting indirect view of that feminism by reviewing the responses to it. Central to the reception of *Three Guineas* is the hostility provoked by the book's endnotes and its photographs. This chapter therefore concludes with a discussion of the scholarly apparatus and the illustrations that together played such an important role in making this ostensible "letter" into something far more. They are not just, as many assume, citations of sources and comic or aggravating pictures.

By 1938 Virginia Woolf was a well established literary figure. *Three Guineas* was her next book after *The Years*, a volume that had added financial to critical success. Predictably, the little book was widely reviewed in England, by publications ranging from the *Times Literary Supplement* and the *New Statesman and Nation* to *Country Life* and *The Queen*. But it seems evident that reviewers by and large did not like the book that they felt obliged to compliment. The *Times Literary Supplement* featured it with a photo of the author. To her pleasure, the reviewer referred to Woolf as "the most brilliant pamphleteer in England." At the same time, however, he concluded his review with the complaint that Woolf should have considered both possessive mothers (bad) and the liberated young women of the 1930s (emancipated and equal). She spoke, he thought, to a small audience, "educated women of a civilised bourgeoisie." For him, as for many who followed, this was a belittling comment; he would have been unresponsive to her insistence that one should begin reforms at the place one was at. He also felt it necessary to say that the book's irony was "sharp but never inhuman."[1] Woolf recorded her disappointment that her friends and intimates were silent about *Three Guineas;* the contrast was their enthusiastic response, that same summer of 1938, to E. M. Forster's first published version of his famous essay "What I Believe" (*D5* 169). Certainly some men both liked and approved of *Three Guineas*, as did many women, but the book has differed from Woolf's other writing, feminist or not, in drawing a notably harsher response from men than from women. In addition, women who considered themselves feminists were among those responding unfavorably.

The relatively hostile reception of *Three Guineas* is, of course, part of the general reception of Woolf's work, an enormous and contested topic. Because the book is both political and polemical, as well as explicitly feminist in spite of the denials in the text, it received—and still receives—the most serious brunt of the attacks on Woolf that caricatured her as the ailing maiden queen of the snobbish Bloomsbury Group. In *Three Guineas*, she had dabbled her dainty privileged fingers in the serious matter of war and peace. Appreciation of Woolf's own, individual politics came only well after her death, when her diaries, letters, and unpublished manuscripts became available in print. And even then, many critics responded with distaste. Initially, in 1938, reviewers recoiled from the necessity of evaluating the political views of a woman best known for rather high-brow fiction and reviews usually not obviously topical. They were comfortable with neither

her arguments about the causes of war nor her ideas about patriarchy, and they ignored or rejected her claims about connections between the two. The book itself encouraged such hostility. *Three Guineas* was written in an oblique and allusive manner and framed, after all, as responses to an imaginary correspondent who wanted to know, not how feminism could change the world, but how women could help prevent war.

Furthermore, *Three Guineas* was presented to potential readers as an antiwar book and also as a sequel to both *A Room of One's Own* and *The Years*. Woolf may have written and in any case certainly approved Hogarth Press's blurb on the book's dust jacket. It was a straightforward-enough summary, but it concluded, "the book further develops certain trains of thought which run through Mrs. Woolf's last novel, *The Years*."[2] Hogarth Press also distributed in 1938 more than five thousand copies of a card that quoted favorable reviews and read: "The author of A ROOM OF ONE'S OWN asks what can a woman do to prevent war?"[3] *A Room of One's Own* had not made as sweeping an argument as *Three Guineas*. That its sequel was also "feminist" meant, for most reviewers, only that *Three Guineas* also defended women's rights—and, as we have noted, Woolf encouraged (and possibly confused) them in such views by the passage in *Three Guineas* where she defined the word *feminist* and said that it was obsolete. If Woolf's feminism could be seen as relatively limited and personal, it was possible to speculate about its biographical origins and evaluate the whole book as yet another dimension of Woolf's persona. The text could then be more easily depoliticized.[4]

Leonard Woolf's recorded responses to *Three Guineas* give a good indication of favorable but limited contemporary analyses made by those who were sympathetic to changes in the status of women but were not actually women's movement activists themselves. His memoirs, published more than a quarter century after Virginia Woolf's death, included the much-cited remark that his wife had been "the least political animal that has lived since Aristotle invented the definition." In the same paragraph he called *A Room of One's Own* and *Three Guineas* "political pamphlets" that fitted into "a long line stretching back" to Mary Wollstonecraft's *Vindication of the Rights of Woman*.[5] But this is not a good comparison, for Wollstonecraft's publications had partitioned her political concerns in a way that Virginia Woolf's did not. The pioneer feminist wrote about women only after her wildly successful first book about the major happening of her day, the now forgotten *Vindication of the Rights of Man* that countered Burke's views on the French Revolution. Reinforced by John Stuart Mill's widely read treatise *The Subjection of Women*, Wollstonecraft's vindication of woman's rights encouraged a later understanding of the political dimension of feminism as the quest for access to education along with equal public rights and especially the vote.

Virginia Woolf's husband was undeniably committed to the egalitarian treatment of women and identified himself as a feminist. For example, in a book published in 1920 he listed as "political evil" slavery, torture, "the subjection of women," and war. More than forty years later, discussing how Margaret Llewelyn Davies' gender had prevented her receiving public recognition for her work with the Women's Co-operative Guild, he wrote that "feminism [is] the belief or policy of all sensible men."[6] But Leonard Woolf used in 1920 Mill's outdated formulation, "subjection of women"—an equalizing rather than a transformative formulation. Carolyn Heilbrun was correct when she gently accused him of "failing to understand, as he seemed uniquely qualified to do, the connection between the subjection of women and the misuse of authority epitomized in fascism."[7]

As contemporary critics pointed out, Virginia Woolf was writing at a time when the legal barriers to gender equality, so substantial in Wollstonecraft's and Mill's time, had been largely removed. How then could *Three Guineas*, looking at women and war, be either feminist or political? Over time, the vocabulary changed, but to the extent that the topic continued to be, in Mill's words, "the subjection of women," the situation of women was considered irrelevant to what were seen to be larger issues. Above all, critics rejected any suggestion that women as such might generate the crucial, necessary changes in the world. In so doing, they rejected *Three Guineas*, and with it Virginia Woolf's feminism. And so the book sunk into disrepute and disregard.

Mainstream responses at the time of the book's publication, when Woolf was a highly visible and successful writer, handled the conundrum presented by *Three Guineas* by applauding Woolf's style. In the process, reviewers implied that this fine writer was incapable of making a reasoned argument. "What to say about [*Three Guineas*]," asked the *New Statesman and Nation* reviewer; "Should one call it simply a work of art, and hold up her method to the despair of all bunglers? Can one discuss its ideas, as though they were not involved with that enchanting presentment?"[8] Woolf understood how such comments trivialized the text's message and feared "the taunt Charm & emptiness" (*D5* 141). Instead she often got the even more disconcerting response where disagreement was sugared over by praise of style. Thus her dear friend Vita Sackville-West, to Woolf's intense annoyance, complimented the book for "lovely prose" while damning it for "misleading arguments"(*L6* 257). Other readers, including most of those critics who commented on *Three Guineas* after Woolf's death, were to find the prose repugnant as well, overlooking surface polish in their response to the anger in the book.[9]

After Woolf's death, *Three Guineas* received little attention, most of it hostile. In general, her reputation declined, and she came to be regarded as a relatively minor novelist.[10] During the postwar period that Marion Shaw calls the "dark ages" of Woolf criticism, critics "rescued Woolf's artistry at the expense of her politics."[11] She continued to be seen as a Bloomsbury aesthete, an artist who was incapable of realistic fiction or reasoned analysis. The most common response to *Three Guineas* specifically was that because Woolf was so well off, her anger (and her feminism) reflected some sort of psychological defect. Not art, not persuasive, but psychologically significant: these were the elements of the standard evaluations of *Three Guineas.* For example, Irma Rantavaara, in 1953, recognized Woolf's praise of women's distinctive qualities but explained it by the death of Julia Stephen when her daughter was a teenager, which had produced a sort of "repressed mother-worship" extended to all women (as well perhaps as a tendency to lesbianism). She considered *Three Guineas* "an aggressively feminist tract, not a work of art."[12]

Assessments both of feminism and Virginia Woolf have changed, of course, since the 1950s. Revived attention to Woolf has, first of all, to be linked with the mainly positive interest in the Bloomsbury Group that was first stimulated by *A Writer's Diary,* excerpted by Leonard Woolf from Virginia's complete diaries and published in 1953. A stream of biographies and autobiographies of members of the group was widely read, beginning with Roy Harrod's reticent account of Maynard Keynes in 1951 and Michael Holroyd's far more explicit biography of Lytton Strachey in 1967.[13] In the case of Virginia Woolf, the resulting attention tended to focus on her novels and, later, on her life. Quentin Bell's lucid and engaging biography, published in 1972, provided an initial view of his aunt that had a powerful influence on the interpretation of her work, nonfiction as well as fiction. He never liked *Three Guineas:* "the product of a very odd mind and . . . of a very odd state of mind." Bell reported that already in 1938, when he was a young leftist, he felt that the connection between women's rights and war was "tenuous"; the positive suggestions struck him as "wholly inadequate."[14] It seemed obvious to him that allowing arms into Spain and supporting the Left's classic remedy, a United Front, would have been a more appropriate response to the siege of Madrid than an attack on patriarchy. But where Leonard Woolf's memoirs simply left silent his views about *Three Guineas* as anything more than a feminist statement, as late as 1995 Bell felt it necessary to add to a book of reminiscences an appendix that declared *A Room of One's Own* "a masterpiece," but added, unforgivably, that "the mothers of Madrid, hunting in the debris of their bombed-out homes for the shattered limbs of their babies," would have rejected the arguments of *Three Guineas*.[15] More important for the critical reception of *Three Guineas*, he insisted with familial authority, beginning with his biography, that the book was best explained by the 1937 death in the Spanish Civil War of his brother, Julian Bell. In this, Bell was partly right. "I was always thinking of Julian when I wrote," reflected Woolf in June 1938, as she summed up her feelings about what she recalled as "six years floundering, striving, much agony, some ecstasy" while she wrote *The Years* and *Three Guineas* (D5 148). But Quentin Bell was one of many who persistently overlooked the lifelong importance for Woolf of both her feminism and her pacifism.

Virginia Woolf's nonfiction writing has continued to draw less attention than her enduring fiction, even though all of her writings have benefited from the rise of feminism, especially in North America. Those involved in the growing field of women's studies soon identified Woolf as a central figure for a new canon that was political as well as literary. Attention specifically to *Three Guineas* continues to be mainly in the context of academic feminism, unlike *A Room of One's Own*, which has pretty consistently appealed to the public. Even in the context of women's studies, the reception of *Three Guineas* was affected by the wider response to Woolf's nonfiction, which has always been colored by views about her novels. If her fiction is valued for experimentalism or damned for remoteness from some sort of socialist-realist model, so too are her expository texts as well as her essays and reviews. And if her novels are mainly of interest as a revelation of her sexual preferences or personal sufferings, then her nonfiction writing has little importance unless it is overtly autobiographical.

When the second wave of feminism made its appearance in the 1960s, its rediscovery and popularization of Virginia Woolf included a renewed attention to *Three Guineas*. Feminist interpretations of *Three Guineas* mirrored faithfully the development of academic women's studies in the United States. Partly because of Woolf's suicide, the very first feminist critics tended to view her as one of the victims of patriarchy, a member of what Phyllis Rose called the "head-in-the-oven school" of women writers.[16] The pioneering feminist critics tended to disregard the harsher and less literary *Three Guineas* or, at the most, to reject its insistence on the value of female experience. Their initially more positive reading of *A Room of One's Own* may in part have been based on a misunderstanding of what Woolf meant by androgyny, which second-wave feminism interpreted in a narrowly psychological sense. Carolyn Heilbrun, the theorist of androgyny who had written disparagingly of *Three Guineas'* "stridency" in 1973, confessed ten years later her "shame" at having preferred the "nicer" *A Room of One's Own* and commended Woolf for having, in her fifties, learned to express anger and value women's qualities.[17] But her more positive evaluation was still a personal, apolitical one.

When a full transcription of Woolf's letters began to appear in print in 1975, it attracted a wide readership, as did her adult diaries, published in the years 1977–84. All of these new books provided full annotations of all individuals whom Woolf encountered or mentioned. In addition, they documented Woolf's psychological fragility and her intense emotional involvement in her work. Although they provided substantial evidence of Woolf's enduring commitment to the views expressed in *Three Guineas*, they also had the incidental result of supporting renewed attention to biographical and therapeutic explanations of her writing. This was the period that saw multiple analyses of Woolf's periods of madness and a widely read volume attributing major influence on her work to (contested) episodes of sexual abuse.[18] Such analyses most often served preconceptions of the value of Woolf's writings, giving the growing body of feminist readers a new basis for valorizing her writing by praise for their author as a victim or a survivor.

Woolf's diaries also encouraged focus on the partial truth that Woolf saw *The Years* and *Three Guineas* as effectively the same book.[19] In 1996 Herbert Marder reexamined critical assessments that he had made some thirty years earlier; in 1968 he had approved of the novel but had seen in the "morbid" *Three Guineas* an image of "the evil patriarch . . . a twisted monster" and a "direct attack on social evil . . . too shrill and self-indulgent to succeed, even as propaganda." The persuasive or polemic essay, he said then, was the failure one would expect from an admired writer of subjective, personal fiction. Now he thought that *The Years* was "self-immolating" and *Three Guineas* "an attempt to rectify that."[20] This grudging statement did not rescind Marder's distaste for *Three Guineas*. Instead, new awareness of Woolf's lengthy, painful production of *The Years* had produced psychological dismissal of the novel and the associated *Three Guineas*.

A few analysts argued for attention to the direct connections to be found between Woolf's writings and the "real world" of conventional politics as she experienced it. The phrase is Alex Zwerdling's, from the title of an important 1986 book that devotes a chapter to "Woolf's Feminism in Historical Perspective" and half of another to *Three Guineas*. As he notes, Woolf was well aware of the differences among suffrage organizations and "the wide range of issues the movement had raised from its beginnings." However, in a sophisticated interpretation that drew critical attention to the political context of Woolf's writings, he nevertheless emphasizes Woolf's personal history: her "twin needs" in writing *A Room of One's Own* and *Three Guineas* were "to vent her anger about the subjection of women and to conciliate the male audience she could never entirely ignore."[21] Predictably, Zwerdling sees Woolf's pacifism as a response to the horrors of the approach to World War Two (which it was) but not as part of her feminism (which it also was). Similarly, Berenice Carroll appreciated the political stance underlying Woolf's work and most clearly expressed in *Three Guineas*. However, Carroll, affiliated with peace studies, also reverted to the earlier (and continuing) interpretation of the book as most centrally concerned with prevention of war. Feminism seemed to her, as to so many other critics, a limited ideology. She included in a perceptive discussion of the whole of Woolf's writing the statement that "properly understood, *Three Guineas* should be read as an essay in peace theory and peace action rather than as 'feminist pamphleteering,' though Woolf's radical pacifism is closely intertwined with her radical feminism." More recently, at the end of 2002, Susan Sontag described *Three Guineas* as Woolf's "brave, unwelcomed reflections on the roots of war." But she finds the book conventional in rhetoric and conclusions, and adds that "after some pages devoted to the feminist point," Woolf reverts to an unreasoned and unpolitical revulsion against war.[22]

It is to be expected that readers unsympathetic to feminism should be baffled or hostile. But even those willing to identify themselves as feminists have sometimes been wary of *Three Guineas*, which does not fit comfortably into those versions of feminism that are generally recognized. For the Left, feminism has historically been acceptable only if it centered on class issues and kept the needs of women deferential to the needs of the communist revolution or, until the Nazi-Soviet Pact, the communist-directed resistance to fascism. In an especially obtuse application of standpoint theory, Q. D. Leavis scolded Woolf in 1938 for her lack of awareness of the real needs of real women, who were from the working class and in any case humbly aware that they were still inferior to men. "Mrs. Woolf is not living in the contemporary world," she wrote, in a review studded with remarks about how Woolf was writing only for the "women of her class."[23] She deplored the massive implied changes; the deconstruction of patriarchy was not, of course, the sort of social reorganization that Leavis approved of.

A generation later, in 1975, Robin Majumdar and Allen McLaurin introduced selected reviews of *Three Guineas* with a summary of Leavis's comments, agreeing that "this book was written for a special, privileged class of women."[24] Strictly speaking, this is an accurate statement, for Woolf was exhorting women like herself to become active rather than passive outsiders. It is also, however, a rejection of Woolf's insistence on a gender-based and women-centered analysis. Even among second-wave feminists, as late as the end of the twentieth century, those who were primarily socialist in orientation had trouble with Woolf's insistence that class analysis was inadequate for understanding the situation of women like herself. Michèle Barrett suggested in 1993 that the "daughters of educated men" whom Woolf hoped to enlist against patriarchy might, over time, have become true bourgeoises in the classic sense once they could in fact acquire control of economically productive resources. For material reasons they would now, in their own right, share the national and class situation of their brothers instead of the emancipatory position that Woolf had attempted to place them in.[25] Socialists including the *Scrutiny* critics (in particular, Q. D. and F. R. Leavis) influenced Woolf's reputation and the reading of her works, especially in England. Well into the revival of feminism in the 1960s, even some liberal-feminist critics agreed that Woolf herself had had such opportunities that her feminism was inappropriate.

In addition, many readers, feminist or not, dislike any valorization of the differences between men and women; they can accept Woolf's feminism only to the extent that it singles out the disadvantages of women as compared to men—disadvantages that are now remedied. When Quentin Bell approvingly described Bloomsbury as "feminist," he based it on the fact that "women were on a completely equal footing with men" there. Such beliefs were, he said, "libertarian," and by contrast he decried the way in which the "puritanical" feminism of the nineteenth century had attempted to exert a domestic influence over male behavior.[26] At the early date of 1965, Cynthia Ozick identified Virginia Woolf herself—but as a writer, not as a feminist—as "the artist-pioneer" of the claim of women to creativity on equal terms with men. "We are far past the grievances Virginia Woolf grappled with in *A Room of One's Own* and *Three Guineas*—books still sneered at as 'feminist,'" she wrote. When she reprinted the essay eight years later, she prefaced it with an uneasy introduction that made it clear that she rejected basic aspects of Woolf's feminism: "Feminism as a literary issue was absent before the women's movement, and now that there is a strong women's movement deliberately defining itself through deliberate segregation, it seems to me that feminism is again absent." Even in *A Room of One's Own*, when she wrote about the incandescence and androgyny of genius, Woolf's views were not on Ozick's side of this argument. But then Ozick still believed in 1983 that "in 1965, there was no glimmer of a women's movement."[27]

At the time of Woolf's centenary in 1982, well after the appearance of women's liberation and the widespread acceptance of at least the liberal-feminist versions of feminism, the distinguished philosopher and novelist Iris Murdoch summed up reactions to Woolf's views:

> Perhaps we both recognise her feminism now and are critical of it. That is, we see, on the one hand, that she's a fighter for the position of women. . . . On the other hand, there's an awful lot in her stories which is to do with portraying a feminine sensibility in contrast to a masculine intellect, or a feminine generosity in comparison with a male egotism.

She did not think "that the liberation of women should be associated with such distinctions."[28] The vocabulary had shifted, and the interpretation of Woolf's views about men and women was one that would not have been made earlier. But the evaluation had not changed; differences between men and women were still not seen as valuable or as relevant to social change.

It is the self-identified radical feminists who have been best able to expand *Three Guineas'* analysis of patriarchy and militarism; such rationales prompted the organization of peace camps at the nuclear base at Greenham Common. Responding to the 1991 Gulf War against Iraq, radical feminist Carol Anne Douglas gave a nuanced interpretation, treating Woolf's feminism and pacifism as inseparable. In a piece titled "Dear Ms. Woolf, We Are Returning Your Guineas," she lamented that Woolf's prescriptions for education were not being followed. Women's integration into public life meant that they increasingly shared the "unreal loyalties" that, according to Woolf, made men willing to go to war. As Douglas noted in something close to despair, women were even serving in the military, with support from feminist theorists and women's organizations.[29]

More recently, the movement of feminism toward appreciation of women's specific and varying histories and experiences has made *Three Guineas* increasingly relevant. Beginning in the 1980s, feminist critics became concerned about issues of diversity and the interaction of systems of domination. For socialists, issues of class had always been paramount, which led to discussions about Woolf's attitudes toward class differences, including whether in *Three Guineas* she was condescending about domestics.[30] In an analysis reflecting growing awareness of the interactions among structures of domination, Mary M. Childers articulated the deserved criticism that Woolf "describes the experience of working-class and middle-class women as completely separate, rather than interlocking in a hierarchical system in which differences connect people through conflict that considerably modifies similarities produced by gender."[31]

Nevertheless, there was increased agreement about the political significance of the themes of *Three Guineas*. By the end of the twentieth century, the consensus was in the direction of accepting Woolf's feminism—especially in *Three Guineas*—as in tune with feminists' historical and present opposition to all forms of hierarchy, now understood as including the oppressive structures of sexism and heterosexism, in addition to class, racism, and imperialism. *Three Guineas* certainly spoke to inequalities of class and race, and also imperialism, even though it made no reference to sexual orientation or to issues of age and bodily condition.[32]

In general, by the beginning of the twenty-first century, critics were more likely to react positively to Woolf's anger and satire in *Three Guineas*. The availability of an extraordinarily wide range of material about Woolf finally generated a more persuasive appreciation of *Three Guineas* as a presentation of deeply felt feminist views. In 1996 a balanced, explicitly feminist biography of Woolf by Hermione Lee, the best received and most widely read of several recent biographies that supplement Quentin Bell's more family- and personally oriented book, included a careful and largely positive assessment of *Three Guineas*. The book is "a radical—and unpalatable—critique of 'Hitler in England,' or 'subconscious Hitlerism,'" Lee concluded.[33] At the end of the millennium, it seemed reasonable to state that, for most readers, *Three Guineas* had ceased to be "odd" or "flawed" and had become an essential document of Virginia Woolf's feminism, which itself was better understood.

At the same time, approval of *Three Guineas* has been far from universal.

The English have remained relatively unimpressed by Virginia Woolf.[34] At the time of her centenary in 1982, Frank Kermode was prepared to dismiss "the revival of interest in Woolf" as "a sort of epiphenomenon of the revival of feminism."[35] A decade later, as series editor for a new paperback edition of her works, including a double volume combining *Three Guineas* with *A Room of One's Own*, he stressed Woolf's literary originality and Bloomsbury connections and did not mention her feminism; the "polemical" *Three Guineas* was merely noted in passing.[36] Jane Marcus wrote, optimistically, in 2001 that "something of the liveliness of the American debate on Woolf in the 1980s appears to be going on now in Britain," but the books she called "a series of excellent and serious historical studies" were Nigel Nicolson's brief biography, which Marcus justly described as "brief, eccentric, self-aggrandizing . . . the zillionth life of Virginia Woolf," yet another edition of *Flush*, an analysis of Woolf's writing in terms of public/private contrasts, a rather schematic decoding of fiction for political subtexts, and an account of Woolf's alleged anorexia. Among the authors reviewed, Anna Snaith, who had transcribed and annotated the letters that Woolf received from readers of *Three Guineas*, was the only one to discuss the book seriously. Even the ever-enthusiastic Marcus had to conclude that these works represented Woolf as something very different from what she rather disparagingly described as "the aggressive feminist created by my generation of American feminist critics."[37] In 2001, the new, massive *Norton Anthology of Theory and Criticism* included a few excerpts from *A Room of One's Own* and no mention of *Three Guineas*.[38] And in 2002, no less than two literary journals in England featured attacks on *Three Guineas* that were essentially attacks on Woolf's politics.[39]

II

We may well wonder why this book has so often been marginalized or, if noticed, so disliked. The reasons seem to start with the tone of *Three Guineas*. It has been variously described. Even as late as 1990 a friendly feminist critic could describe the tone of *Three Guineas* as a "powerful stridency which muddied [Woolf's] argument and earned her charges of naiveté."[40] Woolf wrote to Margaret Llewelyn Davies that she had needed to "secrete a jelly to slip quotations down people's throats," but she told her niece, Philippa Woolf (aged fifteen), that the book was intended to make people angry and to say irritating things (*L6* 251, 360).[41] It is perhaps best described as deliberately teasing. It is not obvious that the tone itself is aggravating. Those who were receptive to the message also responded positively to the tone. Those who do not like or understand the message are also repelled by the tone of the book as well as by its structure and form, particularly the annotations and the photographs. This reaction amounted to a further rejection of the book's feminism, and of Virginia Woolf's feminism more generally.

Three Guineas is at the same time a consciousness-raiser and a fund-raising appeal and program designed to promote middle-class women's activism. Not shrill, not strident, not conventionally charming, the voice in *Three Guineas* is the voice of the daughters of educated men talking to one another. They have grievances, but they laugh—at men—as they work up their indignation together. They are elite women, with less power than their elite brothers, but nevertheless with the potential to produce large-scale social change, even an end to war and to its source, sexism. We can assume Woolf knew her likely audience and what they would find appealing. She was, as well as a novelist, a professional literary journalist who knew that raw facts must be processed if the result was to be published and read. It is important to remember Woolf's continuing experience with magazines and newspapers, including some produced by and for women. How could she be so naive as to think, for example, that her brother-in-law Clive Bell would find the illustrations in *Three Guineas*, let alone the arguments, either comic or telling? He had been a hunting, shooting man, after all, even though he was a pacifist.

The intended audience, persuaded or persuadable of *Three Guineas'* underlying feminism, certainly relished the tone as well as the content of the book. Pippa Strachey, longtime activist with the suffragists and then the London and National Society for Women's Service, wrote optimistically that *Three Guineas'* "amusingness" would make even the hostile read it; her own pleasure was "swollen by all sorts of extraneous currents including the joys of a vent for evil feelings." Shena Simon wrote, "I never imagined that you could write a second 'Room of One's Own' which would equal if not surpass (I haven't quite decided yet) the original." In addition, right from the time of first publication, feminist enthusiasm encompassed the form as well as the content of *Three Guineas*, with particular attention to the notes and the photographs. Pippa loved the notes, "more effective by being collected together at the end instead of creeping in & out around the margins." Lady Simon felt that "the footnotes raise the whole level of references to a height that no other writer can ever hope to reach"—though she hoped that they would not be missed by readers who did not want to turn to the end. Veteran suffragist Emmeline Pethick-Lawrence, who commented that *Three Guineas* was "likely to inaugurate a new era," added in a postscript that "the illustrations are a work of genius—simply delicious!"[42]

But we have already moved from tone to form and structure. *Three Guineas* is more than just a document of feminism or a polemic for it, whatever its intended audience. It is also, like all of Virginia Woolf's publications, a carefully crafted work of art whose form is linked closely and consciously to its content. In this case, the apparatus of scholarship deployed in *Three Guineas* as well as the use of photographs are significant parts of the feminist intentions of the book.

Many critics found what looked like the "scholarly," argumentative dimensions of the book particularly off-putting, both incompetent and offensive. They were impressed by neither the logic nor the array of citations and endnotes. Maynard Keynes's reaction is reported as follows by Quentin Bell, who basically agreed with it: Keynes "found it difficult not to lose his temper with a production that seemed to him so shrill, so foolish, so muddleheaded."[43] In a similar vein, Nigel Nicolson, co-editor with Joanne Trautmann of Woolf's published letters and son of her dear friend Vita Sackville-West, felt the need to use the introduction to the 1932–35 volume of letters to comment critically. Virginia "was an imaginative, emotional writer," he wrote, "and in *Three Guineas* attempted to use for the first time the apparatus of logic, scholarship and politics, and the scope and shape of it were not suited to her particular cast of mind." Furthermore, "her argument was weakened by inconsistency, incoherence, selective quotation and abandoned trails" (*L5* xv, xvii–xviii). In the year 2000, Nicolson explicitly repeated his criticism. Writing of the absence of "intellectual discipline that might have saved [Woolf] from the hyperbole of *Three Guineas*," he invoked once again the similar criticisms made earlier by Quentin Bell and by Nicolson's mother.[44] Even the sympathetic Zwerdling deems the paraded learning a failure: "argument by citation and footnote" was an "alien discourse" for which Woolf "gritted her teeth, determined to beat the enemy at his own game."[45]

The varied responses to the citations and endnotes relate in part to the fact that there are two, somewhat contradictory dimensions to the presentation in *Three Guineas*. Woolf, who sometimes used conventional documentation conventionally, also undercut it in a demonstration of what a feminist approach to scholarship might look like. In this endeavor, she was picking up the task of feminists in the National Union of Women's Suffrage Societies but carrying it a stage further. The activist women closest to Woolf had a strategy of negotiating peacefully with the male political establishment while demonstrating the sort of feminist society that was their aim. Accordingly, in striking contrast to Mrs. Pankhurst's authoritarian rule of the militant suffragettes, the member and successor groups of the National Union nurtured internally a ponderous but genuine democracy. Woolf was telling the truth—up to a point—when she wrote in a letter, "all I wanted was to state a very intricate case as plainly and readable as I can" (*L6* 243). She was also demonstrating what a feminist could do with (and to) the apparatus of scholarship.

It is true that a book relying explicitly on "fact" was a new and somewhat difficult task for Woolf. It was not that she lacked experience in basing a text on sources outside it; her reading notebooks and diaries bear witness to a long-established set of procedures for taking notes and weaving quotations into essays and reviews. She had also published a number of texts that drew on nonliterary sources with varying degrees of acknowledgment and had even supplied notes: eight straightforward footnotes in *A Room of One's Own* and ten endnotes keyed to page references in *Flush*.[46] By the time Woolf was writing *Three Guineas*, she had already compiled a vast amount of extracts from letters and other material that she would use for her biography of Roger Fry. But *Three Guineas* was the only place where she even attempted to join a systematic attribution of sources to the main text. Nor did she ever base any other substantial piece of writing on current periodicals. She used a massive number of sources for the book. Almost a hundred books and half as many periodical items are cited or referred to in *Three Guineas*.[47]

Woolf used her cited sources seriously and with full awareness of the problems involved in integrating them into an effective text. Commenting on a draft of Ethel Smyth's autobiographical *Female Pipings in Eden*, she objected to Smyth's use of "statistics." Her criticism was "largely on aesthetic grounds," she wrote, the risk that "the whole effect of the writing, as a rounded and designed building, is frittered away and teased." It was so difficult to "quote rightly," she wrote to Lady Cecil after *Three Guineas* had been published. "One flies along full tilt on one's own sail: then there's a loathsome lump of fact—some Bishop or Marquess or Mr Baldwin or Whitaker—to be worked in—thats the snag." "I'm suspicious of the vulgarity of the notes: of a certain insistence," she wrote in her journal in April after she had finished them (*L5* 191; *L6* 242; *D5* 134).

It is clear Woolf was critical of the apparatus of scholarship that she used so emphatically in *Three Guineas*. "A Society" has great fun with the process of enquiry, and *A Room of One's Own* gives an ironical account of research in the British Museum, setting the stage for a direct attack in *Three Guineas*. There, some explicit comments grow out of a discussion of the Church of England's rejection of the ordination of women. The narrator summarizes the church's arguments: women are less spiritual, and this is fortunate, for in order to "forsake all worldly cares and studies" a minister needs a wife who will occupy herself with "the cares of the household and the family." The resulting fascist-like separation of women from men has had significant effects:

> we owe to this segregation the immense elaboration of modern instruments and methods of war; the astonishing complexities of theology; the vast deposit of notes at the bottom of Greek, Latin and even English texts; the innumerable carvings, chasings and unnecessary ornamentations of our common furniture and crockery; the myriad distinctions of Debrett and Burke.

She sums it up as the "meaningless but highly ingenious turnings and twistings into which the intellect ties itself" when freed from domestic responsibilities (*3G* 163). Warfare, theology, footnotes, Victorian over-ornamentation, minute and meaningless social distinctions—this is a mixture typical of Woolf, as is her mockery of her own lengthy, well-documented note.

Finally, she generated a mass of notes—124 of them—which make up a fifth of the book.[48] Forty-six of these are simply sources for citations given in the text. Of the remainder, some sixty are essays, sometimes on topics more briefly referred to in the text, sometimes on completely different though related subjects. These note-essays are not a trivial part of the book's argument. As we have seen, the omission of endnotes from the serial "Women Must Weep" creates a major difference in tone and emphasis between the serial and its book version, with the serial far more tightly focused on the issue of prevention of war.

III

The two sorts of notes in *Three Guineas* correspond roughly to the two sorts of cited material to be found in both text and supporting documentation. Some of the evidence is conventional, as when Woolf cites figures of maternal mortality or of the relative number of scholarships or honors awarded to men and women, in the latter case by an ingenious (and accurate) comparison of column inches. Such undeniable and well-documented facts both support and belie Woolf's disingenuous statements such as that "the book is a mere outline, but I wanted to state the case as briefly as possible" (*L6* 238–39). Related arguments are familiar, unambiguous, and largely uncontroversial by the later 1930s, such as that childbirth is a hazardous female occupation that should be treated by doctors in a way responsive to women's needs, or that women should have the same access to all dimensions of postsecondary education as men. Such material is the portion of the book that is liable to be seen as obvious, acceptable, at the worst perhaps a little dated (even though the examples show how much is still left to be done, worldwide, some seventy-five years later).

Even with such seemingly standard reference material, however, the use of "facts" is not entirely straightforward. Woolf usually picks out, or even invents, dramatic dimensions that can serve as symbols. For example, she emphasizes access to the use of chloroform for childbirth pain in order to dramatize the long resistance of the medical profession to the use of analgesics for women in labor, still a significant issue in the interwar period. Chloroform, as she points out, had been first publicly used by Queen Victoria in 1853, over half a century before childbirth anesthesia became widely accepted. In the real world of reproductive politics, however, after the publication of Grantly Dick Read's book in 1933, women activists came to support the unmedicated "natural childbirth" he recommended. Even the medical profession accepted the use of "twilight sleep," which combined the analgesic morphine with the amnesiac scopolamine; it had been available since 1902. Similarly, in relation to women's postsecondary education, the fact that in 1938 Cambridge still did not allow women to receive more than nominal degrees or become professors is indignantly highlighted in *Three Guineas*. Yet the "modern universities" had admitted women in the nineteenth century and treated them in an egalitarian fashion long before they were accepted at the two older ones. In addition, although in the late 1930s there were not yet any women professors at Oxbridge, women both lectured and, more important, conducted tutorials and set examinations at Cambridge as well as Oxford.

In the first example, Woolf was highlighting male resistance to women's desire to control reproduction, and in the second, she was making vivid the boorish reluctance of the male establishment to treat women as equals and equally entitled to share in that education that gives access to power. Q. D. Leavis, herself an early graduate of Girton College, was prepared to state flatly in her 1938 review of *Three Guineas* that "fifty years of experience" have showed that "it is the exceptional and not the average woman student who is the intellectual equal of the average serious undergraduate in the same subject." In the true Oxbridge spirit that Virginia Woolf so disliked, Leavis recommended that women students should be relegated to the far less prestigious red brick universities that had been more hospitable to them.[49]

Most of the remaining documentation of *Three Guineas* is relatively unconventional in both content and form, using, for example, material like quotations from the explorer Mary Kingsley ("All the paid-for education I ever received was lessons in German") and a newspaper account of a man who made his wife call him "sir." A few supportive men are quoted— Bertrand Russell, Julian Huxley, George Bernard Shaw—but examples of male prejudice are far more common, such as the writer William Gerhardie remarking that he has never "committed the error of looking on women writers as serious fellow artists. I enjoy them rather as spiritual helpers [whose] true role is to hold out the sponge to us, cool our brow, while we bleed" (*3G* 161). With such material, a good deal of which is hidden in the endnotes, it is a question less of rational arguments than of demonstrations of the horrors and absurdities of a hierarchical and therefore militaristic world. For this purpose, the endnotes include a large number of essays only loosely connected to the markers in the text, such as a long reflection on the lives of maids, an analysis of the pleasures of domination, and a discussion of Saint Paul's views about the veiling of women, cited as an example of patriarchal ideology.

It is striking to what extent the endnotes include memorable parts of the book. It is in the endnotes, not the main text, that Woolf invokes *Antigone*, derides Mr. Justice McCardie, cites Walter Bagehot's horrible letter about professional women, expounds her views on chastity and veiling and Saint Paul, and quotes Walt Whitman, S. T. Coleridge, and George Sand on the nature of equality and freedom. It is in an endnote that Woolf justifies coining the term "educated man's daughter" on the grounds that "our ideology is still . . . inveterately anthropocentric." Although the clumsy coinage "anthropocentric" never caught on, here is Woolf, in 1938, identifying what we now call androcentrism.[50]

Throughout *Three Guineas*, in both the main text and the endnotes, snippets of the lives of actual women represent both history and future possibilities for a life shaped by women's experience. Leslie Stephen's influence, along with the *Dictionary of National Biography* that he inaugurated and edited, is patent here. But central to his daughter's method is a very different choice and treatment of subjects. The *DNB* has never included many women; up to 1985 only 4 percent of the cumulated entries recounted women's lives. When 1993's "Missing Persons" added accounts of those notables who had been previously and inappropriately omitted from earlier editions, Margaret Llewelyn Davies finally made it into the *DNB*, along with Sylvia Pankhurst and Ray Strachey. But only 12 percent of those retrieved were women.[51] Such notable women do appear in *Three Guineas*, though most often as sources rather than examples. However, even the few undeniably famous women whom Woolf discusses, such as Mary Kingsley and Florence Nightingale, Elizabeth Barrett Browning and Charlotte Brontë and Gertrude Bell, appear basically as daughters and sisters who are not educated, who are prevented from marrying according to their choice, or who cannot go out in London without an escort. Barbara Bodichon is given credit for her work as a supporter of women's education and rights, but hers is hardly a well-known name, and her main function in the text is as an example of what "one father . . . could do by allowing one daughter £300 a year" (*3G* 125). *Three Guineas* gives more attention to women who would never by any possible recalculation be included in any *DNB*. These are the "lives of the obscure": Miss Weeton the governess, Mrs. Rance the mayoress of Woolwich, Mrs. Frankau the wife whom Mr. Justice McCardie thinks so badly of.[52] There is an underlying conviction in *Three Guineas* that powerful men are both wrongheaded and ridiculous; they appear most conspicuously in the mocking photographs. "Laughter as an antidote to dominance is perhaps indicated," Woolf writes at the conclusion of one of the more important of the endnote essays (*3G* 164). And the essays, like the photographs, are often comic, as Woolf puts her own admonition into practice.

In notes connected to an account of the riots that enforced women's continuing formal exclusion from equal participation at Cambridge, Woolf even tells the reader what she is doing. The first note simply gives the main source, a moderately sympathetic eyewitness account she has excerpted from the memoirs of the noted physicist J. J. Thomson, director of the Cavendish Laboratory and Master of Trinity. In her second reference in the text, she adds an effective and provocative detail about the riots: "the gentlemen in authority" watched from their study windows, "without taking the cigars from their lips or ceasing to sip, slowly as its bouquet deserves, their admirable claret." But the appended reference to a newspaper clipping does not refer the reader to Thomson's memoirs. Instead it cites a description of how "Dons in a Senior Common Room after dinner" use a little trolley to move, not claret, but port around the table.[53] "Strict accuracy, here slightly in conflict with rhythm and euphony, requires the word 'port,'" Woolf notes (*3G* 82, 156); do we hear a slight giggle?

Thus, if the first endnote supplies conventional documentation, the second one explicitly undercuts trust in such material. We are warned that she is playing around with details. But she has done more: examination of Thomson's memoirs reveals that really "strict accuracy" about the attacks on women students at Cambridge would also require noting that Woolf has combined comments about two different occasions when the undergraduates were encouraged to resist forcefully the incursion of women into their ranks.[54] Furthermore, the telling, invented detail about the drinking dons is based on an article about Common Room practices at Oxford, not Cambridge, and has nothing to do with antiwoman riots (Oxford, to its credit, had none). In a note to *Flush* she makes a similar comment: Elizabeth Barrett Browning's dog was stolen three times, but because of "the unities" she has compressed the repeated thefts into one.[55]

Woolf was deadly serious about topics such as the marginalization of women in the elite educational system. She nevertheless deliberately used her evidence in ways that were playful and ironic, as she had on a slighter scale in *A Room of One's Own*. Such evidence included the five photographs that are an essential part of *Three Guineas*.

IV

Hostile male readers of *Three Guineas* are particularly liable to react strongly to the photographs and the related material about male public display. (See the illustrations following page 166.) Shena Simon wrote to Woolf in November 1938, reporting a meeting of about fifty middle-class Fabians: "What surprised and amused me, was the reaction of the men to your remarks about their dress."[56] Quentin Bell, again giving his own and Keynes's responses, casts some light on such reactions:

> [Keynes] was particularly cross about the illustrations. . . . They proved, amusingly enough, that women have no monopoly of absurdity in dress; I don't think that they proved very much more than that. But to Maynard they seemed a monstrous addition. They made a mockery, not of men, but of institutions for which he had a real affection. They made a mockery of our history and this he resented.[57]

Bell, whose first book was about English fashion, was able to be dismissive about the photos. But it was the indignant Keynes who sensed what the photographs meant. Like the text itself and its endnotes, they were challenges to the hierarchical structure so comfortably accepted by the patriarchy. Certainly, the five photographs used to illustrate the book are less ambiguous than the endnotes. Given the context, their display of official masculine finery was no more "a crude statement of fact" than were the photographs from the Spanish Civil War to which Woolf's remark originally applied (3G 10). Behind the illustrations to *Three Guineas* lurk the photographs of eminent Victorians that were carefully selected for debunking by Lytton Strachey. We should also remember the straightforwardly admiring Victorian portraits snapped by Woolf's aunt, Julia Margaret Cameron; Virginia Woolf, with Roger Fry, reprinted a selection of these under the appropriate title "famous men and fair women."[58] *Three Guineas'* photographs deserve more attention than they usually get; it is unfortunate that they have been omitted from nearly all of the paperback editions of the book.

Virginia Woolf uses photographs fairly frequently in her nonfiction books, but only in *Roger Fry* are they serious illustrations of the text.[59] The photographs of *Three Guineas* are more than jokes, however, and they are also more than simply illustrations. Looked at in isolation from the surrounding text, they are unremarkable. It is true that they are all photographs of men, but they are of public events in which women are relatively infrequently found. Even today, women are not often generals, heralds, judges, or university chancellors, and there has still not been a woman archbishop. That is the major point being made by *Three Guineas'* photographs: the absence of women from the formal ceremonial contexts that attest to public power.[60]

Furthermore, *Three Guineas'* anonymous photographs, surprising in a heavily documented book, make the point that the eminence of men is generic—that the institutions, not the individuals, are the reason for both the panoply and the reality of power. Radical feminist Robin Morgan suggests that domination and its violent outcomes depend on the depersonalizing effect of certain sorts of publicly assumed garb. She points to similarity of design and function among what men wore in 1938 and in 1989: "costumes, uniforms, disguises [are] worn by the men of the church and the military (as Virginia Woolf noted in *Three Guineas*) *and* by men of the corporation, *and* by the hip-radical or the Yuppie, the biker or the chieftain."[61] For Morgan, these are the emissaries of patriarchy, and they are all potential terrorists. In her bleaker moods, Woolf would agree.

More benignly, concealed by the anonymity, the photographs include

A General

An Archbishop

Heralds

A University Procession

A Judge

jokes not visible to us but likely to be obvious to the first readers of *Three Guineas*. The individuals in the pictures were well known in their day: the general with his dress uniform and honors was the hero of Mafeking and the founder of the Boy Scouts, shown at a levée at St. James's Palace in 1937; the academic procession was headed by a former prime minister, Stanley Baldwin, in his capacity as chancellor of Cambridge University; the judge was Gordon Hewart, lord chief justice of England, leaving a Judges' Service at Westminster Abbey; and the cleric was Cosmo Gordon Lang, archbishop of Canterbury, in a photograph taken in about 1936.[62] Only the mislabeled heralds, actually state trumpeters, were genuinely anonymous, and they were typical of many such seen in 1936, the year when a royal death and two accessions produced a great deal of related pageantry.

The third and major point made by the photographs, but only when they are placed in the context of the arguments of *Three Guineas*, is that men are vain, and arrogant, and besotted with status. The pictures are notable for the display of gorgeous apparel, every piece of which has meaning and indicates rank and power. In 1927 Virginia Woolf wrote: "there may be good reasons for believing in a King or a Judge or a Lord Mayor. When we see them go sweeping by in their robes and their wigs, with their heralds and outriders, our knees begin to shake and our looks to falter."[63] In *Three Guineas*, on the page before the photograph of the general in all his glory of plumes and medals, the narrator observes that "every button, rosette and stripe seems to have some symbolical meaning" (*3G* 17). There is nothing generic about what the general has on. Sir Robert Stephenson Smyth Baden-Powell (1857–1941), first Lord Baden-Powell of Gilwell, is in his full dress uniform as colonel of the Thirteenth Hussars, and draped across his chest are many of the decorations derided in *Three Guineas:* neck decorations of the Order of Merit and of a Knight of the Order of the Bath as well as a sash of a Knight Grand Cross of the Order of Saint Michael and Saint George, a badge of the Order of Saint John, a breast star of the Order of the Bath, and what may be a breast star of the Royal Victorian Order.[64]

Most importantly, the trappings of hierarchy are part of a justification of competition and domination. Nigel Nicolson complained that Woolf "not only overstated the case but muddled it" by the inclusion of the photos: "If [men] wore robes, wigs and uniforms of different ranks . . . it was for historical reasons," he wrote. And he protested, like Keynes, that "her anger was focused not on men of mean attainments but on the successful. Not on the intrusive bureaucrat, the bullying sergeant, or the hack scholar, but on the statesman, the General, the Professor and the Judge" (*L5* xvi). Quite so; it was indeed historical, and it was precisely the successes, not the failures, of masculine civilization that feminists like Woolf objected to.

For contrast, it is worth examining the four photographs that Leonard Woolf used in 1935 for his own antiwar polemic, *Quack, Quack!* Two photographs described as "Effigy of the War-God Kukailimoku from the Hawaiian Islands (British Museum)" are interleaved with "Herr Hitler" and "Signor Mussolini" so that the masks face the dictators side by side for the reader of the book. War-gods and fascist dictators match one another in vicious and slightly comic rage; they are presented as, respectively, survivors of and throwbacks to what Leonard Woolf sees as a less civilized era. Leonard Woolf's analysis is different from his wife's, who had contrasted her own civilization to that of the fathers who were pig butchers. For her, militarism was not any sort of reversion to savagery but instead a logical consequence of patriarchy.

Furthermore, the photographs in *Quack, Quack!* seem to be rather differently selected and used than those in *Three Guineas*. It is difficult to evaluate them so many years later, but if Hitler's photograph is possibly a hostile choice, the picture of Mussolini is relatively characteristic. It is not the images themselves that matter but the juxtapositions—a condemnation by resemblance. The polemical point is obvious even without the text, although the text spells out the implications to make them clearer. By contrast—and this is what can make them so annoying—Virginia Woolf's photographs, in isolation, are simply typical public men, if especially ornamental ones. It is worth noting that her discussions of the dictators of her time have no pictorial accompaniments; Mussolini, Franco, and Hitler could hardly be presented anonymously.

Leonard Woolf's photographic satire has been seriously undercut since 1935. A man like him would be wary today of the Eurocentrism of such a comparison. In addition, although the wars of the Hawai'ians, as reported by the Europeans, were notoriously bloody, more recent anthropological analyses have demonstrated a high degree of structure in such "primitive" combats.[65] In general, war is now most often interpreted as a representation of a given society's cultural and historical situation. "Modern" warfare emerges as the least constrained, the most destructive—not a throwback but a horrible progression. As John Keegan wrote in 1993 in his well received *History of Warfare*, "In the primitive world, [warmaking] was circumscribed by ritual and ceremony. In the postprimitive world, human ingenuity ripped ritual and ceremony, and the restraints they imposed on warmaking, away from warmaking practice, empowering men of violence to press its limits of tolerability beyond the extreme."[66] By contrast, Virginia Woolf's description of martial ornamentation and hierarchy seems more rather than less accurate today. As in civilian life, both regalia and rationale are essentially unchanged, even if a few female faces and bodies are now present.

The photographs in *Three Guineas*, like the arguments, the style, and the notes, demonstrated Woolf's feminism: a radical rejection of much of the society she lived in. Woolf had pilloried Nicolson's statesman, general, and judge in both photographs and text. Her attack on the professor had an additional dimension, the form of *Three Guineas* itself. No wonder professors—and critics—did not approve. But the daughters of educated men continued to like it, possibly because so many of the issues it had identified remained unresolved, possibly also because, like Virginia Woolf, they found the disasters of patriarchy comic as well as appalling.

8

Feminism in the Third Millennium

The problem now is to evaluate Woolf's feminism, still so often rejected by those who do not understand—or do not want to understand—what it is about. Repeatedly, recurrently, Woolf has been charged with being remote from the most immediately compelling problems of her, and now our, time. Yet the writer of *Three Guineas* was transfixed by the Spanish Civil War and the likelihood of a larger war that would grow from the same causes. This is hardly avoiding the obsessive struggles of the day, or the questions of war and of militarism. The problem was, in fact, that even when Woolf targeted a particular combat or even all wars actual and imaginable, what she cared most about were the larger social structures that caused the battles.

Even among feminists, those who are not simply committed pacifists are unlikely to see *Three Guineas* as applicable in more than very vague and unhelpful ways to current problems of war and peace. More generally, recent readers, discouraged by the lack of world change since the eve of World War Two, have been likely to find the arguments presented in *Three Guineas* inadequate, even close to irrelevant. Hierarchy still prevails. The world is still racked by war and poverty, sexism and racism, and the oppression of those of minority religions or sexual orientation. Disasters, terrors, and militarism continue even in those places where feminism has had some hearing and some impact. The ethnic and religious conflicts that have followed us into the early years of this century repeat, in even more dreadful form, the horrors of the 1930s. The dreaded Second World War, not won until after Virginia Woolf's death, has been replaced by seemingly endless struggles unlikely to see the closure of military victory. Even in some few places where the clearest embodiments of patriarchal tyranny have been defeated, shattered societies lie in ruins.

When I was beginning to write this book, in 1999, an Albanian ethnic province of the former Yugoslavia became a symbol of the disasters of war, as Madrid had been for a much earlier generation. In Kosovo, in the twentieth century's last chapter of the unfinished book of the self-destruction of Yugoslavia, murder, rape, and expulsion of an unwanted civilian population provoked from NATO a version of the international military support refused half a century earlier to the republican government of Spain. But the impact of well-intended intervention, itself a reaction against the interwar hesitations of the 1930s, was dubious, and the future of the devastated region is still clouded years later. No women, no women's voices, no women's perspective appear in the media, except when women survive the massacre of their husbands and sons to become a potent symbol of victimization—but without any accompanying vision of how their nation became so pathological. At the end of the twentieth century, "Virginia Woolf at Kosovo" could serve as a symbol of the marginalization of feminism: what comfort could we or the victims of war draw from a parodic imagined image of Virginia Woolf, prim in a long skirt and cardigan, picking her way gingerly over ruins like those she had described in Spain? These are images that make *Three Guineas*, and indeed feminism with its focus on women, look limited, dated.

I do not accept these judgments; we need not accept these judgments. Both feminism and Woolf's specific version of it have been grossly misunderstood and underestimated. The Balkans, and indeed the world, will pull clear of the seemingly endless cycles of domination and violence only if we reimagine and rebuild in a new way. Those who read *Three Guineas* with care will find some answers there. And some few now seem to have done so.

Two years after the NATO intervention in Kosovo, on 11 September 2001, terrorist suicide attacks in New York and Washington killed thousands of civilians inside a country that was not at war. Feminists once again had to ask themselves how to respond. But this time it has been possible to articulate a feminist response compatible with Woolf's feminism, and even one drawing explicitly on her vision. Robin Morgan, who has long written eloquently on the malignancy of masculine violence, ended a widely circulated e-mail report on the tragedy with a reference to *Three Guineas*. Rejecting simple patriotism, unconditional national commitment, and pledges of allegiance, she concluded: "I weep for a city and a world. I cling to a different loyalty . . . the defiant un-pledge of a madwoman who also had mere words as her only tools in a time of ignorance and carnage." And she quoted Virginia Woolf: "As a woman I have no country. As a woman I want no country. As a woman my country is the whole world."[1] Like Woolf, Morgan qualified her disengagement from patriotic chauvinism with a deep devotion to the realities of the place where she lived, in her case the devastated New York City of the attack on the World Trade Center. Morgan's own history of working with the international women's movement, along with her recommendations of possible action—beginning with words—made it clear that she still thought feminism central and vital, and that it was a feminism growing from Woolf's. In 1989 she had invoked "Virginia Woolf's elegant response to male 'pacifist' appeals for aid"— Woolf's refusal to join the peace society and her insistence that women should work for peace in their own way and through their own society.[2]

Morgan was not the only feminist to turn to Virginia Woolf and specifically to *Three Guineas* for a response to violence and militarism. In 1995 a young scholar cited *Three Guineas* in connection to the Gulf War and the recent Oklahoma City bombing and the "difficult quandary" of Bosnia; she found the book "a marvel in precision and clarity."[3] Some twenty years earlier Adrienne Rich had cited Woolf's challenges to "civilization" in the service of a feminism Rich described as seeking "the creation of a society without domination . . . the making new of all relationships."[4] In so doing, she summed up the purposes—and the uses—of *Three Guineas* and the feminism it presents.

Here, in this conclusion, I look at the apparent limits of *Three Guineas* and Virginia Woolf's feminism in general, and at their continuing relevance. Even for Kosovo, even for Ground Zero in New York City. My assumption is that the reader, like all reasonable women or men, has or has had some belief in the value of feminism, but perhaps also has doubts about Virginia Woolf's version of it—particularly as expressed in *Three Guineas*—and doubts also about how it can be relevant to the horrors of our time. This final chapter, therefore, evaluates Woolf's feminism in the context of her own time as well as in that of the present. There is danger of anachronism here, of course. But Virginia Woolf's is a feminism that stands up to the test of time.

I

Let us look again at the title, *Three Guineas*, where the book begins. Those two words suggest that uneasiness with Woolf's feminism might be justified by something about its being possibly culture-linked and class-bound. As we know, the term *guinea* is used only in certain limited elite contexts. Class-linked, guineas certainly are, first of all, because income has always been related to class. So it is jolting to see guineas mentioned so often in Virginia Woolf's own financial references and connections. Thus, in the handwritten notes for the speech that was to become *Three Guineas*, the fictional narrator notes that as a beginning writer she was paid for book reviews at the rate of a guinea per thousand words.[5] Invited donations for the Marsham Street library are referred to as guineas. In 1938 Vanessa Bell was paid five guineas for the cover of *Three Guineas*, and in 1939 Woolf gave her sister "ten Guineas" for her sixtieth birthday present, to be spent on "making masterpieces."[6] And so on.

Yet it is important to note the sources of Woolf's real-life guineas and also what they were spent on. The guineas she spends represent a working literary journalist's income that she uses, among other things, in support of good causes (including a women's library and an equally professional sister). Most often, in the life and writings of the Woolfs, the specific sum of "three guineas" appears as the fee paid for the services of a doctor, as when in 1922 Leonard Woolf recorded paying "the great Dr. Sainsbury" that sum for an unhelpful consultation about his wife's health.[7] More directly relevant, in the draft for *The Years* Woolf has the character then called Elvira ask, "But how is that poor woman there going to Harley Street? with three guineas?"[8] At issue is the financial impossibility of abortions for poor women. Then illegal, they were relatively easily and discreetly purchased by middle- and upper-class women from fashionable doctors at locations such as Harley Street. The back-alley abortionists available, with difficulty, for the poor and working classes might well charge less, but still more than was easily available.

So if the term *guineas* could seem to marginalize anything that could be said by the woman who uses the word so casually both in writing and in everyday life, references to guineas also undercut the conventional meaning of class, by bringing in the usually submerged gender dimension. Class affects women differently than men, and not just those among the poor. Paying for abortions may well be the single most distinctively female economic issue, the one for which family money is least liable to be available. Even for less fraught decisions, as the central argument in *Three Guineas* insists, even women of the privileged classes still have only limited, indirect use of family or class resources. The £250 a year that in *Three Guineas* Woolf reports for a self-supporting woman would give a monthly income of just over £20; a guinea would have been a hefty slice of that, and three of them not a trivial fraction of even the £500 a year recommended in *A Room of One's Own*. Women are therefore fatally constrained and constricted in both their personal development and their chances of influence. As a result, there is little hope of producing a world in which women's issues and women's rights would become human issues and rights.

Three Guineas presents the problem of money, and consequent power, in a typically semi-comic discussion of the "virile" tastes of middle-class women. Assuming they have full responsibility for the spending of the allegedly shared family income, they can be seen to spend "vast sums" on activities from which they are excluded. The list of female-subsidized but predominantly masculine enterprises such as sport, "grouse moors," cricket, football, and exclusive men's clubs also includes "party funds" (*3G* 53). We understand: these are the locales of power and privilege, what we still call the "old boys' club." The entry fees are substantial, and not at women's disposal.

No wonder Woolf identifies the right to earn a living as the crucial right for women, and documents in scathing detail the unequal conditions under which they continue to work and are paid. As *A Room of One's Own* demonstrates, even the daughters of educated men—daughters of the men potentially most enlightened—are happy to have sixpences in their purses, whether earned or unearned. *Three Guineas* shows that they are delighted when they have guineas at their disposal. For women, to be able to lay out guineas for causes that are truly of their own choice symbolizes, not some inherited, unearned membership in the middle class, but an earned degree of standing among the influential. This standing is precisely what their gender prevents for women who would otherwise seem to have every claim to it.

In addition, the word *guineas* and the history of the coin itself invoke the imperialism that made England a world power and that, within that country, empowered those specific elites from which Virginia Stephen, later Woolf, was descended.[9] It was in 1661 that the Royal Mint was authorized to coin gold pieces in the name and for the use of the Company of Royal Adventurers of England trading with the Guinea Coast of West Africa.[10] Made from Guinea gold, it was soon called a guinea.[11] A Guinea ship, a ship of the West Africa trade, was more precisely a slave ship.[12] The guinea therefore represents the English ruling class, whose female members are excluded from power, but it represents as well the exploitation, the corruption that underlies that power. It can therefore also represent the connections between all levels of hierarchy and domination, all condemned by Virginia Woolf's feminism. Guineas were tainted money, if there ever was such. Now, for Woolf, they are turned to women's purposes.

The particular hierarchy that is imperialism is among the themes of *Three Guineas*, presented as a version of the patriarchal structures that oppress women first and most. "Our splendid empire," Woolf quotes Lady Lovelace as saying, "the price of which . . . is mainly paid by women" (*3G* 37). In her original text Lovelace continues: "In our higher classes a large percentage of sons and brothers must always be overseas. Some of them return later, but not all, and meantime most of our women remain." She was, it seems, thinking specifically of the absence of marriageable young men who were sacrificed for the empire. In *Three Guineas* Woolf uses Lovelace's words for wider implications, a condemnation of empire as part of the paraphernalia of patriarchy.[13]

In the last years of the twentieth century, the complexities of women's relationships to European colonialism and to orientalism became a significant feature of feminist analyses. White women often benefited from empire, even abetted it. At the same time, imperialism also added to the burdens of sexism even for them, for it provided yet another justification for hierarchy, including the basic structures of male domination. *Three Guineas* is prescient about such issues. When the narrator challenges the value of British "civilization," she tells women to compare "the testimony of the ruled—the Indians or the Irish, say"—with the claims made by their rulers (*3G* 99). A portrait of a viceroy would have been another fitting addition to *Three Guineas'* photographs of male rulers in their finery.

In recent years, feminists have focused on white women's unwitting complicity in the projects of colonialism. For Woolf, co-option into the ideologies of imperialism—a subset of the ideologies of patriarchy—is the more immediate danger (*3G* 149). The phrase "For God and Empire," the motto of the Order of the British Empire, is prominent in *Three Guineas*. Women can receive the OBE, Virginia Woolf notes, even if with a slightly less impressive set of regalia.[14] "If you succeed in your professions," the OBE's slogan "will very likely be written, like the address on a dog-collar, around your neck," writes the narrator of *Three Guineas* (*3G* 66). Here she echoes a passage in *A Room of One's Own* about men's "instinct" to label their possessions, an instinct "which murmurs if it sees a fine woman go by, or even a dog, Ce chien est à moi." Not by coincidence, one assumes, this phrase had been one of the epigraphs to Leonard Woolf's anti-imperialist *Empire and Commerce in Africa*.[15]

Virginia Woolf certainly knew about the West African slave trade. For a review of Hakluyt's *Voyages* that she first published in 1918, she took notes from the great historian Froude's lectures on "English Seamen in the Sixteenth Century," recording how "an African co. formed by Hawkins . . . got slaves in Sierra Leone & sold them in St Domingo."[16] This section of the notes does not appear in the review, and we should be careful not to read too much into the title of the book. The Stephen family had strong connections with the imperial civil service, and Woolf's grandfather, Sir James Stephen, had been an influential undersecretary of state in the Colonial Office. But although a distant ancestor had some dealings with the slave trade, his descendants, including Sir James, were all actively opposed to it.[17] There is no evidence that Woolf intended this second level of (imperial) symbolism. But it remains true that naming the book after the currency of the slave trade is a fine, hidden flourish.

At the same time, Woolf's reading notes direct our attention to Froude's lectures, and his own judgment on the Guinea merchants is useful for judging Woolf's feminism. In a chapter titled "Sir John Hawkins and the African Slave Trade," Froude writes, "We know to what the slave trade grew." He adds: "We have all learnt to repent of the share which England had in it, and to abhor anyone whose hands were stained by contact with so accursed a business." His assessment of Hawkins is relatively mild: "One regrets that a famous Englishman should have been connected with the slave trade; but we have no right to heap violent censures on him because he was no more enlightened than the wisest of his contemporaries."[18] Froude is too easy on Hawkins; as he also recounts, even in the Elizabethan age, those trading in human beings had to mobilize a lot of specious arguments. But the historian's judgment at the end of the nineteenth century can remind us of the importance of historical context, as we attempt to understand a feminism articulated in the 1920s and 1930s. It is the more difficult to keep this setting—this context—in mind, in that Woolf's feminism has been extended already well beyond her own expression of it in *Three Guineas*, and can legitimately be extended even further.

II

Context, for a piece of writing, most importantly means history, and history itself is a complex and contested notion. We can, all the same, agree that there is some reality in the sequence of recorded events in a given location at a given time. I have already outlined the process that represents Virginia Woolf's composition of *Three Guineas*, as well as discussing the other feminist writings by Woolf that form its feminist literary history. But to understand *Three Guineas* fully (and responses to it) we have also to take account of two sorts of less personal happenings: what was happening in the world as Virginia Woolf wrote about feminism, and what was then happening specifically to women and feminists in England.

When readers of the later twentieth and then the twenty-first centuries fault Woolf's vision in *Three Guineas*, it is often because of the way the book responded to the most visible examples of patriarchy's harm in her own environment and to the feminist traditions of her time. Thus, she illustrated the horrors of militarism by the fascist regimes in Italy and Germany and also by the civil war in Spain that was so immediate for her and her contemporaries. Woolf could hardly write about the wars we now refer to, dying as she did before the Second World War itself revealed its realities of genocide, urban firestorms, and nuclear devastation. In the years following the First World War, trench warfare and the slaughter of young soldiers loomed behind opposition to war. As Woolf was writing the book that would become *Three Guineas*, the unprecedented massive bombing of civilian targets was only a dreadful possibility, imagined (and exaggerated) on the basis of what had happened in Spain when the country town of Guernica was devastated on a market day in 1937; concentration camps had not yet turned into extermination factories. On the other hand, at the end of the 1930s an invasion of England seemed a real possibility, the Nazis' plans for occupation were well known, and Leonard and Virginia Woolf were among many who made provisions for suicide before they could be shipped off like other dissidents and Jews.

Yet Woolf's was not an apocalyptic vision like that of so many of her contemporaries. Her last feminist publication in her lifetime, "Thoughts on Peace in an Air Raid," published in October 1940 at a time when German bombing raids were ferociously under way, is about how "we can think peace into existence."[19] The interwar period's seemingly inexorable descent into catastrophe shadows the analysis that informs *Three Guineas*, but persistent hope for a better postwar future nevertheless inspires the recommendations that so many take for impracticable. After we have seen so many liberation struggles subordinate women to some higher cause, only to create a new society that remains as abhorrent as the old, we can better appreciate Woolf's insight that even self-defense should be egalitarian, nonsexist, transformative in structure and process. Her insistence that symphonies should be reformed and lectures not given at patriarchal Oxbridge, even though war loomed, were not intended to stop or to win the dreadful combats of her day, but instead to establish the basis for a better way of living after the combats had, once again, abated. But the argument was necessarily framed by the battles of Woolf's own era.

Similarly, the feminist issues Woolf discussed were those of her time. Historical context—specifically, changes in the status of English women including Virginia Woolf—explains significant differences in her feminist texts. "A Society" was written before the legislative and economic developments that made assumptions even of women's formal equality plausible, at a time when only women over thirty could vote and before any effect could be felt from legislation mandating access to the professions. The research of the society's members outlines the areas in which changes were needed. *A Room of One's Own*, published the year after British women finally achieved full suffrage, had as its subject the psychological and material conditions not of equality but of autonomy, with a focus on the creative woman artist. In her introduction to *Life as We Have Known It*, Woolf delineated the continuing, larger needs and demands of married women of the working class, the ones whose lives had not yet been changed and for whom neither artistic creativity nor higher education and access to professions were immediately relevant. The 1931 speech seems then to have assumed that, in material as well as political terms, the struggle had been won, at least in legal terms; thanks to the efforts of women such as Ethel Smyth, the vote as well as access to education and professional occupations were assured. The evidence was the group of young professional women to whom Woolf was speaking, whose occupations she had seen impressively listed in the 1930 report of the Junior Council. The lecture therefore focused on those constraints of female psychology and male prejudice that still existed. Woolf's own situation, earning an adequate income in a profession that accepted women, could serve to illustrate both the possibilities and the limits of the best possible case. Then *Three Guineas* laid bare at documented length the continuing inadequacy of both the legal and the social situation of women, spelling out the theoretical links to patriarchy and militarism in a world rapidly descending into global war. "Professions for Women" gave a decade-end summary, centered once more on the relatively small group of professional women whom Woolf had spoken to all those years before. *Three Guineas* had shown how few in number and how powerless those women were. Yet they were the women of the elite, the ones who potentially had the most influence. Now, addressing them once more as she had in her 1931 lecture, Woolf again summarized the situation of women by use of the continuing symbol of the room of one's own. And always from the position of what has to be considered a radical form of feminism. The war once begun, "Thoughts on Peace in an Air Raid" reflected on ideas for a satisfactory peace, as well as the continuing absence of women both from combat and from policy.

All of Woolf's feminist themes and policy issues are to be found among the women's movement in England, because it also adapted to the changing situation of women. It is now accepted that struggles for the vote and the related issues of legal standing and influence were far from being all of the women's movement of Woolf's day, even if they often still serve as convenient markers for stages of women's activism. Those critics who were most hostile to Woolf's feminism based their arguments specifically on women's successive acquisitions of legal rights in the late nineteenth and early twentieth centuries, which were seen as making feminism unnecessary. When we turn our attention to what was going on among feminist activists contemporary to Woolf, the picture is somewhat different. The vote acquired, activists did not return to their knitting or restrict themselves to personal advancement. In fact, the postsuffrage eras in England were full of women's activism. Only the most militant of the suffragette organizers and organizations became inactive, while suffragists such as the former members of the National Union of Women's Suffrage Societies turned to those specific policy issues for which women had sought the vote. In their diversity and diffusion, the interwar campaigns of women's groups were less visible to the public and to historians. Long-standing goals remained, however, even though they were in many cases still unachieved at the time when the second wave of the movement emerged in the 1960s. In fact, the feminists of that generation were amazed to rediscover what they named their "foremothers" and to learn that the questions of social service and justice, and of war and peace, had been alive, if not well, all through the interwar period.

Generally speaking, the goals promoted by Woolf go far to cover those that feminists sought in her time and most that they are seeking even today. Apart from the general, all-encompassing quest for an end to hierarchy and most specifically its embodiment in patriarchy, Woolf demanded a very long list of specific changes for women. "A Society" presented women's claim to control of their children and their children's future, as well as to free enquiry and, more broadly, intellectual activity. *A Room of One's Own* lays out the need for women's economic independence and privacy as well as an education comparable to men's (including the accumulation of experience through leisure and travel). The "Introductory

Letter" supports working-class women's specific demands, including re-formed divorce laws and minimum wages for women, as well as the goal of world peace. *Three Guineas* reiterates the previous program and adds support of a women's party in electoral politics, state subsidies for single women and for wives, childbirth anesthesia, and equal citizenship. Most importantly, it demands equal access and treatment for women in all the institutions that currently serve as a basis of power and influence: the senior professions, including religion, educational establishments, and male-dominated structures such as clubs and associations that support them. In addition, there is consistent, repeated examination and criticism of legal change (the vote, the legislation enabling access to education and the professions) in terms of consequences—or lack of them—in giving women resources equal to men's.

It is a long list, still surprisingly apposite. All the same, the issues of the 1930s were not the issues of the 1960s, when feminism regained a public visibility and a mass of popular support. For example, violence against women goes virtually unmentioned in Virginia Woolf's feminist writing. In *A Room of One's Own* the imaginary Judith Shakespeare is beaten by her loving father, but when she flees to London, she has been more damaged by psychological inhibitions than by physical force. In *Three Guineas* Woolf refers to the historian G. M. Trevelyan for evidence that other Elizabethan women were beaten, but she does not discuss the topic. The fact is, before the postwar revival of the women's movement, neither domestic violence nor rape was yet seen as intrinsic to male dominance, though both were certainly recognized as among the wrongs endured by women. Marital rape, like sexual harassment, was not conceptualized by feminists until well into the second wave of feminism.

The list may seem seriously incomplete in other respects, even when compared only to the feminism of interwar England. In particular, *Three Guineas* has been criticized for absences that are related to sexuality and to class—concerns that are central for the second wave of feminism, but not absent from first-wave feminism either.

III

Even in the context of historical feminism in England, *Three Guineas* seems least radical in relation to issues of sexuality. The nineteenth-century women's movement was concerned about sexually transmitted diseases and about prostitution. One of those most active in this connection was Josephine Butler, who carefully kept her campaigns from contaminating the mainstream "woman movement." Woolf does indeed cite and discuss Butler, one of the heroes of *Three Guineas*—but it is for the purity and universality of her motivation as well as the refusal of the press to cover her group's activities; there is only one passing mention of "the campaign against the sale and purchase of children 'for infamous purposes' " (*3G* 71). Prostitution appears in the book twice: as (rhetorically) preferable to the sexual seductions that were part of the basis of influence for upper-class women in the private house and as a metaphor for subservience to patriarchy. The first comparison, made stronger by the accompanying argument that marriage is like prostitution but worse because hypocritical, is common in the rhetoric of radicals among first-wave feminists anxious to abolish marriage as it then existed. "Free love" was accepted in progressive circles in the 1920s and 1930s; Ann's mother and her friends in "A Society" are quite calm about the extramarital baby. However, *Three Guineas* does not propose doing away with marriage but instead discusses the freedom to marry without the interference of possibly pathological parental demands. Marie Stopes, the famous advocate of birth control, obliquely referred to in *A Room of One's Own*, is not mentioned in *Three Guineas*, nor are any other of the interwar period's sexual radicals. In addition, although lesbian identity was visible in Woolf's time, and she had some sexual involvement and a good deal of close friendship with lesbians, the book lacks the references to women loving women that can be found in *A Room of One's Own* and *The Years*.[20]

Woolf does not seem to have been influenced, in relation to sexual issues, by the rather unusual stance of the Women's Co-operative Guild. At a time when such questions had not yet become central for other women's organizations, the WCG formally supported divorce, family limitation, and abortion. This is the more surprising in that, as Woolf noted, individual members of the WCG were extremely conservative in relation to sexual matters; women in her Richmond branch were distressed, even affronted, by a 1917 lecture (arranged by her) that discussed sexually transmitted diseases. It is perhaps more significant that, on reflection, they admitted the usefulness of such information (*L2* 138–39; *D1* 141). In any case, representatives of the WCG had appeared before the Royal Commission on Divorce and endorsed in 1911 the commission's majority report favoring easier divorce. In May 1913 Woolf herself was involved to the extent of asking Nelly Cecil to join a deputation to the prime minister supporting changes in divorce law; she was writing, she said, "upon compulsion from Miss Llewelyn Davies, who would compel a steam roller to waltz" (*L2* 30). However, neither the word nor the concept of divorce appears in *Three Guineas*, even though Woolf refers in her feminist writings to both George Eliot and "Mrs. Mill." As Woolf notes, Eliot was cut off from society because she was living with a man still married to an insane wife. John Stuart Mill and Harriet Taylor were married only briefly, after the death of her first husband ended a long marriage that cried out for termination. Nor does Woolf discuss abortion, even though at the early date of 1934, the WCG passed resolutions calling for legalized it.[21] Control of reproduction, often called "family planning," was certainly among the goals of some segments of the interwar women's movement in England; it appears in *Three Guineas* only in a passing remark that "when the body seller has sold her momentary pleasure she takes good care that the matter shall end there" (*3G* 86). Abortion, which has some discussion in the drafts of *The Years*, is absent from both the novel and *Three Guineas* itself.[22]

It is a damning list of absences, on the face of it, one that many analysts have retreated to biography to explain: Woolf was sexually molested to a smaller or greater degree by her half brother(s); (perhaps as a result) Woolf was sexually frigid; Woolf's attraction to her husband was less sexual than filial, and his role was nurturant rather than heterosexually active; the Bloomsbury Group was so liberal (even groundbreaking) in its attitudes toward sexuality that the issues did not seem real to Woolf; the reduction of such issues' impact in *The Years* and the related *Three Guineas* are examples of Woolf's self-censoring (that she did not dare to say these things to the audience of men she saw lurking behind her intended women readers).[23]

If we are looking for causality, many—though not all—of these factors seem likely to have played a role. But it is perhaps unhelpful to attempt to look for biographical explanations for what is or is not in *Three Guineas*. Woolf herself, in the famous piece published after her death as "A Sketch of the Past," warns that such enquiries are unlikely to be successful. In it, she wonders about her reluctance to look at her own face in the mirror— "I cannot now powder my nose in public"—and why for her everything to do with dress is frightening. She speculates that she "must have been ashamed or afraid of [her] own body." The possible causes she suggests are not the same as the reasons usually suggested for her (non)treatment of sexual issues in her feminism; they are instead, and equally plausibly, her tomboy youth, a Puritanism inherited from the Clapham sect, and an ancestral revulsion from sensuality (evoked by sexual touching by her older stepbrother but not caused by it). She concludes these reflections, in 1939, as follows: "Though I have done my best to explain why I was ashamed of looking at my own face I have only been able to discover some possible reasons; there may be others; I do not suppose that I have got at the truth; yet this is a simple incident; and it happened to me personally."[24]

Sexual issues serve mainly as metaphors in *Three Guineas*, even though in her first excited mention of what would become *The Years* and *Three Guineas*, Woolf described it as "a sequel to a Room of Ones Own—about the sexual life of women: to be called Professions for Women perhaps" (*D4* 6). But it is not so much that the obvious sexually related topics are absent from Woolf's feminist writing, especially *Three Guineas*, as that they are not discussed as such. Even in her first mention of "the sexual life of women," Woolf links the issue to their "professions"; it has no independent standing. We would not expect that sexual dimension in the lecture that was the first version of *Three Guineas;* surely it would have seemed inappropriate for the intended audience of young professionals. However, even in the drafts that precede *Three Guineas*, sex plays a particular, rather surprising, and limited role.[25] A good example of this is Woolf's treatment of one of the major themes in the first essay-novel construction of the work: "street love, common love, love in general."[26] The central example of "street love," which remains important in *The Years*, is the experience of the youngest daughter, Rose, then aged ten, who slips out alone at dusk to a nearby corner store (as she is forbidden to) and passes a man who exposes himself to her. At no time in the sequence of texts does Woolf draw the conclusion that London streets are dangerous or that women are at risk because of male sexuality. Instead, she stresses the impact of the constraints that society justifies by "street love," as well as the duplicity and secretiveness those constraints encourage. In a similar way, in *Three Guineas* she insists that middle-class women are protected from the appearance of danger rather than its reality. Again, there is an episode in *The Pargiters* when Rose's twelve-year-old brother is accosted by a prostitute. It did not survive into *The Years*, but even in the manuscript the event is used, not to discuss either male or female sexuality or the sex trade, but to stand for Bobby's initiation into "the fellowship of men together—a fellowship which, he began to feel, yielded a great many rights and privileges" and separated him out from his sisters.[27]

In general, apart from the imaginary Judith Shakespeare's accidental pregnancy that provoked her suicide in *A Room of One's Own*, Woolf's feminist writings leave unexamined the risks as well as the possibilities attached to female embodiment. Even that example is a mild one, for the father of Judith's child is not a predator but her protector. What Judith needs is autonomy, and autonomy means education and a job, without any special concern for sexual liberation or even effective contraception. In *Three Guineas*, "facilities for sexual intercourse" are mentioned once, in an endnote glossing "property." Gender relations to possessions can be charted, says Woolf, by mapping out how many acres women own compared to men (red for men, blue for women), and also their patterns of consumption, measured by the number of sheep and cattle they eat, as well as the number of barrels and hogsheads of wine, beer, and tobacco they drink or smoke. Opportunities for copulation appear at the end of the list, after "physical exercise" and "domestic employments," among less quantifiable indicators of property (*3G* 136). A social scientist would find these all admirable indirect indicators of potential power, but the presentation is definitely a de-eroticizing one.

Prostitution and adultery suffer a similar treatment in *Three Guineas*. Redefined to mean contamination by market demands, they have their fullest discussion as images of the co-opted literary life. The "chastity" recommended to the Outsiders consists of a difficult disinterestedness that is not a sexual one. When Woolf does turn at some length in an endnote to "the question of chastity, both of mind and body," once again the subject is power, not sex. The problem is the wider structures of hierarchy and control that constrain women rather than those subsets of them that relate to women's bodies. This is the endnote that presents a rather idiosyncratic interpretation of Saint Paul, including citing Renan slanderously about the saint's possible intimacy with his sister; it is about the ways that men control women and the possessive instincts that produced Saint Paul's prescription of veiled and silent women and modern constraints on the education and employment of women. The note concludes with quoted passages supporting the "psychological argument in favour of chastity" for both men and women (*3G* 153).[28] Here, briefly, chastity has become a sexual matter. Some among the first-wave feminists hoped to end the double standard of morality, not by extending to women the sexual freedoms enjoyed by men, but by requiring of both sexes the limits then seen as appropriate only for women. Virginia Woolf, central to the Bloomsbury Group, can hardly have agreed. She would most likely have hoped to see widely accepted for both sexes her closest associates' tolerance and flexibility about sexuality. But she does not expound her views on this issue in her feminist writings.

Any personal reasons why *Three Guineas* and other texts of Woolf's feminism omit sexually related issues would, finally, seem to be less important than a relatively banal fact: that in this area, though not in her general argument, Woolf presented priorities like those of the mainstream women's movement of her time. Thus, as late as 1937 the National Birth Control Association thought a parliamentary debate on their topic far too risky, and Parliament looked at the issue only in the 1950s.[29]

At the same time, if *Three Guineas* seems, today, too narrow and disembodied in its treatment of sexually related issues, we can respond to Virginia Woolf's emphasis on women's lack of autonomy. In particular, she is concerned with the ways in which male control of moral and, more specifically, sexual standards serves to constrain women in their professional, their personal, and their creative lives. The parental and societal attitudes about female sexuality and domesticity that justified the dreadful Barrett, Jex-Blake, and Brontë fathers, discussed at such length in *Three Guineas*, still exist. Second-wave feminist concerns about heterosexism and the sexual objectification of women follow naturally; we are still trying to "Take Back the Night" that Rose rushed through so anxiously.

And what about class? Here the contrast is to the socialist feminists who had been active since the previous century, and who focused their attention on women of the working class and what socialism could do for them. Leonard Woolf was an advisor and parliamentary candidate for the Labour Party, and Virginia had some involvement with the local party branch; she was not a socialist except in the sense that the British Labour Party was socialist. And it is clear that party politics bored and repelled her—hence her husband's insistence that she was not a political person. All the same, thanks to her feminism, and unusually for her time, Woolf's awareness of class includes sensitivity to the specific material position of women, and not just women working for pay. In *Three Guineas*, "working class experience" is illustrated by a cited account of how much dish, glass, and floor washing the average housewife does, and for information about the working class she refers the reader to *Life as We Have Known It* as well as to the *Life of Joseph Wright* (*3G* 160). Elsewhere she writes indignantly about the lives of maids "in the darkness of the beetle-haunted basement" (*3G* 150), and in the "Introductory Letter" in particular she is clear about the relative independence and advantages of women such as herself, when contrasted with women of the working classes.

Woolf does, it seems, respond to the issue of class as it affects women. What is bothersome to socialist feminists is that she interprets the concept of class itself unconventionally. In a famous endnote in *Three Guineas*, she defines the term "educated man's daughter" as "the class whose fathers have been educated at public schools and universities." This term is so important for *Three Guineas* that variants of it are used 126 times in the book. "Obviously," she adds, "if the term 'bourgeois' fits her brother, it is grossly incorrect to use it of one who differs so profoundly in the two prime characteristics of the bourgeoisie—capital and environment" (*3G* 133).[30] Capital is obvious in meaning. Environment, however, is more problematic; it turns out to mean education and (therefore) professional occupation.

Closer examination of the "Introductory Letter" to *Life as We Have Known It* makes even clearer Woolf's belief that class is defined less by material goods than by educational possibilities. Winifred Holtby, in 1932, thought the "Introductory Letter" Woolf's furthest excursion into "political writing" because of its attention to what she called "the practical material conditions of living."[31] By this she meant the everyday conditions of the lives of working-class women; *A Room of One's Own* had certainly been responsive to the material conditions of life of other sorts of women. In the "Introductory Letter," it seems at first that class is used in a conventional way. Woolf contrasts herself, not with her male counterparts, as she usually does, but with the guildswomen themselves. Even here, however, Woolf, who at first seems to define class in terms of economic situation, also finally defines it in terms of education. The letter writer begins by referring to herself as a "lady," one of those "whose minds . . . fly free at the end of a short length of capital." She has income, she has leisure, she has servants. The writers of the collected memoirs and letters had worked, before marriage, as laborers, shop hands, mill workers, domestics; they clearly lacked capital. She reflects edgily that "if every reform [the WCG sought] was granted this very instant it would not touch one hair of my comfortable capitalistic head."[32] (No such phrase is to be found in the *Yale Review* version.) The usual contrast, in class terms, is clear. But it turns out the guildswomen are also in a different class than the author as regards their education, and therefore also as regards their relationship to that English language the Outsiders will be urged to read and write. That the guildswomen are self-educated, if educated at all, is at least as important as that they are not ladies, or that they are the wives and daughters of uneducated or working-class men. The guildswomen's strongest aspirations had been for literacy itself, and they had then become autodidacts who "read with the indiscriminate greed of a hungry appetite, that crams itself with toffee and beef and tarts and vinegar and champagne all in one gulp." Unassisted by access to the personal library of the editor of the *Dictionary of National Biography*, they relished Mrs. Barclay's novel *The Oracle*—dismissed by Woolf as a "purple pumpkin" in the *Woman's Leader* in 1922—as well as Dickens.

However, for Woolf, some degree of identification with the middle class persists (not just with the class of educated men). Although she obviously recognizes the desirability of education for self-development for women of all classes, she seems to believe that the use of education as a means to power and influence is essentially irrelevant to the women of the WCG. These women, like their men, it seems, will have impact as workers and through the workers' party. At times, Woolf seems actually to consider the "educated man's daughter" like herself less influential than the women of the conventionally defined lower classes. The serial "Women Must Weep" asserts the superior economic leverage of those who work for pay, and the "Introductory Letter" outlines the routes to influence within their own class, as conventionally defined. In 1913, these did not yet include the vote, but there were possibilities in industrial action and labor politics, along with the actions of the Women's Co-operative Guild itself. Today's feminist, socialist or not, will therefore criticize Woolf because she does not analyze the specific gender disabilities of working-class women—their disadvantages relative to their own men. Woolf does not seem to be aware of the limited representation and influence of women even in the Co-operative movement, let alone in the union-dominated labor movement itself.[33] Ironically enough, it was because of the unrelenting support of pacifism that Woolf so admired that guildswomen in the postwar period were to find themselves barred from parliamentary nomination by the Labour Party.

On the same topic of class, an indignant endnote essay in *Three Guineas* addressed the topic of middle-class proletarian wannabes. To them Woolf contrasts "the true-born working man or woman" who lacks middle-class capital—a straightforward example of class analysis. When she enjoins "educated men's daughters" to avoid sentimental identification with the working class, and instead to work in their own class "which stands much in need of improvement," the contrast is with the working class, well served in the nineteenth century by the charitable efforts of women like herself. Now, to the extent that some daughters of educated men have themselves achieved "an expensive education," the lady bountifuls of the past have joined the class of their fathers, husbands, and brothers, and consequently acquired a new set of obligations (*3G* 159). Education—expensive education—has reappeared as a basis of class distinctions.

At the same time, the specific measures advocated in *Three Guineas*, not to mention its general argument, would benefit working-class women along with their more prosperous sisters: childbed anesthesia, mothers' allowance, lifting of the marriage ban, adequate pay, equal access to education. And surely, given the composition of modern armies, peace would benefit these women the most of all, as would *Three Guineas*' insistence that activist women must be responsive to all issues of exclusion: "You will swear that you will do all in your power to insist that any woman who enters any profession shall in no way hinder any other human being, whether man or woman, white or black . . . from entering it, but shall do all in her power to help them" (*3G* 63).

This statement was written well before any significant influx of immigrants of color to Britain. Even in the 1930s, however, issues of race were closely linked to issues of class, in all senses of the word, whatever its definition. Woolf's feminism, in its critique of hierarchy, its search for women's autonomy and influence, responded to such concerns in spite of its focus on the conditions of its own day.

IV

I have been stressing the ways in which Woolf's feminism, as she presents it, falls short of what we might expect. *Three Guineas* and the wider feminism it demonstrates continue to be valid, however, and it is in part because of the ways they can be extended. In the narrowest literary sense, there are two offspring of Woolf's (nonfiction) feminism. In a wider sense, as I demonstrate in the last part of this chapter and book, there continues to be guidance for ongoing activism, most specifically in *Three Guineas*. But first let us look at the literary daughters of Woolf's feminism.

A Room of One's Own inspired a widely read book that appeared in 1978, Tillie Olsen's *Silences*. Olsen's book itself, in conjunction with the draft for Woolf's 1931 speech, then stimulated an important essay by the well-known feminist science fiction writer Ursula Le Guin. The two works together show the far-reaching implication of Woolf's beliefs. Olsen's *Silences* is an extension of *A Room of One's Own* from the perspective of women less well-off than the implicitly middle-class narrator of that book. They are that majority of women who, historically, have moved into marriage as the expected occupation for women, and one that had motherhood as a central consequence and responsibility. Olsen's topic is how childrearing and home maintenance have interfered with women's possibilities for artistic creativity. The book's argument was enthusiastically received by

American feminists in the 1970s. So, indeed, was Tilly Olsen, and I remember seeing her at a conference on Virginia Woolf, insisting that Woolf's views were not "classist" but instead an inspiration to working-class feminists like herself.

In *Silences*, the clash between marriage and literary creativity is the issue. Olsen is not interested in the plight of the dependent unmarried daughter, nor does she discuss the desperation of Shakespeare's imaginary sister, unable to obtain the work she wants, pregnant and isolated. Domesticity is inevitable and valuable, Olsen feels, but incompatible with self-development. She thus closely follows the underlying logic of both *A Room of One's Own* and *Three Guineas*—that domestic conditions and responsibilities have fatally handicapped women. Her main contribution to the ongoing discussion is to examine in detail just how being a wife and, specifically, a mother affects the creative woman. She adds a dimension that, implicit in Woolf's life, does not appear in her writing: every artist, it seems, needs a "wife," someone to fill the nurturant role that Leonard Woolf played. Olsen believes that for the literary man, such a role is most often performed by a woman who otherwise might herself have been creative. Following Woolf, Olsen focuses on the negative impact of domestic life and women's poverty.

Q. D. Leavis, reviewing *Three Guineas* in 1938, was unkind to accuse the childless Woolf of not knowing which end of a cradle to rock. But it is true that child care and cooking were seen by Woolf as ancillary tasks that could interfere with reading or thinking or writing done by women. In the "Introductory Letter," the WCG is seen as a "refuge" from "boiling saucepans and crying children."[34] Woolf never presents women's experience as child bearers and child rearers as a potentially valuable influence on society. She praises, instead of domestic achievements, the austere negative qualities of a metaphorical chastity and an active disinterestedness that she sees as the educational results of confinement and exclusion. The reforms she argues for are therefore ones that would end women's confinement and exclusion and would also provide independence and privacy for them. "Professions for Women" does indeed end with the statement that the rented room must be shared. But this is, clearly enough, still the room rented by a single woman, and there is no implication that she will be raising a family there. Marriage bars are abominable, but there is not even a mention of what the positive impact might be of having children.

The popular and much admired science fiction writer Ursula Le Guin takes the discussion to the next stage. In 1976 she wrote: "I considered myself a feminist [in the mid-1960s]; I didn't see how you could be a thinking woman and not be a feminist; but I had never taken a step beyond the ground gained for us by Emmeline Pankhurst and Virginia Woolf." In 1987 she commented, referring to her earlier remarks, "Feminism has enlarged its ground and extended its theory and practice immensely, and enduringly, in these past twenty years; but has anyone actually taken a step 'beyond' Virginia Woolf?" In the same essay she makes a remark suggesting the influence of *Three Guineas* on her famous novel *The Left Hand of Darkness*: "At the very inception of the whole book, I was interested in writing a novel about people in a society that had never had a war."[35] Her solution was to make them androgynous, perhaps an echo of both *A Room of One's Own* and *Orlando*. Le Guin is an admirer of *Silences* and also of *Three Guineas*, but, unlike Woolf and Olsen, she claims that the domestic experience of women can be not just educational through a discipline of suffering, not just necessary but painful, but also a source of empowerment and creativity.

Woolf could perhaps have made a positive argument about maternity on the basis of her sister's experience as matriarch, presiding over a large unconventional family, as well as artist. But she did not make it. And indeed Vanessa Bell was, at least metaphorically, able to close that door to the room where she painted, though she did share it with her partner, the painter Duncan Grant. We have records of how important the ability to create a private sphere was to her: her children, unlike Darwin children, did not play where their parents were working, and one of her objections to Maynard Keynes's relationship to Lydia Lopokova was that Lydia persistently invaded Vanessa's working time and space.[36] By contrast, Le Guin builds on Woolf's arguments to claim that the presence of children, including the responsibilities and awareness that result, is a positive influence on the woman worker or artist. Here she includes graphic artists (with the example of Käthe Kollwitz), and it is clear that the argument can be expanded more generally so that maternal and domestic qualities enrich all of life.

As the title of "The Fisherwoman's Daughter" suggests, in this essay Le Guin appropriates and extends Woolf's image of the imaginative artist as fisher. She draws on Woolf's notes for her 1931 lecture, and especially its image of the woman writer struggling to reel in inspiration from the water of remembered experience. In this fragment, the author's imagination was personified as a rather choleric young woman who emerged soaking wet to express Woolf's own indignation that society prevents her from writing about women's bodies. The fisherwoman survives from this first text into

"Professions for Women," less detailed but equally frustrated and distressed. Le Guin makes the writer's imagination into a baby-sitting "auntie" who assures the artist's daughter that the best possible situation for a woman artist is to be both creator and mother; this is very different from the image of the lecture and "Professions for Women," and indeed from *Three Guineas* itself.

However, Woolf has another and somewhat different use of the fisherwoman image, and that is the one that Le Guin's reinterpretation is closest to. In *A Room of Own*, Woolf's narrator describes herself as sitting "lost in thought" on the banks of an Oxbridge river during her visit to "Fernham" and then adds: "Thought . . . had let its line down into the stream." Soon a little tug on the line indicates "the sudden conglomeration of an idea" that can be carefully hauled out and, like a hooked fish, laid out on the grass for inspection. The idea for *A Room of One's Own*, she thinks, looks small and insignificant, like something a good fisherman would throw back to grow bigger. Then, shifting images, the fish/idea is "put back into the mind," where it generates a dazzling, exciting tumult of further ideas.[37] The fisherwoman is thus hoping to catch the source for a text, instead of the mermaid-like figure that embodies her inspiration. The writer's fishing line has been dropped down to hook the basis of a piece of writing.

Just such a fisherwoman, in Le Guin's tale, has a daughter, and a sister, Imagination, who can watch over the child. Unlike the young women of "A Society," this little girl will not have to choose between making good people and making good books, for the two enterprises will be mutually supportive. "The Fisherwoman's Daughter" ends with these words: " 'Auntie,' says the little girl, 'can I go fishing with you now?' " "A Society" ended with a weeping child; Ann's mother regrets that she is learning to read, to make judgments, and to be discontented. Le Guin's little girl is smiling as she too sits down to fish, assisted by her mother's imagination while her mother waits in (temporary) solitude, her fishing line slack, for thoughts to come. Le Guin ends, finally, with something implicit both in Woolf's own life and in her brief discussions of reasonable and supportive men: the writer does not need a "child-free space" or even, "speaking strictly on the evidence, a room of her own, though that is an amazing help," but instead "the goodwill and cooperation of the opposite sex, or at least the local, in-house representative of it." Echoing Woolf's first comments to the Junior Council of the L&NSWS, Le Guin concludes that "the one thing that a writer has to have is a pencil and some paper." And, above all, to be "responsible . . . autonomous . . . free" in her use of them.[38]

Woolf's great insight in *A Room of One's Own*, which Le Guin dances around, is the role that material conditions and social relations play in the possibility of being "responsible . . . autonomous . . . free." Extended to include children as a central feature of life, Woolf's analysis implies that for the fisherwoman to be free, there has to be someone to share and support child care. *Three Guineas* adds a larger message about social context. For the artist and her daughter to both metaphorically and literally sit safely on the bank and fish in their different ways, there has to be peace. Peace, however, means equality and respect as well as the absence of the threat of armed conflict. It also means absence of the structural violence of abuse and exploitation. This set of beliefs is a recognizable, if recognizably radical, version of feminism, one that has mobilized many women and continues to do so. Such feminism can certainly include the positive value of the maternity that Woolf discusses so little in her feminist work. Accordingly, Le Guin, like many others, finds that Virginia Woolf was and is always "the greatest enabler." *Three Guineas*, she says, was her "treasure in the days of poverty" before the rebirth of the women's movement.[39]

v

The problem, of course, then as now, was how to forward the feminist project, how to put into practice the profound transformation of society that it implied. For the answer, we turn to the third guinea. Feminist analysts of *Three Guineas* have, understandably, been inclined to focus attention on the first two guineas, so innovatively donated to support women's education and their professional advancement, as promoted through their own single-sex organizations. Then there is the Outsiders' Society, which is intended to summarize women's unstructured acts of continuing resistance. But a major part of the arguments of the book is directed toward a "peace" society—its president is the addressee of the framing letter, after all—and if the author will not join his group, she will nevertheless give him as much money as she gives to each of the two others. The goals of that mixed-membership society are crucial to Woolf's feminism.

Woolf's feminism, most clearly stated in *Three Guineas*, gives us an image of the desirable, spells out its logic, and justifies the still necessary first steps toward making it possible. The donated three guineas go, together, to provide the necessary conditions for effective change: women's education, professional empowerment for women, and one more thing—a free and open society. The first two go to women's groups, because society as a whole, even after the enabling legal changes, has not been diligent in promoting women's education and their economic self-sufficiency and influence. The third guinea, donated "to protect culture and intellectual liberty," has in view the sort of society in which the third women's organization, the Outsiders' Society, can prosper and be influential. Perhaps feminists have tended to underestimate the importance of this final guinea, which represents the best part of the ambiguous tradition that made possible Virginia Woolf herself and her *Three Guineas*.

At this point we should look more closely at the "peace society" to whose president its author addressed *Three Guineas*. Its slogan is close to phrases used by the group that called itself For Intellectual Liberty (FIL), founded in February 1936 to support French intellectuals against the rightist pressures in that country.[40] Groups like FIL did not envision any particular role for women or make any connection between the situation of women and the struggles to prevent war and defeat fascism. Virginia Woolf, a relatively inactive founding member, was impatient with FIL and soon ceased to play any role in the organization. However, *Three Guineas* makes it clear that she recognized that the conditions the group sought to advance were crucial for the possible impact of her feminism. "Women Must Weep," lacking so much of the material about the women's groups destined to receive the first two guineas, in the process obscures the fact that the mere existence of women's groups and women's influences depends on the conditions that the final guinea makes possible. These are conditions that, for all Woolf's criticism of the exclusionary and oppressive nature of patriarchal England, already existed there to a considerable extent. What she calls "experiments" in constructing a new society have already started, and they provide models for future action.

In 1940, in the letter to Shena Simon already quoted, Woolf wrote about what would be needed for "sharing life after the war." We should be thinking, she suggested, about combining men's and women's works, about "removing men's disabilities." Can we change sex characteristics? she asks. And she concludes with another question: "How far is the women's movement a remarkable experiment in that transformation?" (*L6* 379). The reference to the women's movement reminds us of the role of the historical women's movement in creating in England as elsewhere that degree of equality and freedom that women, specifically, now have. In *Three Guineas*, with the Outsiders, Woolf makes a somewhat different, but related argument, supporting anonymous and unorganized efforts at change. In fact, she cites three individual examples of what unrecognized individual women are already doing: the mayoress of Woolwich has refused to endorse the war effort, women's sports organizations operate without prizes or other encouragement of competition, and educated young women have decreased their participation in the Church of England. "An extraordinarily interesting experiment," she says of the second of these, echoing her comment about the women's movement (3G 106).

Once again, these are examples that can easily be dismissed as trivial (one thinks of de Gaulle's probably apocryphal response to the suggestion to create a Ministry for the Status of Women: why not a Ministry for Knitting?). And certainly Woolf has played her usual games with the accounts on which she based her narrative. Thus, she seizes on a remark by the wife of the mayor of Woolwich (a borough that depended on armament factories) that she would "not so much as darn a sock to help in a war," changing it into "the prevention of war by not knitting socks," and then interpreting the statement as public opposition to war. The real situation was, as usual, more complicated, for the full text of the newspaper article cited by Woolf states that the lady in question, a member of the Peace Pledge Union, is "frequently present in an official capacity at military functions in Woolwich" and that her son is "making good progress" in the R.A.F.[41]

But the "mayoress" persisted, and publicly, in expressing unpopular views, and this Woolf suggests is exemplary behavior. Woolf's other *Three Guineas* "experiments" can also be seen as having larger meaning than their immediate characteristics, for they amount to the provision of non-competitive models and a more general withdrawal from sexist, hierarchical institutions. Such actions are dependent on the possibility that women have of attempting, organized or not, to live a different sort of life. In a totalitarian state, of course, no independent women's movement was possible. As the third guinea reminds us, in Nazi Germany the wife of a mayor would not be allowed to make public statements against official policy, sports would be organized to train girls in their proper domestic roles (and boys in the necessary competitiveness that patriarchy requires), and the church would give women no choice but to be dutiful acolytes. Under the most blatantly fascist regimes of Woolf's time, women (and most men) were unable to experiment with freedom by refusing to cooperate with war preparation or resisting incorporation into the established religions or devising educational modes and organizations of their own choice. In England, individuals were free to try all these approaches, as indeed, not just the arguments, but the very publication, distribution, and reviews of *Three Guineas* demonstrated.

Here are the mandates we need. The model supplied by *Three Guineas* is not some vast mobilization of women (and perhaps men). Instead the book recommends a relatively loose and unstructured series of actions by individual women or women banding together on occasion for specific purposes that are part of the larger project of destroying the hierarchies that govern and deform our lives. For this to be possible, women need be educated and to have access to the economic resources needed to participate in public life as workers and political beings. The women's groups that receive the first two guineas have such goals. The third guinea, however, goes to a group that is working to enhance those conditions of intellectual and other freedom that are necessary for the empowerment of women. Only under such conditions will it be possible for women to respond to specific situations of violence and war, both as individuals and as groups.

Virginia Woolf reminds us that women's responses will vary, given the context, given their situation. Today, we can see that groups such as the Mothers of the Plaza Mayor and the Women in Black provide an innovative model based on women's experiences, using the discourse that has constrained them in the past as a basis for action. But there are other legitimate ways for free citizens to respond. *Three Guineas*, although its preferences are pacifist, also makes clear that perhaps at some times (in Spain, in Kosovo, against terrorism directed toward civilians) those involved may not prefer nonviolent alternatives. And if they are women, like the Spanish Republican woman warrior cited in *Three Guineas*, they are no less entitled than men to make such decisions for themselves. Sergeant Amalia Bonilla is presented as an example of how women also may develop "the fighting instinct" more common in men. The excerpt from the account of the sergeant is a sympathetic one. Asked why she has joined the army, Bonilla replies that two of her daughters were militiawomen, and the younger has been killed; she has joined to replace her "and to avenge her" (*3G* 160). We have noted that Woolf herself had supported lifting the arms embargo in Spain.

In *Three Guineas*, the narrator notes that "pacifism is enforced upon women" (because they are not allowed to serve in the armed forces). "Men are still allowed liberty of choice" (*3G* 160). And this is the goal of the so-called peace society: liberty of choice, and for a choice based on reason, not instinct. Autonomy depends, for women, on the end of the structure of sexism. But they cannot bring about those necessary changes in attitude without the conditions of free expression and activism that the last guinea will support.

Given peace—in the largest sense—it will be possible to construct and to learn from "experiments" in nonhierarchical modes of making decisions and taking action, as the women's movement in its different generations has done. The young feminists of the 1960s were not the first members of women's groups to be dubious about an unquestioning acceptance of authority. It is easy to be scornful of the "lady" officers of nineteenth-century temperance and social reform organizations, and of their successors in the National Councils of Women and the League of Women Voters. These leaders were, however, elected and on occasion rebuked or rejected. If their organizations were all too often unable to move swiftly or change rapidly, it was in part because of the operation of a genuine consultative process. The "nonhierarchical" women's liberation groups in turn came to realize that the absence of formal rules and structures was itself likely to generate domination by a single leader or a small self-selected elite. We are, it seems, only now beginning to learn how to facilitate rather than dominate. The crucial necessary element is an awareness of the risks that any form of organization entails, that, above all, structure must be matched to function and not merely derived from tradition.

Given the freedom to choose, it is of course necessary to resist co-optation into the structuring hierarchies of our current society. But here *Three Guineas* moderates an apparently implausible call for withdrawal from all positions of actual or potential influence, arguing instead for participation modified by remembrance of the ends for which power, the means, is to be used. It is possible to "enter the professions and yet remain civilized human beings, human beings who discourage war," writes the narrator of *Three Guineas*. You must hold on to the integrity and disdain for accumulation and fame that women have developed, powerless and confined to the private realm, but you must also acquire "some wealth, some knowledge, and some service to real loyalties" (*3G* 74).

Virginia Woolf's argument for a diffuse and decentralized movement of women that will somehow deconstruct the hierarchy is weakest when it comes to the link between individual and group action, and uninformative about what will move women to even individual action. What indeed is the role of feminism and the women's movement in all this? Increasingly, I have come to agree with Woolf that out of the actions of individual women—feminists whatever they call themselves—comes a sort of everyday feminism that produces, cumulatively, at least the beginning of the changes we hope for. From Afghanistan, this new century's most vivid example of a misogynistic regime that, when overthrown, left behind chaos, comes the encouraging example of the impact of both individuals and organized groups of women. Accounts in 2001 were able to list activities that have mobilized thousands of Afghan women under conditions in which women were not expected to be visible, let alone vocal.[42] Even before the existence of these groups was known—the most extreme example of diffuse and secretive action under unpropitious conditions—the international women's movement, based in places where the third guinea's success gave them a chance of influence, had been able to insist on the inclusion of women's rights in a new interim structure of governance and the inclusion of women among the new governors. We do not yet know how this will work out; we know in any case that there are narrowly opportunistic reasons for even temporary successes. But we can nevertheless be hopeful. *Three Guineas'* recommendations seem relevant, as women avoid involvement in hierarchy and war, focusing instead on democratization, education, and public professional activity—the goals of the three guineas. Although Afghan women have had no choice in the past about whether to be fighters or pacifists, perhaps both they and their society will have that choice in the future, and the more so because of the role they are beginning to play.

Let us conclude by again emphasizing the role of the third guinea, but without losing sight of the other two. From Chechnya, in 2001, in the course of yet another interminable dirty little war, this time amid the festering remains of the former Soviet Union, comes the tale of two Russian mothers who went to the battle zone to find their young soldier sons who had been kidnapped with the complicity of their commanders. One of the boys, successfully rescued, spoke to a reporter "about how shocked he was when the Chechens told them their mothers had come. 'They said the only reason our commanders were starting to speak of exchange or ransom was on account of our mothers.' "[43] It is a murky story, and a saddening one, for the sons of the women of Chechnya are still being treated with the same lack of concern as are the sons of the Russians, and the war against Chechnya has, if anything, heated up as I write. But Yelena Arefieva and Masha Chernikova, battling patriarchy in the form of postcommunist bureaucracy and a crazed military hierarchy, are surely part of the hopeful experimentation of the Outsiders' Society. Their heroism seems to have rescued only one of their children, but the revulsion to the war that they epitomize ended the first Chechen war and will, if anything does, end the second also.

Russian mothers Arefieva and Chernikova grew up in a society that, deeply flawed as it was and is, provided equal educational opportunity for women and was committed, even if for ignoble reasons, to having them earn their living. Woolf's beliefs that such things matter—and that, particularly if so enabled, women's experience and values will drive them to change, even to challenge the male, public world—seem to be true. In a society that is responsive to the opinions of its citizens, including the women among them, as even the ex–Soviet Union is beginning to be, there is hope for change, even if we can expect it to be no more than gradual and unintended. All three of the guineas matter.

On the typed draft she left us of her speech of January 1931, Virginia Woolf wrote in the margin, in her difficult, spiky handwriting, "Men too can be emancipated." This remark has been misread as "Men too can be manipulated." That was not Woolf's point, for she was writing about her hopes for the future. All the same, men and women alike, we are manipulated by a sexist and oppressive world that we support without knowing it. But we can also hope to be emancipated, to create what Woolf described in the typed phrase she was commenting on: "perfect freedom, without fear."[44]

Notes

CHAPTER 1. Finding Feminism in Virginia Woolf

1. Woolf had been asked to write an article on the same lines as E. M. Forster's famous essay, first published as "Two Cheers for Democracy" in the *Nation* in June 1938, then republished with some changes as "Credo" in the *London Mercury* in September 1938; see B. J. Kirkpatrick, *A Bibliography of E. M. Forster*, 2d ed. (Oxford: Clarendon Press, 1985), 50. The citation is from an unpublished letter dated 30 November 1938, to R. A. Scott James, editor of the *London Mercury*, held at the Harry Ransom Humanities Research Center, University of Texas, Austin.

2. This phrase is taken from Woolf's closely related novel, *The Years* (London: Hogarth Press, 1937), 314, 340.

3. Noel Annan, *Leslie Stephen: The Godless Victorian* (London: Weidenfeld and Nicolson: 1984), 109, 110, 293–94; also Leslie Stephen, *Selected Letters*, 2 vols., ed. John W. Bicknell (London: Macmillan, 1996), 103 and 213–15.

4. Stephen, *Selected Letters*, especially Stephen's letter to his wife (413–14, 414 n. 1), as well as his letter of sympathy on the death of Mrs. Green's friend Mary Kingsley (507–8), and his last, affectionate letter to her shortly before his death (543). Stephen became chair of the London Library committee in 1892.

5. Quentin Bell, "Bloomsbury and 'the Vulgar Passions,'" *Critical Inquiry* 6.2 (1979): 249–50, 251.

6. Hermione Lee, *Virginia Woolf* (London: Chatto and Windus, 1996), 681.

7. Nigel Nicolson, *Virginia Woolf* (London: Weidenfeld and Nicolson, 2000), 132.

8. Alison Light, "Harnessed to a Shark," *London Review of Books*, 21 March 2002, 31; Theodore Dalrymple, "Virginia Woolf and the Triumph of Narcissism," *Guardian Review*, 17 August 2002, 4–6.

9. Q. D. Leavis, "Caterpillars of the Commonwealth, Unite!" *Scrutiny* 7 (September 1938): 203–15. Leavis was of course echoing Marx, but also perhaps picking up on Woolf's discussion of professional men being like caterpillars going "head to tail" about the sacred tree of property (*3G* 70). For other possible sources of this image, see *3G* 198.

10. For summaries and a recent example examining images of Woolf, see Brenda Silver, *Virginia Woolf Icon* (Chicago: University of Chicago Press, 1999).

11. Laura Marcus, "Virginia Woolf's Feminism and Feminism's Virginia Woolf," in *The Cambridge Companion to Virginia Woolf*, ed. Sue Roe and Susan Sellers (Cambridge: Cambridge University Press, 2000). Her perceptive article lacks the space to explicate *Three Guineas* fully.

12. I deliberately use the term *gender* here rather than *sex* in order to include so-

cially created distinctions as well as what are thought of as simply biological ones. Women are not, of course, the only gender-defined group, but their relationship to the gender-defined group "men" is unique. See Naomi Black, *Social Feminism* (Ithaca, N.Y.: Cornell University Press, 1989), chaps. 1–3, for fuller discussion of the issues raised in this section.

13. It also seems reasonable to consider antifeminist or at most nonfeminist those groups and individuals, of whatever gender, who deny that any women are disadvantaged as such.

14. United Nations, *Report of the World Conference of the International Women's Year,* E/CONF. 66 (New York, 1980), 34.

15. Teresa de Lauretis, "Feminist Studies/Critical Studies: Issues, Terms and Contexts," in *Feminist Studies/Critical Studies*, ed. T. de Lauretis (Bloomington: Indiana University Press, 1986), 9.

16. The latter group has also been called "cultural" feminists, but they never accepted this derogatory term. The best source on radical feminism is still Carol Anne Douglas, *Love and Politics: Radical Feminist and Lesbian Theories* (San Francisco: Ism Press, 1990).

17. See Jo Freeman, *The Politics of Women's Liberation* (New York: David McKay Co., 1975); Alice Echols, *Daring to Be Bad: Radical Feminism in America, 1967–1975* (Minneapolis: University of Minnesota Press, 1989); Susan Brownmiller, *In Our Time: Memoir of a Revolution* (New York: Dial Press, 1999); and Alison M. Jaggar, *Feminist Politics and Human Nature* (Totowa, N.J.: Rowman and Allanheld, 1983). Jaggar defined these categories most authoritatively and co-edited an influential anthology that outlined and then expanded the categories for a generation of women's studies students; see Jaggar and Paula Rothenberg Struhl, eds., *Feminist Frameworks: Alternate Theoretical Accounts of the Relations between Women and Men* (New York: McGraw-Hill, 1978), and the second edition, edited by Jaggar and Paula S. Rothenberg (McGraw-Hill, 1984).

18. The contrast has also been framed, less accurately, as between feminisms of similarity and difference. Karen Offen makes a similar argument, using the terms *individualistic* and *relational.* We agree about the importance of Woolf's feminism. Offen includes the 1938 publication of *Three Guineas* in the chronology at the start of her recent, massive study of European feminisms, Karen Offen, *European Feminisms, 1750–1950: A Political History* (Stanford, Calif.; Stanford University Press, 2000), xxvii.

19. For a fuller discussion of Woolf as "political," see Naomi Black, "Virginia Woolf and the Women's Movement," in *Virginia Woolf: A Feminist Slant*, ed. Jane Marcus, 180–97 (Lincoln: University of Nebraska Press, 1983).

20. Linden Peach, *Virginia Woolf* (London: Palgrave, 2000), 12, 35.

21. E. M. Forster, "The Rede Lecture," reprinted in *The Bloomsbury Group: A Collection of Memoirs and Commentary*, rev. ed., ed. S. P. Rosenbaum (Toronto: University of Toronto Press, 1995), 233. We may speculate that Forster's hostility was in part because feminism made use of the heterosexist privilege that enabled straight women to claim rights for themselves as a class in a way not possible for homosexual men like

himself. More likely, he identified feminism with the man-hating aggression attributed to the suffragettes.

22. See discussions in Lee, *Virginia Woolf*. For an earlier assessment, see Sue Roe, *Writing and Gender: Virginia Woolf's Writing Practice* (London: Harvester Wheatsheaf, 1990), 171: "To the extent that Woolf's writing is feminist, it is so because she attempts to re-formulate meaning within fictitious forms, rather than because she harbored any long-term strategies for political change."

23. See Natania Rosenfeld, *Outsiders Together: Virginia and Leonard Woolf* (Princeton, N.J.: Princeton University Press, 2000), 159, who judges fiction and nonfiction alike as "radical" when it is relatively modernist, and overlooks even the formal radicalism of *Three Guineas*.

24. One exception is Beth Carole Rosenberg and Jeanne Dubino, eds., *Virginia Woolf and the Essay* (New York: St. Martin's Press, 1997), especially the chapter by Catherine Sandbach-Dahlstrom, " 'Que Scais-je': Virginia Woolf and the Essay as Feminist Critique." Sandbach-Dahlstrom sees Woolf's use of the essay as "a vehicle for processes of exploration rather determinacy . . . a collage of vacillating viewpoints and shifting inconclusive perspectives" and therefore feminist because "questioning and resistance are inseparable" (280).

25. See Rachel Bowlby's editions of selections among the essays and reviews, *A Woman's Essays: Selected Essays*, vol. 1, and *The Crowded Dance of Modern Life: Selected Essays*, vol. 2 (London: Penguin, 1992, 1993).

26. Anne Thackeray Ritchie, *Letters*, ed. Hester Ritchie (London: John Murray Ritchie, 1924), 144.

27. Leonard Woolf was excused from war service in the First World War for physical reasons, but many of Woolf's friends were conscientious objectors, Lytton Strachey famously so. Only Clive Bell continued to be a pacifist as the Second World War approached, publishing for the Peace Pledge Union in 1938 his uncompromisingly pacifist *War Mongers*.

28. This invitation was from the Cambridge English Society; she had earlier refused the offer of the prestigious Clark Lectures. See S. P. Rosenbaum, "Virginia Woolf and the Clark Lectures," *Charleston Magazine* 22 (autumn/winter 2000): 5–10.

CHAPTER 2. Feminism and the Women's Movement

1. Karen Offen, *European Feminisms, 1750–1950: A Political History* (Stanford, Calif.; Stanford University Press 2000), 283.

2. This definition is presumably based on the one found in the *Oxford English Dictionary* (1931): "Advocacy of the rights of women (based on the theory of the equality of the sexes)."

3. A draft, probably written in 1937, had burned the word *patriarch* along with *feminist*. *The Virginia Woolf Manuscripts: From the Henry W. and Albert A. Berg Collection at the New York Public Library* (Woodbridge, Conn.: Research Publication International, 1994), microfilm, reel 7, M28.

4. See Naomi Black and Gail Cuthbert Brandt, *Feminist Politics on the Farm: Rural*

Catholic Women in Southern Quebec and Southwestern France (Montreal: McGill-Queen's University Press, 1999), 119–20.

5. The Contagious Diseases Acts infringed the civil liberties of all British women, both in the homeland and in imperial outposts as remote as British North America. Although, in practice, class and race protected the majority of them, all women, without exception, were considered potential whores. The logical next policy step, already in place in Europe, would be registration and medical regulation of prostitutes, but this was not the subject of the Acts themselves.

6. Butler was careful to dissociate her activism related to sexually transmitted diseases and prostitution from the more respectable mainstream efforts to obtain education, employment, and the vote for women.

7. Josephine Butler, *Personal Reminiscences of a Great Crusade* (London: Horace Marshall and Sons, 1896), 80. The emphasis in the second citation is in the original.

8. Ibid., 83.

9. In the interwar period, women were accordingly admitted to the legal profession and to closed corporations such as the Society of Chartered Accountants as well as to jury duty and the civil service.

10. Woolf used Whitaker's *Almanack* for 1936, as a major source for *Three Guineas*. See *3G* 170.

11. Cambridge granted full academic standing to women only in 1948.

12. Test cases brought in the 1920s found that "although marriage did not of itself disqualify a woman from employment, there was nothing in the Act to prevent an employer from refusing to employ her on this account." Vera Douie, *The Lesser Half: A Survey of the Laws, Regulations and Practices Introduced during the Present War Which Embody Discrimination against Women* (London: Swindon Press for the Women's Publicity Planning Association, 1943), 12. Douie was the librarian at the London and National Society for Women's Service and a major source of facts and figures for *Three Guineas*. The marriage bar was ended in the civil service only in 1946.

13. Clive Bell, *Old Friends* (Chicago: University of Chicago Press, 1956), 101.

14. Virginia Woolf, *"Women & Fiction": The Manuscript Versions of "A Room of One's Own,"* ed. S. P. Rosenbaum (Oxford: Shakespeare Head Press for Basil Blackwell, 1992), 213.

15. Virginia Woolf wrote an obituary essay about Jane Maria Strachey when she died in 1928 at the age of eighty-eight. In it, extensive involvement in the women's movement is summed up as "keen interest in public questions, particularly in the education and emancipation of women." *The Essays of Virginia Woolf*, vol. 4, ed. Andrew McNeillie (London: Hogarth Press, 1994), 574. On Lady Strachey, see her own remarks in "Some Recollections of a Long Life," part 4, *Nation and Athenaeum*, 30 August 1924, and Nupur Chaudhuri, "Bloomsbury Ancestry: Jane Maria Strachey, Feminism, and Younger Strachey Women," in *Women in the Milieu of Leonard and Virginia Woolf: Peace, Politics, and Education*, ed. Wayne K. Chapman and Janet M. Manson (New York: Pace University Press, 1998). Meg A. Meneghel gives a useful summary of daughter-in-law Ray Strachey's feminist career, which included major roles in the National Union of Women's Suffrage Societies, the London and National Society for

Women's Service, and the Women's Employment Federation: "'Dear Mother': Ray Strachey's Role in Feminism and the League of Nations as Seen from the Lilly Library," also in *Women in the Milieu of Leonard and Virginia Woolf*. Neither Pippa nor Pernel Strachey have yet received the biographical and analytical attention they deserve, though Brian Harrison has a chapter on Ray Strachey that also includes some material on Pippa, in *Prudent Revolutionaries: Portraits of British Feminists between the Wars* (Oxford: Clarendon Press, 1987).

16. Leslie Stephen's letters reflect tense discussions between Woolf's parents about women's education and professionalism, with Leslie distressed at Julia's responses and the pain he had caused her. Noel Annan, *Leslie Stephen: The Godless Victorian* (London: Weidenfeld and Nicolson, 1984), 109, 110, 293–94; and Leslie Stephen, *Selected Letters*, ed. John W. Bicknell (London: Macmillan, 1996), 1:103, 213–15.

17. We also know that Woolf attended classes in history at King's College, and also, less common for girls, was taught Latin and Greek there, the Greek followed up in private lessons. This was not a usual subject for girls, nor was it usual to have, as she did, unfettered access to her father's large library.

18. George Dangerfield, *The Strange Death of Liberal England* (New York: Capricorn, 1961), 163. The group is sometimes referred to as the People's Suffrage Federation for Adult Suffrage, although this was not the name on its letterhead. Founding members included, along with the Women's Co-operative Guild, the Women's Labour League and the Women's Trade Union League.

19. The PSF's executive board included Davies and Janet Case (Virginia Stephen's former Latin teacher) as well as other representatives of women's groups, male supporters from the British Labour Party and the Co-operative movement, and some of the more "social-democratic" Liberals. Its address, as shown on its letterhead, was in Mecklenburgh Square, close to where Virginia Stephen lived. *The Suffrage Annual and Women's Who's Who*, ed. A. J. R. (London: Stanley Paul, 1913), 99–102; Margherita Rendel, "The Contribution of the Women's Labour League to the Winning of the Franchise," in *Women in the Labour Movement*, ed. Lucy Middleton (London: Croom Helm, 1977), 70. I refer to Margaret Llewelyn Davies as "Davies," although some sources use Llewelyn Davies.

20. The response to "Miss Stephen" came from another PSF board member, Rosalind Vaughan Nash, a Co-operative movement figure but not a Bloomsbury one.

21. Quentin Bell, *Virginia Woolf: A Biography* (London: Hogarth Press, 1972), 1:161; PSF pamphlets in the National Women's Library; letter from Rosalind Nash in the library of the University of Sussex.

22. Barbara Strachey Halpern, "Ray Strachey—A Memoir," in Chapman and Manson, *Women in the Milieu of Leonard and Virginia Woolf*, 78, 79–80, 86 n. 2.

23. On this occasion, she was not impressed by Mrs. Pethick-Lawrence but thought that the "Russian speaker" had "imagination."

24. Virginia Stephen referred to "Adult Suffrage" in at least three letters in 1910 related to her activism with the PSF (*L1* 421, 422, 426). On the reputation of the PSF, see Martin Pugh, *The March of the Women: A Revisionist Account of the Campaign for Women's Suffrage, 1866–1914* (Oxford: Oxford University Press, 2000) 28–29, 266;

also Constance Rover, *Women's Suffrage and Party Politics in Britain, 1866–1914* (London: Routledge and Kegan Paul, 1967); Jill Liddington and Jill Norris, *One Hand Tied behind Us: The Rise of the Women's Suffrage Movement* (London: Virago Press, 1978).

25. Virginia Woolf, *Moments of Being*, rev. and enlarged ed., ed. Jeanne Schulkind (London: Hogarth Press, 1985), 181.

26. In a 1909 sketch, Stephen refers to meeting a "Miss Margaret Davies" who has "organised a great co-operative movement in the north." Virginia Woolf, "Hampstead," in *Carlyle's House and Other Sketches*, ed. David Bradshaw (London: Hesperus Press, 2003), 10, 11. Leonard Woolf met Davies in 1912, on the occasion of his engagement to Virginia. See Sybil Oldfield, "Margaret Llewelyn Davies and Leonard Woolf," in Chapman and Manson, *Women in the Milieu of Leonard and Virginia Woolf*, 3. Leonard notes that his wife's association with Davies brought him into the Co-operative movement. He became active with the Fabian Society after the Webbs noticed his article about the 1913 Congress of the WCG, the one described in Virginia Woolf's "Introductory Letter" to *Life as We Have Known It*. See Leonard Woolf, *Beginning Again: An Autobiography of the Years 1911–1918* (London: Hogarth Press, 1964), 101–2, 106–8.

27. Sandra Stanley Holton gives a detailed account of the Women's Co-operative Guild's suffragism and outlines usefully the founding and operation of the PSF in *Women's Suffrage and Reform Politics in Britain, 1910–1918* (Cambridge: Cambridge University Press, 1986); see esp. 63–64 on Davies' role there.

28. Consumer, as opposed to producer, co-operation hoped to produce socialism by means of purchases through co-operatively owned stores as well as, later, factories and other forms of public service such as banks and insurance. Co-op stores generated a form of savings in dividends that were paid out at intervals; prices were correspondingly higher, although quality and service were supposed to be both ethically and materially superior. Working-class women, who controlled family pocketbooks, were crucial to the success of the project. The best account of the Women's Co-operative Guild remains its centennial history, Jean Gaffin and David Thoms, *Caring and Sharing: The Centenary History of the Co-operative Women's Guild* (Manchester: Co-operative Union, 1983).

29. References by Virginia Woolf to WCG membership include *L2* 90, 138–40, 152, 155, 157, 356; *L3* 53, 54.

30. Mary Lawrenson was the first general secretary of the Women's Co-operative Guild; Sarah Reddish was its first paid employee, organizing branches in the years 1893–95.

31. Virginia Woolf's contacts with Co-operation are referred to in her letters as follows: reading manuals and traveling to inspect sites with Leonard in 1913 and 1914: *L2* 19, 41, 44, 45; letters for *Maternity* (1914): *L2* 54; 1916 WCG Congress: *L2* 28, 99, 105; *Life as We Have Known It*, first references: *L3* 166, *L4* 191; 1933 WCG Jubilee Congress: *D5* 165.

32. See Naomi Black, *Social Feminism* (Ithaca, N.Y.: Cornell University Press, 1989), 116.

33. See ibid., 109–59, for fuller discussion.

34. From a pamphlet in the Women's Library, London Guildhall University.

35. These white peace poppies were adopted by the Peace Pledge Union and in 2002 were still being distributed by them and by a number of other peace groups, such as Canada's Voice of Women for Peace.

36. The Women's Co-operative Guild changed its name to the Co-operative Women's Guild, reflecting a turn away from the feminism of earlier years. Clearly a dying organization, the guild is today in even worse shape than the rest of the declining English Consumer Co-operative movement as a whole. Its membership in 2001 was 2,591. Information by phone from the Co-operative Women's Guild, London, September 2002.

37. See Pugh, *The March of the Women*, for a demonstration of the relatively limited impact of the Women's Social and Political Union.

38. Ray Strachey, *The Cause: A Short History of the Women's Movement in Great Britain*, was published in 1928 by G. Bell and Co., not Hogarth; a revised version of the first edition was published in facsimile by Cedric Chivers in 1974. Brian Harrison notes that both Millicent Garrett Fawcett (to whom it was dedicated) and Pippa Strachey "were scrutinizing her drafts" (*Prudent Revolutionaries*, 173).

39. Strachey, *The Cause*, 304.

40. Ray Strachey, *Millicent Garrett Fawcett* (London: John Murray, 1931), 289 (my translation).

41. Prominent members of the NUWSS, including its secretary and editor of its journal, Helena Swanwick, eventually withdrew from the war effort; Swanwick herself was to become steadily more pacifist, finally committing suicide at the outbreak of the Second World War. The Pankhursts' Women's Social and Political Union, by contrast, greeted with enthusiasm the opportunity in 1914 to demonstrate women's fitness for those armed forms of civil service for which they had been thought unfit— an argument often used by antisuffragists.

42. This article appeared in *Ius Suffragii*, the journal of the International Women's Suffrage Alliance, and signed by Helena Swanwick as secretary of the NUWSS. Cited in Arnold Whittick, *Woman into Citizen* (London: Athenaeum with Frederick Muller, 1979), 296; emphases in the original.

43. In 1911 Mrs. Pankhurst was sent to Holloway Prison after conviction for "conspiracy and incitement to riot" when she and two companions broke the windows of Number 10 Downing Street while 150 other militants simultaneously broke plate-glass windows in shops, post offices, and government departments. The famous hunger strikes started as attempts to gain treatment as political prisoners rather than common criminals.

44. Ethel Smyth was among the models for Rose Pargiter, the suffragette in *The Years;* the character also resembles "General" Drummond, who is cited in *Three Guineas (3G 148)*.

45. The WFL pioneered such innovative tactics as the withholding of taxes and active noncooperation with the Census. See Harrison, *Prudent Revolutionaries,* for the history and relationship of the suffrage groups and of the NUWSS's successors in the interwar period; there is a helpful diagram on 4–5.

46. Two versions of *The Cause* were published, both dated 1928, with identical title pages and no indication that they were different. In one of these Strachey remarks intemperately and inaccurately that there had been no accounts or audits of the "enormous sums of money" that "passed through the hands of the society" because the Women's Social and Political Union "spent no time on 'formalities'" (311). The other version replaces the comments on WSPU finances with figures for the organization's income—which Virginia Woolf cites in *Three Guineas* and mistakenly identifies as the income of the much smaller Women's Freedom League (*3G* 145). It seems likely that a lawsuit was threatened and a substitute page inserted. (Harrison mentions in connection with *The Cause* "the customary gauntlet of threatened Pankhurstian lawsuits" [*Prudent Revolutionaries*, 173]). The unexpurgated version, without WSPU figures, was reprinted by Cedric Chivers in 1974. See the copies of *The Cause* in the Women's Library; for more detail about suffrage finances and their misstatement in *Three Guineas*, see *3G* 224. Ray Strachey's rather confusing description of the origins of the WFL, the same in both "first" editions, seems to have been responsible in part for Woolf's substituting the WFL for the organization that its leaders had left.

47. Woolf mentioned seeing Mrs. Pethick-Lawrence speak at the Kingsway Hall celebration of the achievement of the vote in March 1918 (*D1* 125).

48. Anna Snaith, "*Three Guineas* Letters," *Woolf Studies Annual* 6 (2000): 34; *L6* 239; Emmeline Pethick-Lawrence, *My Part in a Changing World* (London: Victor Gollancz, 1938), 177.

49. This is a simplification of a more complicated history, for which see Harrison, *Prudent Revolutionaries*; Harrison is one of those who use for convenience's sake the name assumed after women's enfranchisement, the London Society for Women's Service; I use the name of the group at the time Virginia Woolf was involved with it. In 2002 its successor, the Fawcett Society, was running two campaigns: "Equality? Get Real" and the Women's Representation Bill (http://www.fawcettsociety.org).

50. *L5* 136; *L6* 231, 234, 236; and *D5* 144. See also nine unpublished postcards and two letters in the possession of the Women's Library that attest to Woolf's appeals for research help and her donation of books, identified in the actual volumes as "presented by Mrs Woolf." See also Vera Douie, "Women's Service Library: The First Sixteen Years, 1925–42," typescript, n.d., 7–8, in the Women's Library, London. In 1933 there was an unsuccessful attempt to sell the manuscript of *A Room of One's Own* to benefit the library; see Hermione Lee, *Virginia Woolf* (London: Chatto and Windus, 1996), 602 and 847–88 nn. 129, 130. Also see *L5* 136.

51. Strachey, *Millicent Garrett Fawcett*, 336.

52. In 1941 Woolf agreed to serve on some sort of committee and received material about the L&NSWS's various campaigns, such as the one related to the differential insurance provisions for women workers in 1937. On solicitation of subscriptions, see *L6* 232, 234, 236, 239; on the committee, *L6* 473; on the Pensions Bill, *L6* 145, *3G* 147.

53. The Finance Minutes of the WEF (in the Women's Library) record a series of appeals to donors and two fund-raising dinners, in 1934 and 1935.

54. The letter the narrator of *Three Guineas* claims to be answering asked, she says, for "books, fruit or cast-off clothing that can be sold in a bazaar" (*3G* 40). The first

endnote for chapter 2 is inserted at this point. It begins, "To quote the exact words of one such appeal" and ends with the parenthetical note, "(Extract from a letter received from the London and National Society for Women's Service. (1938)" (*3G* 144).

55. WEF Annual Report, 1938, Women's Library.

56. Harrison has a full chapter on Eleanor Rathbone; writing at the end of the 1980s, he describes her as "a heroine," "perhaps the most distinguished British feminist the twentieth century has so far seen" (*Prudent Revolutionaries*, 9).

57. Eleanor Rathbone, "Changes in Public Life," in *Our Freedom and Its Results*, ed. Ray Strachey (London: Hogarth Press, 1936), 58.

58. J. H. Willis, Jr., *Leonard and Virginia Woolf as Publishers* (Charlottesville: University of Virginia Press, 1992), 248–49.

59. For an early but still solid account of the politics of mothers' allowances in England, see Jane Lewis, *The Politics of Motherhood: Child and Maternal Welfare in England, 1900–1939* (London: Croom Helm, 1980).

60. Virginia Woolf, *A Room of One's Own* (London: Hogarth Press, 1929), 149.

61. Joanne Trautmann Banks, "Some New Woolf Letters," *Modern Fiction Studies* 30.2 (1984): 189.

62. She also provided substitute terms for soldier ("gutsgruzzler") as well as heroism and hero ("botulism" and "bottle"). Monk's House Papers, University of Sussex Library, Brighton; partially reproduced in *N56* 253.

CHAPTER 3. The Evolution of *Three Guineas*

1. The essay was first published in *The Death of the Moth*, the first collection of Virginia Woolf's essays that Leonard Woolf put together for publication after her death (London: Hogarth Press, 1942). In his introduction to the volume, he describes the contents as corresponding roughly to a planned third series of *The Common Reader* (7).

2. The notebooks cover the years 1905–41. Brenda R. Silver, *Virginia Woolf's Reading Notebooks* (Princeton, N.J.: Princeton University Press, 1983), xi. Silver sorted out the reading notes that are mixed up with manuscript drafts in the Woolf material held at the New York Public Library (Berg Collection) and the University of Sussex Library (Monk's House Papers); more of Woolf's reading notes are in the library of Smith College, but they are not relevant to the composition of *Three Guineas*. See *3G*, Appendices D and E, for a detailed list of periodical and book sources of *Three Guineas*.

3. Silver, *Reading Notebooks*, 32–33, provides a description of the "notebooks"; she comments repeatedly on "Woolf's haphazard approach to binding her reading notes" (69). The catalog of the New York Public Library's microfilmed Woolf material notes the difficulty of deciphering the texts: "Virginia Woolf often wrote in her notebooks in more than one direction," including reversing directions in notebooks and writing on both sides of the paper. Preface to *The Virginia Woolf Manuscripts: From the Henry W. and Albert A. Berg Collection at The New York Public Library* (Woodbridge, Conn.: Research Publication International, 1994), n.p.

4. These scrapbooks are in the Monk's House Papers; the handlist describes them as "3 bound volumes containing Press Cuttings & extracts collected or copied by VW relative to *3Gs*." Silver gives this description of a scrapbook: "a loose-leafed two-ringed notebook, with a hard cover" (*Reading Notebooks*, 259).

5. J. C. Squire, *Reflections and Memories* (London: Heinemann, 1935).

6. It is widely believed that the manuscript of *Three Guineas* that was sold in 1939 "for the Refugees society" later ended up in the Berg Collection of the New York Public Library. See Hermione Lee, *Virginia Woolf* (London: Chatto and Windus, 1996), 687, relying on *L6* 314 and 319; see also the notes to these two letters. May Sarton did solicit a manuscript on behalf of the American Guild for German Cultural Freedom, which, along with the League of American Writers and the Book-sellers Guild of America, co-sponsored an auction, held at the Hotel Delmonico on 19 February 1939, to benefit exiled anti-Nazi writers and the Rehabilitation Fund of the Abraham Lincoln Brigade. The auction catalogue includes only one item by Virginia Woolf, a signed copy of *Jacob's Room*. Communications from Sylvia Asmus of the Deutsche Bibliothek, Deutsches Exilarchiv 1933–1945, 10 and 11 December 2002. For the auction, see *Deutsche Intellektuelle im Exil: ihre Akademie und die "American Guild for German Cultural Freedom": eine Ausstellung der Deutschen Exilarchivs 1933–45 des Deutschen Bibliothek, Frankfurt am Main* (Munich: K. G. Saur, 1993), 247–49.

7. The material that the Berg acquired from Leonard Woolf was described correctly at the time of sale as "loose sheets, some typed." Communication from Isaac Gewirtz, curator of the Berg Collection, 10 September 2002.

8. Virginia Woolf, *A Writer's Diary*, ed. Leonard Woolf (London: Hogarth Press, 1953), 165n.

9. Titles used briefly also include "P & P" and "my P. P. little book," and "What are we to do." For a full list of titles and references, with dates, see *3G* lviii.

10. Vera Brittain, "A Woman's Notebook," *Nation and Athenaeum*, 31 January 1931, 571.

11. For details on Brittain's column and Keynes's review, see *3G* xx–xxi, 137, 220.

12. London and National Society for Women's Service, Junior Council, Annual Report, 1931, p. 8, Women's Library, London Guildhall University.

13. See Lee, *Virginia Woolf*, 601.

14. These are reprinted in Virginia Woolf, *The Pargiters*, ed. Mitchell Leaska (London: Hogarth Press, 1977), xxvii–xliv and 163–67.

15. Ibid., xliv, 164.

16. Ibid., 167, xliii, 7. Six occupations appear in the typescript but not the holo-graph, including "Aero-Engineer," the occupation of one of the men on the list. London and National Society for Women's Service, Junior Council, List of Members, in Annual Report (1930), 6.

17. Woolf, *The Pargiters*, xli and xliv, corrected by *Virginia Woolf Manuscripts*, reel 11, M70.

18. Figures about the dates of topics and the sources of clippings are approximate. Not all items clipped for the scrapbooks had dates on them or could be dated. For *3G*

we attempted to trace, among undated items, only those actually used in *Three Guineas*.

19. From an unpublished letter in the Winifred Holtby Collection, Hull Public Library, cited by Marion Shaw, "From *A Room of One's Own* to *A Literature of One's Own*," *South Carolina Review* 19.1 (1996): 61.

20. Woolf, *The Pargiters*. According to Grace Radin, Leaska's transcription represents most of the first two volumes of the holograph. Radin, *Virginia Woolf's "The Years": The Evolution of a Novel* (Knoxville: University of Tennessee Press, 1981), xii.

21. Woolf, *The Pargiters*, xiv n. 2; but see the communication to Michèle Barrett referred to at xiv n. 1. For Newbolt, I am relying on a communication by Bell to S. P. Rosenbaum; see Henry Newbolt, *My World as in My Time* (London: Faber and Faber, 1932), including the picture of "Pargiters, Yattenden" opposite p. 186. There are many family and other connections here: Newbolt was a friend and favorite author of Leslie Stephen; Poet Laureate Bridges was a cousin by marriage and close associate of Roger Fry, as well as a patron of Gerard Manley Hopkins, whose work he introduced to Fry and through him to Virginia Woolf.

22. Woolf, *The Pargiters*, 8.

23. Merry M. Pawlowski, "Toward a Feminist Theory of the State: Virginia Woolf and Wyndham Lewis on Art, Gender, and Politics," in *Virginia Woolf and Fascism: Resisting the Dictators' Seduction*, ed. M. M. Pawlowski (London: Palgrave, 2001), 41, suggests that the new title was a reaction to Wyndham Lewis's virulent attack on Woolf in the previous October (in his *Men without Art*). Woolf recorded her pain in her diary on 14 October 1934: "I have taken the arrow of W.L. to my heart," adding that it was "fatal" to answer back to attacks or "to arrange the P[argiter]s so as to meet his criticisms" (*D4* 251, 252).

24. Radin, *Woolf's "The Years,"* 34, calls this "Sketch for Professions," but as in much of this text, the scrawled writing is difficult to decipher. *Virginia Woolf Manuscripts*, reel 4, M1.4.

25. H. G. Wells, *Experiment in Autobiography: Discoveries and Conclusions of a Very Ordinary Brain (since 1866)* (London: Victor Gollancz and Cresset Press, 1934).

26. *Virginia Woolf Manuscripts*, reel 4, M1.4.

27. For Woolf's involvement (by invitation) in male-organized left-wing opposition to fascism during the 1930s, see David Bradshaw, "British Writers and Anti-Fascism in the 1930s. Part I: 'The Bray and Drone of Tortured Voices,'" *Woolf Studies Annual* 3 (1997): 3–27; and Bradshaw, "British Writers and Anti-Fascism in the 1930s. Part II: 'Under the Hawk's Wings,'" *Woolf Studies Annual* 4 (1998): 41–66.

28. Quentin Bell, *Virginia Woolf: A Biography* (London: Hogarth Press, 1972), 2:186–87.

29. The main business at the Labour Party congress in Brighton had been crushing the anti-imperialist and pacifist views of Alfred Salter, with whom Woolf recorded her sympathies in her diary.

30. There is a sum in the margin subtracting from 1919 (date of the Sex Disqualification [Removal] Act that is featured in *Three Guineas*) from 1937, although the fragment itself is dated only 21 September. *Virginia Woolf Manuscripts*, reel 7, M28.

31. Bell, *Virginia Woolf*, 2: Appendix C, 258, 259.

32. On 12 March 1938, Woolf recorded that after three other U.S. journals had rejected *Three Guineas*, the *Atlantic Monthly* was willing to pay £120 for 12,000 words; the text (without notes) therefore had to be cut to about a quarter of its original length (*D5* 130).

33. Leonard Woolf had printed 16,250 copies and about 6,000 were sold in the ten weeks after publication (*D5* 155). There were 1,000 copies of the first English edition left to be rebound in 1943 for the second issue and some 7,250 more for the Uniform Edition probably issued in 1947. The first American edition had a print run of 7,500. See B. J. Kirkpatrick and Stuart N. Clarke, *A Bibliography of Virginia Woolf*, 4th ed. (Oxford: Clarendon Press, 1997), 107–8.

34. Brenda R. Silver, "Three Guineas Before and After," in *Virginia Woolf: A Feminist Slant*, ed. Jane Marcus (Lincoln: University of Nebraska Press, 1983), 255. For transcriptions and annotations of the letters, see Anna Snaith, "*Three Guineas* Letters," *Woolf Studies Annual* 6 (2000): 17–168.

35. *The Collected Essays of Virginia Woolf*, ed. Leonard Woolf (London: Hogarth Press, 1966), 2:289, 288, 289.

CHAPTER 4. The Argument in *Three Guineas*

1. Michèle Barrett, introduction to *"A Room of One's Own" and "Three Guineas,"* ed. M. Barrett (London: Penguin Books, 1993), xxviii.

2. For example, Thomas Jackson Rice, *Virginia Woolf: A Guide to Research* (New York: Garland Publishing, 1984), 176–80.

3. Leonard Woolf, *Downhill All the Way: An Autobiography of the Years 1919–1939* (London: Hogarth Press, 1967), 27.

4. Forster's "Credo" was published in the same series by the Hogarth Press in 1939 under its final title "What I Believe"; Woolf could presumably have reduced *Three Guineas* to something comparable in scale, though, as we have seen, she did not wish to do so for the *London Mercury*.

5. S. P. Rosenbaum, "Bloomsbury Letters," in *Aspects of Bloomsbury: Studies in Modern English Literary and Intellectual History* (New York: Macmillan and St. Martin's Press, 1998), 64.

6. Frank and Anita Kermode footnote Virginia Woolf's remarks that letter writing is "an occupation one could carry on at odd moments . . . anonymously as it were." Kermode and Kermode, *The Oxford Book of Letters* (Oxford: Oxford University Press, 1995), xxi, xxii.

7. The following letters or letter drafts appear in *Three Guineas*: (1) framing letter sent to the representative of a peace society, signing a manifesto and enclosing one guinea but refusing to join the society; (2) letter received from the peace society; (3) letter received from the Spanish government, with photographs; (4) peace society manifesto, for newspaper publication; (5) letter received from the honorary treasurer of the building fund for a women's college; (6) draft response, not sent: alternative education, the "poor college"; (7) draft response, not sent: burn down the college; (8)

letter sent to the building fund for a college, enclosing one guinea with no conditions; (9) letter received from the honorary treasurer of a group supporting professional women; (10) draft response, not sent: burn down the building; (11) letter of conditional support sent to a group supporting professional women, enclosing one guinea, with conditions; (12) draft letter to daughters of educated men, not sent: sign the manifesto of the peace society.

8. A total of 16,500 copies were published in the United Kingdom and 7,500 in the United States. See B. J. Kirkpatrick and Stuart N. Clarke, *A Bibliography of Virginia Woolf,* 4th ed. (Oxford: Clarendon Press, 1997), 65, 66.

9. A number of those who wrote to Virginia Woolf about *Three Guineas* expressed the wish that it could be reprinted more cheaply so it could be circulated more widely. See Anna Snaith, *"Three Guineas* Letters," *Woolf Studies Annual* 6 (2000): esp. 5–6.

10. Quentin Bell, *Elders and Betters* (London: John Murray, 1995), Appendix I, 212–20.

11. Ray Strachey, *The Cause: A Short History of the Women's Movement in Great Britain* (London: G. Bell and Co., 1928; facsimile edition by Cedric Chivers, 1974), 379; Arnold Whittick, *Woman into Citizen* (London: Athenaeum with Frederick Muller, 1979), 113. Ray Strachey had worked closely with Cecil in 1921–23; see Meg A. Meneghel, "'Dear Mother': Ray Strachey's Role in Feminism and the League of Nations as Seen from the Lilly Library," in *Women in the Milieu of Leonard and Virginia Woolf: Peace, Politics, and Education,* ed. Wayne K. Chapman and Janet M. Manson (New York: Pace University Press, 1998).

12. Snaith, *"Three Guineas* Letters," 35.

13. Virginia Woolf, *The London Scene* (London: Hogarth Press, 1975) 40; on Duckworth and pigs, *D3* 293–94; on Keynes and pigs, see "JMK," in *The Bloomsbury Group: A Collection of Memoirs and Commentary,* rev. ed., ed. S. P. Rosenbaum (Toronto: University of Toronto Press, 1995), 274.

14. In that book, the narrator was warned off the grass by a "Beadle" and forbidden access to the manuscript of Thackeray's *Henry Esmond,* donated to Trinity College, Cambridge, by Woolf's father, Leslie Stephen; see Virginia Woolf, *"Women & Fiction": The Manuscript Versions of "A Room of One's Own,"* ed. S. P. Rosenbaum (Oxford: Shakespeare Head Press for Basil Blackwell, 1992), 205.

15. See S. P. Rosenbaum, "Virginia Woolf and the Clark Lectures," *Charleston Magazine* 22 (autumn/winter 2000): 5–10.

16. See Elizabeth Abel, *Virginia Woolf and Fictions of Psychoanalysis* (Chicago: University of Chicago Press, 1989), 103. The letter was first published in Paris by the Institute of International Cooperation; the text and related writings by Freud were published by Hogarth Press in 1939 in the collection *Civilisation, War, and Death,* edited by John Rickman. About the original exchange, beginning with a letter dated 30 June 1932, see Ronald W. Clark, *Einstein: The Life and Times* (New York: Avon, 1984), 444–46.

17. Q. D. Leavis, "Caterpillars of the Commonwealth, Unite!" *Scrutiny* 7 (September 1938): 210.

18. Pierre Cot (1895–1977) was a prominent French opponent of fascism, one of the organizers of the Popular Front, and minister of aviation from 1933 through 1938.

19. *N59* 280; quotation from Monk's House Papers, University of Sussex Library, Brighton.

20. The WEF changed its name to the National Advisory Centre on Careers for Women and then simply Careers for Women, and went into voluntary liquidation only in 1993. In the 1930s it served as the liaison for a number of national women's organizations concerned with employment and training of women, including the Association of Head Mistresses, the Midwives' Institute, the National Association of Women Pharmacists, the Council of Women Civil Servants, as well as women's schools and universities. Letters from Menon dated 20 October 1998 and 12 August 2002; see also the WEF Annual Report, 1938, and Finance and Executive Committee Minutes as well as Minutes of the Joint Meetings of the Executives of the Junior and Senior L&NSWS; and information from the Women's Library, London Guildhall University, "collection level description."

21. Baldwin's talk on that occasion is not to be found in the scrapbooks or daily newspapers; perhaps there was some sort of handout that was passed on to Woolf but did not make its way into her scrapbooks.

22. Snaith, "*Three Guineas* Letters," 20.

23. The remark was made by "Mrs. Nansen," who was probably Sigrun Nansen, widow of the Nobel laureate, the great explorer and humanitarian.

24. Snaith, "*Three Guineas* Letters," 20, 35, 23. Brian Harrison cites a letter from Ray Strachey to Lady Astor in which she describes *Three Guineas* as a "glorious attack on the pomposity of men." See Harrison, *Prudent Revolutionaries: Portraits of British Feminists between the Wars* (Oxford: Clarendon Press, 1987), 181.

25. See Naomi Black and Gail Cuthbert Brandt, *Feminist Politics on the Farm* (Montreal: McGill-Queen's University Press, 1999), 125.

26. Prestigious, even posh, as well as a desirable amount of money, the sum of three guineas was the prize awarded in a 1904 contest to name a record-breaking train of the Great Western Railway. The Three Guineas pub, next to the railway station in Reading, has three golden guineas on its sign in memory of this story. The pub is now badly run down and louche. "What a hole," says a Web site that evaluates pubs in Reading (http://www. readingpubs.co.uk/pubs-clubs-pages/3-guineas.htm).

27. See Dolf Mootham, "Appendix A: The Comparative Values of the Pound," in *The Interior Castle: A Life of Gerald Brenan*, by Jonathan Gathorne-Hardy (London: Sinclair-Stevenson, 1992), 611. This is in 1990s dollars but is still pretty accurate.

28. In earlier publications, I did not count separately the letter and the manifesto of the peace society.

29. The Junior Council also had a few men as members, as many as ten of them in 1930. The gender count cannot be exact as there are a few cases of doctors whose names cannot be assigned one way or the other.

30. David Bradshaw, "British Writers and Anti-Fascism in the 1930s. Part II: 'Under the Hawk's Wings,'" *Woolf Studies Annual* 4 (1998): 44, discusses Woolf's re-

luctance, as a "pacifist," to support sanctions against Italy in relation to the invasion of Abyssinia. With Spain, the issue was refraining from policy that would support the aggressors. Bradshaw quotes the letter in question on p. 50.

31. The organization For Intellectual Liberty was begun by a group of British intellectuals, including Aldous Huxley and, initially, both the Woolfs; FIL tended to use the word *defend* rather than *protect*. For FIL and, more generally, Virginia Woolf's relationship to interwar antifascist organizing, see David Bradshaw, "British Writers and Anti-Fascism in the 1930s. Part I: 'The Bray and Drone of Tortured Voices,'" *Woolf Studies Annual* 3 (1997): 3–27; and Bradshaw, "British Writers and Anti-Fascism in the 1930s. Part II."

32. Monk's House Papers.

33. Virginia Woolf, *Collected Essays*, ed. Leonard Woolf, vol. 2 (London: Hogarth Press, 1966), 278–83.

34. The appeal is not for today's fragile nylons but for sturdy woolen and cotton hose that could be darned and reused at a time when respectable women still did not wear trousers to work.

CHAPTER 5. Other Feminist Publications by Virginia Woolf

1. Virginia Woolf may also have written but not published at least one more feminist piece. Its only trace is a note that Margaret Llewelyn Davies jotted on a 1916 letter to Leonard Woolf: "Virginia has written charmingly about our Congress in the Suff. Mag." The *Common Cause*, the only suffragist publication that regularly reported Guild happenings, had only three brief notes about the 1916 Westminster congress that both the Woolfs attended, although the issue of June 30 had announced that the next week would have complete coverage; see "A 'Working Women's Parliament,'" *Common Cause*, 30 June 1916, 150. The undated letter by Davies refers to a dispute that Leonard Woolf was having with a publisher in 1916; it has been misdated with an added note "c. October 1917" (Monk's House Papers, University of Sussex, Brighton). As Sybil Oldfield discovered, it was Leonard Woolf who published a report on the 1916 guild congress: "The Women's Co-operative Guild," *Ius Suffragii*, 1 September 1916, 171.

2. B. J. Kirkpatrick's exhaustive search of the suffragette and suffragist publications found two previously unknown publications by Woolf in the *Woman's Leader* but no other material identifiably by her. See B. J. Kirkpatrick, "Two Contributions by Virginia Woolf to the Suffragette Press," *Charleston Magazine* 12 (autumn/winter 1995): 25–29; Kirkpatrick later examined the Women's Freedom League publication *The Vote*. Letter from B. J. Kirkpatrick, 21 July 2001.

3. See J. H. Willis, Jr., *Leonard and Virginia Woolf as Publishers: The Hogarth Press, 1917–41* (Charlottesville: University of Virginia Press, 1992), 244–51.

4. The two Russian reviews referred to, one of them concerning a performance of *The Cherry Orchard*, were published in the *New Statesman* on 24 July and 7 August 1920 (D2 53 n. 4).

5. It is only fair to cite a later diary account of a visit from MacCarthy, recorded in

February 1938, which lasted from one o'clock to 7:15. "Nor did we stop talking all that time. Nor was I once bored or wished it to stop . . . dear old Desmond" (*D5* 62).

6. *The Essays of Virginia Woolf*, ed. Andrew McNeillie (London: Hogarth Press, 1988), 3:243.

7. Ibid., 3:245.

8. Bennett was later to become an important focus for Woolf's views about the proper form and nature of fiction. See "Mr. Bennett and Mrs. Brown," first published in 1923, in *Essays of Virginia Woolf*, 3:384–89.

9. Desmond MacCarthy [Affable Hawk], "Current Literature: Books in General," *New Statesman* 2 October 1920, 704; "The Intellectual Status of Women," *New Statesman*, 9 October 1929, 15, 16; 16 October 1920, 45, 46.

10. Arnold Bennett, *Our Women: Chapters on the Sex Discord* (London: Cassell, 1920), 102.

11. Woolf had refused Beaton's request to photograph her and was very angry that he included the sketches instead; she referred to him in letters to Ethel Smyth as "the horrid worm" and "that bloody bounder" (*L4* 258, 375). When she complained in her initial letter to the editor that she had not authorized her inclusion in the book, Beaton wrote back that caricaturists never ask permission, and his publication was after all something agreeable. Woolf replied that she objected precisely because this was not an issue of caricature but of a sort of representation that implies co-operation on the part of the subject. Virginia Woolf, "The Book of Beauty: A Protest," and "The Book of Beauty," letters to the editor, *Nation and Athenaeum*, 29 November and 20 December 1930. Also Cecil Beaton, "The Book of Beauty," letters to the editor, *Nation and Athenaeum*, 18 December 1930. There seems to be an issue about vanity; friends had perhaps teased her. Cristabel McLaren, Lady Aberconway, an old friend and well-known society figure, wrote to the *Nation and Athenaeum* a letter published along with Woolf's final defensive response on 20 December, accusing Woolf of keeping her beauty "very much the monopoly of her friends and relations," with only Vanessa Bell's "rather muddy" depiction made available to the public. McLaren, *Nation and Athenaeum*, letters to the editor, 20 December 1930, 373.

12. Julia Margaret Cameron, *Victorian Photographs of Famous Men and Fair Women*, with introductions by Virginia Woolf and Roger Fry (London: Hogarth Press, 1926).

13. This letter may possibly explain the mysterious initials "P&P" and then "P.P." that were used by Woolf to refer to the future *Three Guineas* in diary references two years later, in August and September 1935 (*D4* 335, 341). An entry in Woolf's reading notes includes the phrase "P & P": "P & P. The story of Simon in the home interesting: We are changing the conditions of nurses lives. But are we changing doctors." This might just possibly be a reference to public versus private spheres. In the notebook, the item is in the middle of notes on Marryat, about whom Woolf wrote "The Captain's Deathbed," which she completed on 22 August 1935 (*N10* 71; *D4* 335). It has also been suggested that the initials might refer to *Pride and Prejudice*.

14. Kirkpatrick, "Two Contributions by Virginia Woolf to the Suffragette Press," 28. This review has left no trace in diary or published letter.

15. The piece is mentioned in a letter to Clive Bell dated 26 April 1922, where

Woolf notes in passing, "Here come this moment some remarks upon Princess Bibesco, not very profound, but in payment of 17/6 which I owed Ray [Strachey] for her damnable sheet" (*L2* 523). There is no reference by name to the *Woman's Leader* or any other suffragist publication in Woolf's diaries.

16. Kirkpatrick, "Two Contributions by Virginia Woolf to the Suffragette Press," 26.

17. It has not been possible to identify any book from which the material about an imagined correspondent might have come. The London Library's list of acquisitions for the start of the 1920s supplies no plausible memoir or travel book about South America. Nor does the material correspond to anything in or used as sources for Woolf's first novel, *The Voyage Out*, even though that book takes its protagonists to an imagined South American setting. A letter to Lytton Strachey in February 1922 makes it clear that Woolf did in fact read Bibesco during the long 1922 illness (*L2* 503); she took notes on Chauncey Brewster Tinker's *Young Boswell*, apparently in 1922, the year it was published by Putnam's (*N49* 238).

18. Barclay reappears in a summary list of reading by guildswomen in the "Intro-ductory Letter" to *Life as We Have Known It*, cited as an example of their omnivorous and undiscriminating taste for reading matter, and again, in 1940, in a review of a life of Marie Corelli, where Woolf describes Barclay and Corelli more positively: "glori-ous geese" who "lived with such gusto that no one can fail to share it." Virginia Woolf, *The Crowded Dance of Modern Life: Selected Essays, Volume 2*, ed. Rachel Bowlby (London: Penguin Books, 1993), 164.

19. Woolf wrote in her diary in September 1920 that she was "making up a paper upon Woman, as a counterblast to Mr Bennett's adverse views reported in the paper" (*D2* 69 n. 12).

20. The posthumous collection *A Haunted House and Other Short Stories* (London: Hogarth Press, 1942) included most of the stories from *Monday or Tuesday*, but Leonard Woolf, who edited it, noted (p. 7) that Virginia Woolf had decided not to in-clude "A Society" in the collection of short stories that they had been planning before her death. The other story cut was a slight sketch.

21. *The Complete Shorter Fiction of Virginia Woolf*, ed. Susan Dick (London: Ho-garth Press, 1985), 125, 127, 130, 128.

22. Virginia Woolf, *A Room of One's Own* (London: Hogarth Press, 1929), 41, 13–14.

23. *Complete Shorter Fiction*, 131, 134, 136.

24. *A Room of One's Own*, 52.

25. *Complete Shorter Fiction*, 136.

26. Unpublished letter from Virginia Woolf described by S. P. Rosenbaum in his introduction to Virginia Woolf, *"Women & Fiction": The Manuscript Versions of "A Room of One's Own,"* ed. S. P. Rosenbaum (Oxford: Shakespeare Head Press for Basil Blackwell, 1992), xvii.

27. The chapter is very different in *Jacob's Room*. See Edward L. Bishop, *Virginia Woolf's "Jacob's Room": The Holograph Draft, Transcribed and Edited* (New York: Pace University Press, 1998), 50–54.

28. Edinburgh Women's Union Editorial Committee, "Prefatory Note," in *Ata-lanta's Garland: Being the Book of the Edinburgh Women's Union* (Edinburgh: T. and A.

Constable, 1926), v. Middleton Murry sent two unpublished sketches by Katherine Mansfield, and there were contributions by Hillaire Belloc, Walter De La Mare, W. H. Davies, Edwin Muir, Charlotte Mew, Naomi Mitchison, and many others, not all in English; some items were related to women or the status of women (such as an account of the pioneering medical students), but most were not.

29. The students rage against the chastity imposed by college authorities; they discuss the subterfuges that bypass the college's "utterly and intolerably damnable" restrictive regulations about contacts with young men. The question of women's friendships, even intimate friendships, is raised: "Alice" kisses Angela, sending her into raptures of joy. *Complete Shorter Fiction*, 146, 147.

30. *A Room of One's Own*, 7.

31. "*Women & Fiction*," 200.

32. Ibid., 201.

33. *A Room of One's Own*, 113 n. 1. MacCarthy had cited Woolf along with Jane Austen as examples of female novelists "courageously acknowledging the limitations of their sex'"; he apparently intended this as praise.

34. Appropriately, *A Room of One's Own* raised Woolf's income for 1929 to the very substantial income of just over £3,000, which she described in her diary as "the salary of a civil servant." If this was her estimate of a bureaucrat's salary, it is not surprising that she was indignant when, researching material for *Three Guineas*, she discovered in Whitaker's *Almanack* that the actual pay of women employees was rather closer to the £200 a year she said she had previously been content with (D3 285).

35. *A Room of One's Own*, 157, 13, 37.

36. Quentin Bell, *Bloomsbury*, rev. ed. (London: Omega, 1974), 71.

37. *A Room of One's Own*, 37.

38. The Hogarth Press title page of the piece reads "Introductory Letter to Margaret Llewelyn Davies. By Virginia Woolf"; Woolf, "Introductory Letter," in *Life As We Have Known It: By Co-operative Working Women*, ed. M. L. Davies (London: Hogarth Press, 1931), xv.

39. Ibid., xxviii, xxix.

40. Margaret Llewelyn Davies, *The Women's Co-operative Guild, 1883–1904* (Kirkby Lonsdale: Women's Co-operative Guild, 1904), first page, 10. The next, fuller history of the text, by Catherine Webb, *The Woman with a Basket: The Story of the Women's Co-operative Guild* (Manchester: Co-operative Wholesale Society, 1927), does not supply the text of Mrs. Acland's column that Woolf cites.

41. See Leonard Woolf, "Social Types: A Parliament of Women," *Nation* 21 (June 1913): 456; Leonard Woolf, *Beginning Again: An Autobiography of the Years 1911–1918* (London: Hogarth Press, 1964), 108; Virginia Woolf, *Collected Essays*, ed. Leonard Woolf (London: Hogarth Press, 1966–67), 4:138; Virginia Woolf, "Introductory Letter," xxii–xxiii. Writing about the 1916 guild congress, Leonard uses two phrases that have some echo in the "Introductory Letter": "one speaker imitated the mincing manner of a lady" and "without votes they are without a weapon." See "The Women's Co-operative Guild," *Ius Suffragii*, 1 September 1916, 171.

42. The Women's Co-operative Guild was at the forefront of efforts to create a

political role for the Consumer Co-operative movement, which eventually produced a partisan wing that became part of the Labour Party. Leonard Woolf's accounts of the congresses also include references to the specific reforms that Virginia lists as wanted by congress delegates: "baths and ovens and education and seventeen shillings instead of sixteen" ("Introductory Letter," xxii). The amount of seventeen shillings was the weekly minimum wage that delegates at the WCG's 1913 congress proposed for women in the employ of the Co-operative societies; it was part of an important campaign that achieved success in 1914.

43. A brief explanatory note had been supplied for North American readers. Leonard Woolf retained its first sentence when he reprinted the piece in Virginia Woolf's *Collected Essays* as "Memories of a Working Women's Guild," but he dropped the specification that the piece referred to the "English" Women's Co-operative Guild and added that the text had been written in 1930. The *Yale Review* note, signed by "The Editors," continued, "The Guild, which now has an enrolment of some 70,000 and is the largest association of its kind in England, was founded in 1883 to stimulate the ideas and activities of working women. It holds important annual Congresses, and it is of one of these which met in Manchester, in 1913, that Mrs. Woolf gives her impressions in the early part of her article." *Yale Review* n.s. 20 (September 1930): 121. For Hogarth Press, Davies supplied a four-page "Note on the Women's Co-operative Guild," in which she stressed that guildswomen were *married* working women.

44. *Collected Essays*, 4:147; "Introductory Letter," xxxix.

45. She suggested her cousin Barbara Stephen, who had written a history of the founding of Girton College by Davies' aunt, Emily Davies. Woolf had reviewed the book in 1927 and was to rely heavily on it for *Three Guineas*.

46. *Collected Essays*, 4:140; Introductory Letter," xxxi.

47. Writing about changes in the status of women: "your daughters play games, walk in Bond Street, unattended, wear shorts, smoke cigarettes in the streets." *The Virginia Woolf Manuscripts: From the Henry W. and Albert A. Berg Collection at the New York Public Library* (Woodbridge, Conn.: Research Publication International, 1994), microfilm, reel 7, M28.

48. *Collected Essays*, 4:146; "Introductory Letter," xxxv–xxxvi. There are a number of other moderately interesting changes that can be linked to guildswomen's comments directly. For example, although annoyed that the guildswomen were "shocked by the word 'impure,'" Woolf seems to have yielded the point: the *Yale Review*'s observation that "writing is an impure art much infected by life" is replaced in the "Introductory Letter" by "writing is a complex art, much infected by life." *L4* 228; *Collected Essays*, 4:147; "Introductory Letter," xxxvii.

49. *Collected Essays*, 4:140; "Introductory Letter," xxvi.

50. See S. P. Rosenbaum, *Victorian Bloomsbury: The Early Literary History of the Bloomsbury Group* (London: Macmillan, 1987), esp. 1:39–40.

51. After his 1919 articulation of the general theory of relativity, Einstein became the most famous scientist in the world. In addition, Einstein's pacifism, a constant since the First World War, had a formidable reputation until, in 1933, he renounced it

in response to the renascent German militarism. It is possible that these beliefs, as well as his scientific standing, explain why he appears in the "Introductory Letter."

52. Yale University Press had asked to see proofs in view of a possible North American edition but finally rejected them, according to a letter cited by Virginia Woolf: "Since there is no organization in the U.S. like the Working Womens Guild, the letters prove to deal with matters rather far from the experience and interests of possible readers here" (*L4* 341). There was to be no North American edition.

53. *Collected Essays,* 2:181.

54. The essay's first title appears to have been "Why Lectures etcetera?" *Virginia Woolf Manuscripts,* reel 4, M1.7. For a slightly more detailed discussion of "Why?" see Naomi Black, " 'Not a novel, they said': Editing Virginia Woolf's *Three Guineas,*" in *Editing Women,* ed. Ann Hutchison (Toronto: University of Toronto Press, 1998), 48–49.

55. The editors of the *New Republic* announced when the essay appeared that it was "to be published shortly in 'Women's Forum,' a symposium on current matters concerning women"; it has not been possible to trace this "forum," or "Mrs. Motier Harris Fisher of Oberlin, Ohio," whom the editors of the *New Republic* said was to edit it. See Virginia Woolf, "Thoughts on Peace in an Air Raid," *New Republic,* 21 October 1940, 549n; when Leonard Woolf reprinted the piece, he added a note "Written in August, 1940, for an American symposium on current matters concerning women." Collected *Essays,* 4:173n.

56. *Collected Essays,* 4:176.

57. "Introductory Letter," xix.

58. *Collected Essays,* 4:173, 174.

59. Ibid., 4:175, 176–77.

CHAPTER 6. Versioning Feminism

1. Judging from what we know about Woolf's preparation of other manuscripts, we can speculate that she marked up three sets of proofs, one for each 1938 version, including the serial she called "Women Must Weep," but to what extent she copied from one to another we can only guess. The editors of *The Waves* argue persuasively that for this book Woolf corrected both sets of proofs virtually at the same time, copying corrections from the English proofs to the one intended for the United States. Such a process is certainly plausible for *Three Guineas* as well, but for this book we lack the evidence found in relation to the earlier novel. See Virginia Woolf, *The Waves,* ed. James M. Haule and Philip M. Smith, Jr. (Oxford: Shakespeare Head Press for Basil Blackwell, 1993), xxxii–xxxiii.

2. Thus, although both editions have the same mistaken diacritical marks on the Greek for Antigone's crucial comments, the first American edition also gets three of the Greek letters wrong. Woolf's citation in Greek from *Antigone* is a notorious minefield. *The Years'* version of the Greek is correct; it looks as if we are dealing with printers' errors here, missed by Woolf in one or more sets of proofs or inserted after she

returned the marked-up proofs. For a discussion of the texts of *Three Guineas*, see *3G* lxiii–lxvi; for a list of variants between first editions, *3G* 241–43.

3. The American edition regularizes the few inconsistencies in the Hogarth Press version. Thus, in the Harcourt Brace as contrasted to the Hogarth edition, Princess "Anne" always has the correct terminal *e*, and the motto of the Order of the British Empire is cited accurately both times it appears. But though such alterations are usually helpful, they are sometimes unnecessary, and sometimes dead wrong. For example, in a description of the border of the cross in the regalia of the Order of the British Empire "fimbriated or" becomes "fimbriated, or," a change that shows unawareness of the heraldic meaning of *or* as gold. We can infer, then, that regularization—especially when unnecessary or incorrect—most likely came from American editors or typesetters.

4. For the full text of the passages found only in the Harcourt Brace edition, see *3G* 244–45.

5. *3G* 168; 326 in the Hogarth edition; 282–83 in the Harcourt Brace (first American) edition.

6. This helpful possibility was suggested by Sarah Priddy at the Parliamentary Information Office.

7. *Times*, 2 May 1938. This sounds a bit late for adding material to notes for the Hogarth edition, but, to repeat, we do not have clear dates for the final revisions or proofreading of either edition.

8. This item, overall, is unhelpful in respect to establishing the sequence of texts. There is no relevant clipping in the scrapbook, but the *Times* announced on 19 March 1938 the resignation, in part for family reasons, of M.P. Michael Beaumont. However, a week later Woolf was still adding endnote material that appears identically in both first editions. On 26 April, she noted in her diary that she was reading Mandeville's *The Bees* (*D5* 135), which she cites in both editions. One of the four "American" passages—the single sentence noting our ignorance about the nature of delicacy, chastity, and marriage—in fact comes immediately after the reference to Mandeville.

9. B. J. Kirkpatrick, *A Bibliography of Virginia Woolf*, 3d ed. (Oxford: Clarendon Press, 1980), 175; Kirkpatrick and Stuart N. Clarke, *A Bibliography of Virginia Woolf*, 4th ed. (Oxford: Clarendon Press, 1997), 294.

10. Unpublished letter from the Berg Collection, New York Public Library, dated 10 February 1931. Pearn represented the firm Pearn, Polling, and Higham; in a published letter dated 11 March 1931. In a list of activities, Woolf noted "heres Miss Pearn with a project" (*L4* 297).

11. Archives of the *Atlantic Monthly*, Boston, Mass.

12. *Flush*, only 190 pages long, had been published uncut by the magazine.

13. The text was printed in the same font as the first English edition, so the word limits set by the *Atlantic Monthly* meant reducing 261 pages of text to the equivalent of fewer than 70. The two installments took the form of 20 double-column pages with no more than 650 words on each page; the title pages and the conclusion were somewhat shorter.

14. Perhaps Woolf fitted in work on "Women Must Weep" after the galley proofs

of the main text of *Three Guineas* went back to the printer and before she tackled the notes; there is no way of telling. A marked-up set of galley proofs was sent off to the *Atlantic Monthly* early enough that her American agent was able to write on 4 April to request its return. See Sussex MSS. 13, Ad 18, Leonard Woolf Papers, University of Sussex Library, Brighton.

15. The second page is merely a list of numbers in the same hand as the instructions at the start of the first, relevant page, which seems to be that of the copy editor's. The two sheets are part of the Harcourt Brace Archives, held by the Massachusetts Historical Society, Boston.

16. At the top of this page is written, not in Woolf's handwriting, "All sections to be used are indicated by brackets in the margin." Notes by the same person indicate page numbers of galley proofs and locations for inclusions and omissions in a way that corresponds to the differences between the book and the serial. Two cut-out piece of paper in Woolf's familiar eccentric typewriting are stuck on, giving instructions for substitutions or inserts that appear in the serial; another altered passage has been entered by the copy editor. For a fuller discussion of these proof changes, see Naomi Black, " 'Women Must Weep': The Serialization of *Three Guineas*," in *Editing Virginia Woolf: Interpreting the Modernist Text*, ed. James M. Haule and J. H. Stape (London: Palgrave, 2001), 77–78.

17. Thus "spillikins" becomes "matches" and "wireless becomes "radio," while "tattoos" are omitted from the list of militaristic events to boycott. In all of these cases, the two texts are otherwise identical in the two first editions of the book.

18. For *Flush*, the sequence of serial and book editions was different than for *Three Guineas;* the last installment of *Flush* appeared in the October issue of the magazine, while the book itself was issued in both Britain and the United States on 5 October. See Kirkpatrick and Clarke, *Bibliography*, 292–93.

19. These acts, applicable in English garrison towns, used fear of sexually transmitted disease as a justification for treating all women as potential prostitutes liable to medical inspection and registration, on pain of jail sentences.

20. Josephine Butler, *Personal Reminiscences of a Great Crusade* (London: Horace Marshall and Sons, 1896), 82, 83; Millicent G. Fawcett and E. M. Turner, *Josephine Butler, Her Work and Principles* (London: Association for Moral and Social Hygiene, 1927), 100–101.

21. Arnold Whittick, *Woman into Citizen* (London: Athenaeum with Frederick Muller, 1979), Appendix 2, 296. In *Three Guineas* Woolf quotes Swanwick's memoirs to amplify the suffrage history she drew from the account provided by Ray Strachey, who was also secretary of the NUWSS (*3G* 286). Strachey, *The Cause: A Short History of the Women's Movement in Great Britain* (London: G. Bell and Co: 1928; facsimile ed., Cedric Chivers, 1974).

22. Unpaginated insert at the start of the volume of the *Atlantic Monthly;* there are no such sections earlier or later, and it seems to have been tried out this once by a new editor. He adds, "[Mrs. Woolf] has a definite and trenchant programme, elaborated in her book, *Three Guineas*, which is to be published by Harcourt, Brace and Company, and from which our essay has been extracted." It is interesting to see how Virginia Woolf is

then identified to her American audience: "The daughter of Sir Leslie Stephen and the wife of Leonard Woolf, a London economist and man of letters, Mrs. Woolf is the moving spirit of 'the Bloomsbury Group.'" Their home, we are told, is a "literary center" where are to be met a list of individuals that adds to Keynes "his Russian wife Lydia Lopokova" as well as Lytton Strachey, Desmond MacCarthy, E. M. Forster, Arthur Waley, V. Sackville-West, and Lord Berners. It concludes: "Mrs. Woolf's novels, *The Voyage Out, Jacob's Room, Mrs. Dalloway*, and *Flush*, and her essays, *The Common Reader* and *A Room of One's Own*, have earned her high rank in contemporary letters."

23. The differences between book and serial became clear as I worked with an assistant, comparing the two versions by reading "Women Must Weep" aloud.

24. The passage about the penny candle in *Three Guineas* is also the only place where the peace society is described as "new"; the letter writer started the book by saying that the group's appeal has waited three years for an answer.

25. In one manuscript draft, Sir Sampson, at this point also a Right Honourable, gives an address on "Women in the Civil Service," which makes him sound a bit like Stanley Baldwin and a bit less simply comic. *The Virginia Woolf Manuscripts: From the Henry W. and Albert A. Berg Collection at the New York Public Library* (Woodbridge, Conn.: Research Publication International, 1994), microfilm, reel 7, M28.

26. See *3G* 144 for the requested donations of stockings; for the Strachey letter, Anna Snaith, "*Three Guineas* Letters," *Woolf Studies Annual* 6 (2000): 20, corrected by the original letter in the Monk's House Papers, University of Sussex Library.

27. *Three Guineas* had suggested, again in an unsent draft letter, that since "the whole of what was called 'the woman's movement' has proved itself a failure" by not managing to prevent war, the donated guinea should go not for rent "but to burning your building" (*3G* 42).

28. The *Atlantic Monthly* text is divided into sections headed by Roman numerals; this is section III of the second part.

29. This is the wife of the mayor; although a member of the Peace Pledge Union, she was "frequently present in an official capacity at military functions in Woolwich," and her son was "making good progress" in the R.A.F. See the *Evening Standard*, 20 December 1937.

30. *Virginia Woolf Manuscripts*, reel 7, M28.

31. Strachey, *The Cause*, 342.

32. Leonard Woolf does not report the discussion, but a note in the *Common Cause* states that the congress was planning to consider a proposal for a modest five-pence hourly minimum wage for women munitions workers, or twenty shillings a week. See "Working Women in Conference," *Common Cause*, 23 June 1916, 138; "A 'Working Women's Parliament,'" *Common Cause*, 30 June 1916, 150; and Leonard Woolf, "Women's Wages," *New Statesman*, 4 December 1916.

CHAPTER 7. Scholarship and Subversion

1. The *TLS* review appeared on 4 June 1938; the reviewer was Orlo Williams (1883–1967), a critic and regular reviewer for the *TLS*.

2. The Hogarth Press blurb is reprinted, along with the Harcourt Brace blurb, which Woolf would not have seen, in Stephen Barkway, "Virginia Woolf's Blurbs: *Three Guineas*," *Virginia Woolf Bulletin* 5 (September 2000): 39. See also Hogarth Press's spring books, 1938, Hogarth Press archives in the library of the University of Reading.

3. Hogarth Press archives in the library of the University of Reading.

4. This point has been discussed by a number of feminist critics. See, in particular, Deirdre Lashgari, *Violence, Silence and Anger: Women's Writing as Transgression* (Charlottesville: University of Virginia Press, 1995), esp. 110–12.

5. Leonard Woolf, *Downhill All the Way: An Autobiography of the Years 1919–1939* (London: Hogarth Press, 1967), 27.

6. Leonard Woolf, *Empire and Commerce in Africa: A Study in Economic Imperialism* (London: George Allen and Unwin, 1920), 8; Woolf, *Beginning Again: An Autobiography of the Years 1911–1918* (London: Hogarth Press, 1964), 101.

7. Carolyn Heilbrun, *Writing a Woman's Life* (New York: W. W. Norton, l988), 90.

8. Katherine John (author of *The Prince Imperial* and a translator for Hogarth Press), excerpted in Robin Majumdar and Allen McLaurin, eds., *Virginia Woolf: The Critical Legacy* (London: Routledge and Kegan Paul, 1975), 405.

9. Alex Zwerdling, *Virginia Woolf and the Real World* (Berkeley: University of California Press, 1986), provides a useful summary, although early, of feminist discussions of the nature and purposes of anger in Virginia Woolf's writing, including the debates about whether her published work was harmed or enhanced by her careful reworking of raw material. See also Brenda Silver, "The Authority of Anger: *Three Guineas* as Case Study," *Signs* 16.2 (1991): 340–70, as well as the interesting discussion of the strategic use of angry rhetoric by feminists in Barbara Tomlinson, "The Politics of Textual Vehemence, or, Go to Your Room until You Learn How to Act," *Signs* 22.1 (1996): 86–114.

10. An honorable and very early exception is David Daiches, *Virginia Woolf* (New York: New Directions, 1942; rev. ed., 1963).

11. Marion Shaw, "From *A Room of One's Own* to *A Literature of One's Own*," *South Carolina Review* 19.1 (1996): 264.

12. Irma Rantavaara, *Virginia Woolf and Bloomsbury* (Helsinki: Suomalaisen Kirjallisuuden Seuran Kirjapainon Oy, 1953), 147, 142.

13. Roy Harrod, *The Life of John Maynard Keynes* (New York: Harcourt Brace, 1951); Michael Holroyd, *Lytton Strachey: A Critical Biography*, 2 vols. (London: Heinemann, 1967–68).

14. Quentin Bell, *Virginia Woolf: A Biography* (London: Hogarth Press, 1972), 2:204, 186–87, 205.

15. Quentin Bell, *Elders and Betters* (London: John Murray, 1995), 213, 217, 219. He also included a second appendix, "Maynard Keynes and His Early Beliefs."

16. Phyllis Rose, *Woman of Letters: A Life of Virginia Woolf* (London: Routledge and Kegan Paul, 1978), xii, 223, 218.

17. Carolyn Heilbrun, *Toward a Recognition of Androgyny* (New York: Knopf, 1973), 164; and Heilbrun, "Virginia Woolf in Her Fifties," in *Virginia Woolf: A Feminist Slant*, ed. Jane Marcus (Lincoln: University of Nebraska Press, 1983), 241.

18. For example, Louise A. DeSalvo, *Virginia Woolf: The Impact of Childhood Sexual Abuse on Her Life and Work* (London York: Women's Press, 1989).

19. Leonard Woolf had first set off such interpretations with a comment in *A Writer's Diary* (London: Hogarth, 1953), 165n.

20. Marder's second assessment was made at a conference panel reviewing critical treatments of Woolf's work in the 1960s and 1970s, as cited in *Virginia Woolf: Texts and Contexts. Selected Papers from the Fifth Annual Conference on Virginia Woolf*, ed. Beth Rigel Daugherty and Eileen Barrett (New York: Pace University Press, 1996), xxv. His recent volume on Woolf's later years is more positive about *The Years* but presents essentially the same analysis. See Herbert Marder, *Feminism and Art: A Study of Virginia Woolf* (Chicago: University of Chicago Press, 1968), 91, 175; and Marder, *The Measure of Life: Virginia Woolf's Last Years* (Ithaca, N.Y.: Cornell University Press, 1968).

21. Zwerdling, *Virginia Woolf and the Real World*, 214, 243.

22. Berenice Carroll, "'To Crush Him in Our Own Country': The Political Thought of Virginia Woolf," *Feminist Studies*, February 1978, 126. Susan Sontag, "Looking at War: Photography's View of Devastation and Death," *New Yorker*, 9 December 2002, 82, 83.

23. Q. D. Leavis, "Caterpillars of the Commonwealth, Unite!" *Scrutiny* 7 (September 1938): 203.

24. Majumdar and McLaurin, *Critical Legacy*, 29.

25. Michèle Barrett, introduction to Virginia Woolf, *"A Room of One's Own" and "Three Guineas,"* ed. M. Barrett (London: Penguin Books, 1993), xlii.

26. Quentin Bell, *Bloomsbury*, rev. ed. (London: Omega, 1974), 30, 31.

27. Cynthia Ozick, "Previsions of the Demise of the Dancing Dog," and "Justice to Feminism," reprinted in Ozick, *Art and Ardor* (New York: Knopf, 1983), 272, 261.

28. Murdoch was speaking in "Panel Discussion 2," in *Virginia Woolf: A Centenary Perspective*, ed. Eric Warner (London: Macmillan, 1984), 127.

29. Carol Anne Douglas, "Dear Ms. Woolf, We Are Returning Your Guineas," *off our backs*, February 1991, 5.

30. For contrasting interpretations, see Christine Darrohn, "'In a third class railway carriage': Class, the Great War, and *Mrs. Dalloway*," 99–103; and Debra L. Cumberland, "'A Voice Answering a Voice': Elizabeth Barrett Browning, Virginia Woolf, and Margaret Forster's Literary Friendship," 193–98, both in Daugherty and Barrett, *Texts and Contexts*.

31. Mary M. Childers, "Virginia Woolf on the Outside Looking Down: Reflections on the Class of Women," *Modern Fiction Studies* 38.1 (1992): 66.

32. Interestingly enough, Kathy J. Phillips's *Virginia Woolf against Empire* (Knoxville: University of Tennessee Press, 1994) gives relatively little attention to *Three Guineas*, though she painstakingly decodes the tiniest possible detail of implied attention to imperialism in Woolf's fiction.

33. Hermione Lee, *Virginia Woolf* (London: Chatto and Windus, 1996), 680.

34. See Hermione Lee's account of the different English and North American responses to her 1996 biography of Virginia Woolf: "Responses to a Life of Virginia

Woolf," in *Virginia Woolf and Her Influence*, ed. Laura Davis and Jeanette McVicker (New York: Pace University Press, 1998).

35. Frank Kermode, "Panel Discussion 2," in Warner, *Virginia Woolf*, 150.

36. Frank Kermode, preface to Virginia Woolf, *"A Room of One's Own" and "Three Guineas*," ed. Morag Shiach (Oxford: Oxford University Press, 1992), x.

37. Jane Marcus, "Putting Woolf in Her Place," *Women's Review of Books*, March 2001, 4, 5. The books reviewed are *Flush: A Biography*, ed. Alison Light (London: Penguin, 2000); Anna Snaith, *Virginia Woolf: Public and Private Negotiations* (London: Palgrave, 2000); Nigel Nicolson, *Virginia Woolf* (London: Weidenfeld and Nicolson, 2000); Linden Peach, *Virginia Woolf* (London: Palgrave, 2000); Allie Glenny, *Ravenous Identity: Eating and Eating Distress in the Life and Work of Virginia Woolf* (London: Palgrave, 2000).

38. *The Norton Anthology of Theory and Criticism*, gen. ed. Vincent B. Leitch (New York: Norton, 2001). The selections included are "Shakespeare's Sister," "Chloe Liked Olivia," and "Androgyny."

39. Alison Light, "Harnessed to a Shark," *London Review of Books*, 21 March 2002, 29–31; Theodore Dalrymple, "Virginia Woolf and the Triumph of Narcissism," *Guardian Review*, 17 August 2002, 4–6.

40. Sue Roe, *Writing and Gender: Virginia Woolf's Writing Practice* (London: Harvester Wheatsheaf, 1990), 9.

41. See also Woolf's letters to Vita Sackville-West (*L6* 242, 256, 257). She told another correspondent that *Three Guineas* was "meant to stir, not to charm; to suggest, not to conclude." Joanne Trautmann Banks, "Some New Woolf Letters," *Modern Fiction Studies* 30:2 (summer 1984), 199.

42. Jane Harriet Walker, who reviewed *Three Guineas* for the *Quarterly Journal of the Medical Women's Federation*, wrote that "it ought to be read and reread by every grown man & woman in the English speaking world"; she also thought that the notes should be at the end of each chapter. See Anna Snaith, *"Three Guineas* Letters," *Woolf Studies Annual* 6 (2000): 73–74, 20, 29, 64.

43. Quentin Bell, "Recollections and Reflections on Maynard Keynes," in *Keynes and the Bloomsbury Group*, ed. Derek Crabtree and Anthony Philip Thirlwall (London: Macmillan, 1980), 78.

44. Nicolson, *Virginia Woolf*, 134.

45. Zwerdling, *Virginia Woolf and the Real World*, 257, 258.

46. *Orlando* had included a preface parodying customary appreciations of learned assistance, and for *Flush*, as befits its mock-biographical genre, Woolf went so far as to provide an authentic list of works consulted.

47. *Three Guineas* includes citations or references to 99 books, including the Bible and six other reference books. The 50 periodical references include one item found only in the first American edition; see *3G*, Appendices D and E and lxi. For *Three Guineas*, Virginia Woolf clipped items from the following newspapers: the *Times* (both daily and Sunday), *the Daily Herald*, the *Daily Telegraph*, the *Evening Standard*, and the *Times Literary Supplement*. She also used material from the *Listener* and the *Spectator* plus two magazines, *Everyman* and the *Nation and Athenaeum*. A consid-

erable number of the more recent items cited did not even make their way into the scrapbooks. Woolf notes in a letter that "half [of the facts] had to be struck out of the notes in proof. to keep some slimness, and not repeat inordinately." In the same letter, referring specifically to endnotes, she added, "I had a mass more and still have" (*L6* 234, 235).

48. In the first English edition, there were 66 pages of endnotes out of 322 pages of text, or 20 percent of the text. In the first American edition, there were 64 and 282 pages, respectively, or 23 percent of the text. The unnumbered notes at the bottom of pages give the date of the comments about photos of the Spanish Civil War ("winter of 1936–7," *3G* 10) and state that Baldwin had "ceased to be Prime Minister and become an Earl" since making his cited comments about women in the civil service (*3G* 46). There are twenty-two essays in the notes for chapter 1, fifteen for chapter 2, and twenty-three for chapter 3. The other endnotes consist of cited passages provided without comment.

49. Leavis, "Caterpillars," 212.

50. *A Room of One's Own's* "androgynous" has obviously done better. In drafts Woolf experimented with the biological term *gunandrous;* see S. P. Rosenbaum, "Introduction: Towards the Literary History of *A Room of One's Own*," in Virginia Woolf, *"Women & Fiction": The Manuscript Versions of "A Room of One's Own*," ed. S. P. Rosenbaum (Oxford: Shakespeare Head Press for Basil Blackwell, 1992), xxxix.

51. C. S. Nicholls, introduction to *The Dictionary of National Biography: Missing Persons* (Oxford: Oxford University Press, 1993), vii. In Nicholls' words, "for the years 1850 to the present day" there are "large numbers of businessmen, engineers, scientists, and women—all categories which had suffered some neglect" (vi–vii).

52. "Lives of the Obscure" is the title of one section of Woolf's *The Common Reader* (first published in 1925). The majority of the subjects of those essays are women.

53. The clipping, which Woolf marked only "1937" in her scrapbook, is reproduced in Barrett, *"A Room of One's Own" and "Three Guineas,"* 349. Monk's House Papers, University of Sussex Library, Brighton.

54. Virginia Woolf combined Thomson's accounts of two attempts to normalize the situation of women at Cambridge. In 1897, when an exceptionally large turnout of voters defeated a proposal to allow degree titles to women, it was followed not by a riot but by what Thomson calls "a stupendous 'rag.'" The historian of women at Cambridge gives somewhat different figures for the 1897 vote: 1,713 to 662. After a more complex vote, with the same outcome, on 20 October 1921, students damaged Newnham's bronze gates. Shortly afterward, a compromise arranged that qualified women were to be eligible for degree titles though not for membership or any form of authority in the university. See Rita McWilliams-Tullborg, *Women at Cambridge: A Men's University—Though of a Mixed Type* (London: Victor Gollancz, 1975), 139, 193.

55. Virginia Woolf, *Flush*, ed. Elizabeth Steele (Oxford: Shakespeare Head Press for Basil Blackwell, 1999), 85.

56. Snaith, *"Three Guineas* Letters," 104.

57. Bell, "Keynes," 78. Bell himself used Veblen's theory of conspicuous consumption to explain the vagaries of ornamental dress, both male and female. He too sin-

gled out the army and the Church as striking examples of what he called "sumptuosity," which he labeled, in this case, "archaism"; see Quentin Bell, *On Human Finery* (London: Hogarth Press, 1947), 95.

58. Julia Margaret Cameron, *Victorian Photographs of Famous Men and Fair Women*, with introductions by Virginia Woolf and Roger Fry (London: Hogarth Press, 1926). Woolf and Roger Fry are presumably responsible for the title, which sums up the conventional roles of Victorian men and women.

59. There are four photographs among the eight parody illustrations to *Orlando*. *Flush*, also partly parodic, includes a frontispiece in which the Woolfs' cocker spaniel sits in for Elizabeth Barrett Browning's; each of the first editions also has a dust-jacket photograph of another, unidentified dog. For a useful discussion of Woolf's relationship to photography, including the use of photographs in Hogarth Press books, see Diane F. Gillespie, "'Her Kodak Pointed at His Head': Virginia Woolf and Photography," in *The Multiple Muses of Virginia Woolf*, ed. D. F. Gillespie (Columbia: University of Missouri Press, 1993).

60. I once tried to replicate this visual statement of women's absence, putting into a university status-of-women newsletter some photos of ceremonial events with women (in my view) conspicuously missing. This was in the 1980s; no one got the point I was trying to make.

61. Robin Morgan, *The Demon Lover: The Roots of Terrorism* (New York: Washington Square Press, 2001), 57; emphases in original.

62. As noted in the acknowledgments, the subjects of the photographs were identified individually in 1997, with confirmation by a letter from the firm Garratt and Atkinson ("Engravers and Artists") submitting a bid to reproduce the photographs, to be found in the Hogarth Press archives in the library at the University of Reading (also cited by Alice Stavely, "Name That Face," *Virginia Woolf Miscellany* 51 [spring 1998]: 4–5).

63. *The Essays of Virginia Woolf*, ed. Andrew McNeillie (London: Hogarth, 1994), 4:449.

64. The identical photograph appears in Tim Jeal, *The Boy-Man: The Life of Lord Baden-Powell* (London: Hutchinson, 1987), facing 452.

65. A 1965 discussion of ancient Hawai'ian warfare describes it as "the warfare of feudalism, with its recognised rules and formalities, its prayers, invocations, and ceremonial preparation," concluding that Hawai'ian warfare itself was "highly developed and . . . far removed from savagery in its conduct and regulations." See Kenneth P. Emory, "Warfare," in *Ancient Hawaiian Civilization*, ed. Handy Craighill and K. P. Emory (Rutland, Vt.: Charles E. Tuttle, 1965), 240.

66. See John Keegan, *A History of Warfare* (New York: Vintage, 1994), 385.

CHAPTER 8. Feminism in the Third Millennium

1. Robin Morgan, *The Demon Lover: The Roots of Terrorism* (New York: Washington Square Press, 2001), 410. This is a post–9/11 reprint with a new introduction and an afterword consisting of Morgan's "Letters from Ground Zero." *The Demon Lover* was originally published by Norton in 1989 with the subtitle *On the Sexuality of Terrorism*.

2. Morgan, *Demon Lover*, 337.

3. Stephanie Zappa, "Woolf, Women, and War," in *Virginia Woolf: Texts and Contexts. Selected Papers from the Fifth Annual Conference on Virginia Woolf*, ed. Beth Rigel Daugherty and Eileen Barrett (New York: Pace University Press, 1996), 277, 279.

4. Adrienne Rich, "Disloyal to Civilization: Feminism, Racism, Gynephobia," in *On Lies, Secrets, and Silence: Selected Prose, 1966–1978* (New York: Norton, 1979), 303; Rich, "Notes towards a Politics of Location," in *Blood, Bread, and Poetry: Selected Prose, 1979–1986*, 211–12 (New York: Norton, 1986).

5. Fifty guineas her first year, with the first check for one pound ten and six, presumably for 1,500 words; in the typed version she earns the less plausible one pound seven and sixpence, which would mean 1,357 words; Virginia Woolf, *The Pargiters*, ed. Mitchell Leaska (London: Hogarth Press, 1977), 163, 166, xxix.

6. J. H. Willis, Jr., *Leonard and Virginia Woolf as Publishers: The Hogarth Press, 1917–41* (Charlottesville: University of Virginia Press, 1992), 334. The gift to Vanessa was worth about $350 (US) in 1990s currency. The letter in 1939 is from Joanne Trautmann Banks, "Some New Woolf Letters," *Modern Fiction Studies* 30.2 (1984): 200; Banks notes that the money was to be spent on hiring models.

7. Leonard Woolf, *Downhill All the Way: An Autobiography of the Years 1919–1939* (London: Hogarth Press, 1967), 51. It was the standard amount charged by a doctor in 1935 for advice or for a visit (Whitaker's *Almanack*, under "Professional Fees").

8. Cited by Grace Radin, *Virginia Woolf's "The Years": The Evolution of a Novel* (Knoxville: University of Tennessee Press, 1981), 51.

9. Christine Froula may have been the earliest to pick up this reference. See "St. Virginia's Epistle to an English Gentleman; or, Sex, Violence, and the Public Sphere in Virginia Woolf's *Three Guineas*," *Tulsa Studies in Women's Literature* 13:1 (1994): 53 n. 26; also Pierre-Eric Villeneuve, "Modalités épistolaires chez Virginia Woolf: Vers une économie politique de l'aveu" (Ph.D. dissertation, Université du Québec à Montréal, 1996), 419.

10. The "Guinea Coast" refers either to all of West Africa or to just the part of it that extends from Sierra Leone to Benin.

11. Its specified gold content, priced against the silver standard, fluctuated between 20 and 30 shillings, but was fixed at 21 shillings in 1717.

12. Leonard Woolf's 1920 book on imperialism in Africa focuses on a selected group of areas, including East but not West Africa; he discusses the slave trade in the former at length but has only a brief reference to the latter. See Woolf, *Empire and Commerce in Africa: A Study in Economic Imperialism* (London: George Allen and Unwin, 1920), 232.

13. In a draft for *The Years*, Woolf gives a longer quotation from the article and comments dryly that "since sexual intercourse was then in their class impossible, [middle-class women's] contribution to the British Empire was a very high one" (*The Pargiters*, 111).

14. Debrett's *Peerage, Baronetage, Knightage, and Companionage*, which Woolf cites as her source there, does not give details about honors and orders. What she quotes in her description of the badge is the somewhat similar volume, Burke's *Genealogical*

and Heraldic History of the Peerage and Baronetage, the Privy Council, and Knightage.
Burke's mentions the narrower ribbon for Dames (purple for both, with a red stripe down the middle that is also narrower for women) but states that women wear the same star as men and must pin the ribbon in a bow on the left shoulder rather than hang it around the neck as Woolf says they do.

15. Virginia Woolf, *A Room of One's Own* (London: Hogarth Press, 1929), 76. The original source is Blaise Pascal's *Pensées.*

16. *The Essays of Virginia Woolf,* ed. Andrew McNeillie (London: Hogarth Press, 1987), 2:360; Woolf's reading notes are included as an appendix. The reference is to Sir John Hawkins (1432–95). Woolf's review essay is on James Anthony Froude, *English Seamen in the Sixteenth Century* (London: Longman's Green, 1895), and on Richard Hakluyt's *Collection of the Early Voyages, Travels and Discoveries of the English Nation,* 5 vols., new ed., with additions (London: R. H. Evans, 1809–12).

17. Quentin Bell, *Virginia Woolf: A Biography* (London: Hogarth Press, 1972), 1:1–3.

18. Froude, *English Seamen,* 36, 40.

19. *The Collected Essays of Virginia Woolf,* ed. Leonard Woolf (London: Hogarth Press, 1966), 4:173.

20. See Judith Roof, "Hocus Crocus," in *Virginia Woolf: Turning the Centuries. Selected Papers from the Ninth Annual Conference on Virginia Woolf,* ed. Ann Ardis and Bonnie Kime Scott, 93–102 (New York: Pace University Press, 2000), for a perceptive discussion of the issues relating to lesbian sexuality and lesbian identity in analyses of Woolf's writing.

21. At this time there was very little public support for legalizing abortion. Jean Gaffin was the first to point out the radicalism of the Women's Co-operative Guild in relation to abortion and divorce: see "Women and Co-operation," in *Women in the Labour Movement,* ed. Lucy Middleton, 113–42 (London: Croom Helm, 1977); also Jean Gaffin and David Thoms, *Caring and Sharing: The Centenary History of the Co-operative Women's Guild* (Manchester: Co-operative Union, 1983), 107–8.

22. Radin, *Virginia Woolf's "The Years,"* 51.

23. For a sensible assessment of such analyses, see Hermione Lee, *Virginia Woolf* (London: Chatto and Windus, 1996), esp. 153–59 and 786–87 n. 68.

24. Virginia Woolf, *Moments of Being,* ed. Jeanne Schulkind, introduced and revised by Hermione Lee (London: Pimlico, 2002), 68, 69.

25. Grace Radin's analysis of the relevant manuscripts demonstrates that, as Woolf worked on *The Years,* the sexual dimension was systematically reduced. See Radin, *Virginia Woolf's "The Years,"* esp. 35, 149.

26. *The Pargiters,* 36.

27. Ibid., 54.

28. Adultery in the more usual sense appears only in this note: "a woman . . . can have intercourse with someone other than her husband" (*3G* 153); the context is still the psychological barriers imposed by male-dominated morality.

29. Brian Harrison, *Prudent Revolutionaries: Portraits of British Feminists between the Wars* (Oxford: Clarendon Press, 1987), 313.

30. An earlier draft, probably written in 1935, uses instead the formula "force &

capital." *The Virginia Woolf Manuscripts: From the Henry W. and Albert A. Berg Collection at the New York Public Library* (Woodbridge, Conn.: Research Publication International, 1994), microfilm, reel 7, M40.

31. Winifred Holtby, *Virginia Woolf: A Critical Memoir* (Chicago: Cassandra, 1978), 186.

32. Virginia Woolf, "Introductory Letter to Margaret Llewelyn Davies," in *Life as We Have Known It: By Co-operative Working Women*, ed. Margaret Llewelyn Davies (London: Hogarth Press, 1931), xxv, xix.

33. "Introductory Letter," xxxiv.

34. Ibid., xxxv–vi.

35. Ursula K. Le Guin, "Is Gender Necessary Redux," in *Dancing at the Edge of the World: Thoughts on Words, Women, Places* (New York: Grove Press, 1989), 7–8, 11.

36. The reference here is not to the great Charles Darwin, though he was certainly generous in his attention to his children, but to his sons and their relationships with his grandchildren, including Gwen Raverat; see her *Period Piece: A Cambridge Childhood* (London: Faber and Faber, 1960), 187–88. On Vanessa Bell's working practices, see the book by her son, Quentin Bell, *Elders and Betters* (London: John Murray, 1995), esp. 92.

37. *A Room of One's Own*, 8, 9.

38. Ursula K. Le Guin, "Fisherwoman's Daughter," in *Dancing at the Edge of the World*, 236.

39. Ibid., 234.

40. FIL tended to use the word *defend* rather than *protect*. The title and slogan of the group were suggested by Leonard Woolf. See David Bradshaw, "British Writers and Anti-Fascism in the 1930s. Part II: 'Under the Hawk's Wings,'" *Woolf Studies Annual* 4 (1998): 58.

41. *Evening Standard*, 20 December 1937.

42. See Sharon Groves, "Afghan Women Speak Out," a report prepared for *Feminist Studies* 27.3 (2001): 753–59.

43. Elizabeth Rubin, "Down the Dark Hole of Chechnya," *New York Times Magazine*, 8 July 2001, 54.

44. *Virginia Woolf Manuscripts*, reel 11, M70.

Bibliography

Abel, Elizabeth. *Virginia Woolf and Fictions of Psychoanalysis*. Chicago: University of Chicago Press, 1989.

Annan, Noel. *Leslie Stephen: The Godless Victorian*. London: Weidenfeld and Nicolson, 1984.

Banks, Joanne Trautmann. "Some New Woolf Letters." *Modern Fiction Studies* 30.2 (1984): 175–202.

Barclay, Florence L. *Life of Florence Barclay, by One of Her Daughters*. London: G. P. Putnam's Sons, 1921.

Barkway, Stephen. "Virginia Woolf's Blurbs: *Three Guineas*." *Virginia Woolf Bulletin* 5 (September 2000): 39–40.

Barrett, Eileen, and Patricia Cramer, eds. *Virginia Woolf: Lesbian Readings*. New York: New York University Press, 1997.

Beaton, Cecil. *The Book of Beauty*. London: Duckworth, 1930.

———. "The Book of Beauty." Letter to the editor. *Nation and Athenaeum*, 18 December 1930, 373.

Bell, Clive. *Old Friends*. Chicago: University of Chicago Press, 1973.

———. *War Mongers*. London: Peace Pledge Union, 1938.

Bell, Quentin. *Bloomsbury*. Rev. ed. London: Omega, 1974.

———. "Bloomsbury and 'the Vulgar Passions.'" *Critical Inquiry* 6.2 (1979): 239–52.

———. *Elders and Betters*. London: John Murray, 1995.

———. *On Human Finery*. London: Hogarth Press, 1947; new ed. revised and enlarged, 1976.

———. "Recollections and Reflections on Maynard Keynes." In *Keynes and the Bloomsbury Group*, ed. Derek Crabtree and Anthony Philip Thirlwall, 69–86. London: Macmillan, 1980.

———. *Virginia Woolf: A Biography*. 2 vols. London: Hogarth Press, 1972.

Bennett, Arnold. *Our Women: Chapters on the Sex Discord*. London: Cassell, 1920.

Bishop, Edward L. *Virginia Woolf's "Jacob's Room": The Holograph Draft, Transcribed and Edited*. New York: Pace University Press, 1998.

Black, Naomi. "'Not a novel, they said': Editing Virginia Woolf's *Three Guineas*." In *Editing Women*, ed. Ann Hutchison, 27–54. Toronto: University of Toronto Press, 1998.

———. "A Note on the Feminist Politics of Virginia Woolf." *Virginia Woolf Miscellany* (spring 1980): 5–6.

———. *Social Feminism*. Ithaca, N.Y.: Cornell University Press, 1989.

———. "Virginia Woolf: The Life of Natural Happiness." In *Feminist Theorists: Three*

Centuries of Key Women Thinkers, ed. Dale Spender, 296–313. New York: Pantheon Press, 1983.

———. "Virginia Woolf and the Women's Movement." In *Virginia Woolf: A Feminist Slant*, ed. Jane Marcus, 180–97. Nebraska: University of Nebraska Press, 1983.

———. "'Women Must Weep': The Serialization of *Three Guineas*." In *Editing Virginia Woolf: Interpreting the Modernist Text*, ed. James M. Haule and J. H. Stape, 74–90. London: Palgrave, 2001.

Black, Naomi, and Gail Cuthbert Brandt. *Feminist Politics on the Farm: Rural Catholic Women in Southern Quebec and Southwestern France*. Montreal and Kingston: McGill-Queen's University Press, 1999.

Bowlby, Rachel. "Meet Me in St. Louis: Virginia Woolf and Community." In *Virginia Woolf and Communities*, ed. Jeanette McVicker and Laura Davis, 147–60. New York: Pace University Press, 1999.

Bradshaw, David. "British Writers and Anti-Fascism in the 1930s. Part I: 'The Bray and Drone of Tortured Voices.'" *Woolf Studies Annual* 3 (1997): 3–27.

———. "British Writers and Anti-Fascism in the 1930s. Part II: 'Under the Hawk's Wings.'" *Woolf Studies Annual* 4 (1998): 41–66.

Brittain, Vera. "A Woman's Notebook." *Nation and Athenaeum*, 31 January 1931, 571–72.

Brownmiller, Susan. *In Our Time: Memoir of a Revolution*. New York: Dial Press, 1999.

Butler, Josephine. *Personal Reminiscences of a Great Crusade*. London: Horace Marshall and Sons, 1896.

Cameron, Julia Margaret. *Victorian Photographs of Famous Men and Fair Women*. With introductions by Virginia Woolf and Roger Fry. London: Hogarth Press, 1926.

Carroll, Berenice. "'To Crush Him in Our Own Country': The Political Thought of Virginia Woolf." *Feminist Studies*, February 1978, 99–131.

Chaudhuri, Nupur. "Bloomsbury Ancestry: Jane Maria Strachey, Feminism, and Younger Strachey Women." In *Women in the Milieu of Leonard and Virginia Woolf: Peace, Politics, and Education*, ed. Wayne K. Chapman and Janet M. Manson, 59–73. New York: Pace University Press, 1998.

Childers, Mary M. "Virginia Woolf on the Outside Looking Down: Reflections on the Class of Women." *Modern Fiction Studies* 38.1 (1992): 61–79.

Clark, Ronald W. *Einstein: The Life and Times*. New York: Avon, 1984.

Cumberland, Debra L. "'A Voice Answering a Voice': Elizabeth Barrett Browning, Virginia Woolf, and Margaret Forster's Literary Friendship." In *Virginia Woolf: Texts and Contexts. Selected Papers from the Fifth Annual Conference on Virginia Woolf*, ed. Beth Rigel Daugherty and Eileen Barrett, 193–98. New York: Pace University Press, 1996.

Daiches, David. *Virginia Woolf*. New York: New Directions, 1942; rev. ed., 1963.

Dalrymple, Theodore. "Virginia Woolf and the Triumph of Narcissism." *Guardian Review*, 17 August 2002, 4–6.

Dangerfield, George. *The Strange Death of Liberal England*. New York: Capricorn, 1961.

Darrohn, Christine. "'In a third class railway carriage': Class, the Great War, and *Mrs. Dalloway*." In *Virginia Woolf: Texts and Contexts. Selected Papers from the Fifth Annual Conference on Virginia Woolf*, ed. Beth Rigel Daugherty and Eileen Barrett, 99–103. New York: Pace University Press, 1996.

Davies, Margaret Llewelyn. *The Women's Co-operative Guild, 1883–1904*. Kirkby Lonsdale: Women's Co-operative Guild, 1904.

——, ed. *Life as We Have Known It: By Co-operative Working Women*. London: Hogarth Press, 1931.

——, ed. *Maternity: Letters from Working Women*. London: G. Bell, 1915.

de Lauretis, Teresa. "Feminist Studies/Critical Studies: Issues, Terms and Contexts. In *Feminist Studies/Critical Studies*, ed. T. de Lauretis, 1–30. Bloomington: Indiana University Press, 1986.

DeSalvo, Louise A. *Virginia Woolf: The Impact of Childhood Sexual Abuse on Her Life and Work*. London: Women's Press, 1989.

Deutsche Intellektuelle im Exil: ihre Akademie und die "American Guild for German Cultural Freedom": eine Ausstellung der Deutschen Exilarchivs 1933–45 des Deutschen Bibliothek, Frankfurt am Main. Munich: K. G. Saur, 1993.

Dick, Susan. "'What fools we were': Virginia Woolf's 'A Society.'" *Twentieth Century Literature* 33.1 (1987): 51–66.

Douglas, Carol Anne. "Dear Ms. Woolf, We Are Returning Your Guineas." *off our backs*, February 1991, 5.

——. *Love and Politics: Radical Feminist and Lesbian Theories*. San Francisco: Ism Press, 1990.

Douie, Vera. *The Lesser Half: A Survey of the Laws, Regulations and Practices Introduced during the Present War Which Embody Discrimination against Women*. London: Swindon Press for the Women's Publicity Planning Association, 1943.

——. "Women's Service Library: The First Sixteen Years, 1925–42." Typescript, n.d. Women's Library, London Guildhall University.

Echols, Alice. *Daring to Be Bad: Radical Feminism in America, 1967–1975*. Minneapolis: University of Minnesota Press, 1989.

Edinburgh Women's Union Editorial Committee. *Atalanta's Garland: Being the Book of the Edinburgh Women's Union*. Edinburgh: T. and A. Constable, 1926.

Emory, Kenneth P. "Warfare." In *Ancient Hawaiian Civilization*, ed. Handy Craighill and K. P. Emory. Rutland, Vt.: Charles E. Tuttle, 1965.

Fawcett, Millicent G., and E. M. Turner. *Josephine Butler, Her Work and Principles*. London: Association for Moral and Social Hygiene, 1927.

Forster, E. M. "Virginia Woolf by E. M. Forster." In *The Bloomsbury Group: A Collection of Memoirs and Commentary*, rev. ed., ed. S. P. Rosenbaum, 222–36. Toronto: University of Toronto Press, 1995.

Freeman, Jo. *The Politics of Women's Liberation*. New York: David McKay Co., 1975.

Froude, James Anthony. *English Seamen in the Sixteenth Century*. London: Longman's Green, 1895.

Froula, Christine. "St. Virginia's Epistle to an English Gentleman; or, Sex, Violence, and the Public Sphere in Virginia Woolf's *Three Guineas.*" *Tulsa Studies in Women's Literature* 13.1 (1994): 27–56.

Gaffin, Jean. "Women and Co-operation." In *Women in the Labour Movement*, ed. Lucy Middleton, 113–42. London: Croom Helm, 1977.

Gaffin, Jean, and David Thoms. *Caring and Sharing: The Centenary History of the Co-operative Women's Guild.* Manchester: Co-operative Union, 1983.

Gillespie, Diane F. " 'Her Kodak Pointed at His Head': Virginia Woolf and Photography." In *The Multiple Muses of Virginia Woolf,* ed. D. F. Gillespie, 111–47. Columbia: University of Missouri Press, 1993.

Glennie, Allie. *Ravenous Identity: Eating and Eating Distress in the Life and Work of Virginia Woolf.* London: Palgrave, 2000.

Graves, Pamela. *Labour Women: Women in British Working-Class Politics, 1918–1939.* Cambridge: Cambridge University Press, 1994.

Groves, Sharon. "Afghan Women Speak Out." *Feminist Studies* 27.3 (2001): 753–59.

Hakluyt, Richard. *Collection of the Early Voyages, Travels and Discoveries of the English Nation.* 5 vols. New ed., with additions. London: R. H. Evans, 1809–12.

Halpern, Barbara Strachey. "Ray Strachey—A Memoir." In *Women in the Milieu of Leonard and Virginia Woolf: Peace, Politics, and Education,* ed. Wayne K. Chapman and Janet M. Manson, 77–86. New York: Pace University Press, 1998.

Harrison, Brian. *Prudent Revolutionaries: Portraits of British Feminists between the Wars.* Oxford: Clarendon Press, 1987.

Harrod, R. F. *The Life of John Maynard Keynes.* New York: Harcourt Brace, 1951.

Heilbrun, Carolyn. *Toward a Recognition of Androgyny.* New York: Knopf, 1973.

——. "Virginia Woolf in Her Fifties." In *Virginia Woolf: A Feminist Slant,* ed. Jane Marcus, 236–53. Lincoln: University of Nebraska Press, 1983.

——. *Writing a Woman's Life.* New York: Norton, 1988.

Holroyd, Michael. *Lytton Strachey: A Critical Biography.* 2 vols. London: Heinemann, 1967–68.

Holtby, Winifred. *Virginia Woolf: A Critical Memoir.* Reprint. Chicago: Cassandra, 1978.

Holton, Sandra Stanley. *Women's Suffrage and Reform Politics in Britain, 1910–1918.* Cambridge: Cambridge University Press, 1986.

Jaggar, Alison. *Feminist Politics and Human Nature.* Totowa, N.J.: Rowman and Allanheld, 1983.

Jaggar, Alison M., and Paula S. Rothenberg, eds. *Feminist Frameworks: Alternate Theoretical Accounts of the Relations between Women and Men.* 2d ed. New York: McGraw-Hill, 1984.

Jaggar, Alison M., and Paula Rothenberg Struhl, eds. *Feminist Frameworks: Alternate Theoretical Accounts of the Relations between Women and Men.* New York: McGraw-Hill, 1978.

Jeal, Tim. *The Boy-Man: The Life of Lord Baden-Powell.* London: Hutchinson, 1987.

Joad, C. E. M. "Women of To-day and To-morrow—By a Man." *Everyman,* 12 January 1934, 12.

Keegan, John. *A History of Warfare*. New York: Vintage, 1994.

Kermode, Frank, and Anita Kermode, eds. *The Oxford Book of Letters*. Oxford: Oxford University Press, 1995.

Keynes, John Maynard. Review of Mansfield D. Forbes, ed., *Clare College, 1326–1926* (printed for the college). *Nation and Athenaeum*, 31 January 1995, 512–13.

Kirkpatrick, B. J. *A Bibliography of E. M. Forster.* 2d ed. Oxford: Clarendon Press, 1985.

——. *A Bibliography of Virginia Woolf.* 3d ed. Oxford: Clarendon Press, 1980.

——. "Two Contributions by Virginia Woolf to the Suffragette Press." *Charleston Magazine* 12 (autumn/winter 1995): 25–29.

Kirkpatrick, B. J., and Stuart N. Clarke. *A Bibliography of Virginia Woolf.* 4th ed. Oxford: Clarendon Press, 1997.

Lashgari, Deirdre. *Violence, Silence and Anger: Women's Writing as Transgression.* Charlottesville: University of Virginia Press, 1995.

Leavis, Q. D. "Caterpillars of the Commonwealth, Unite!" *Scrutiny* 7 (September 1938): 203–15.

Lee, Hermione. "Responses to a Life of Virginia Woolf." In *Virginia Woolf and Her Influence*, ed. Laura Davis and Jeanette McVicker, 13–19. New York: Pace University Press, 1998.

——. *Virginia Woolf.* London: Chatto and Windus, 1996.

——. "Virginia Woolf's Essays." In *The Cambridge Companion to Virginia Woolf*, ed. Sue Roe and Susan Sellers, 91–108. Cambridge: Cambridge University Press, 2000.

Le Guin, Ursula K. "The Fisherwoman's Daughter." In *Dancing at the Edge of the World: Thoughts on Words, Women, Places*, 212–37. New York: Grove Press, 1989.

——. "Is Gender Necessary Redux." In *Dancing at the Edge of the World: Thoughts on Words, Women, Places*, 7–16. New York: Grove Press, 1989.

Leitch, Vincent B., gen. ed. *The Norton Anthology of Theory and Criticism*. New York: Norton, 2001.

Lewis, Jane. *The Politics of Motherhood: Child and Maternal Welfare in England, 1900–1939.* London: Croom Helm, 1980.

Lewis, Wyndham. *Men without Art.* London: Cassell, 1934.

Liddington, Jill, and Jill Norris. *One Hand Tied behind Us: The Rise of the Women's Suffrage Movement.* London: Virago Press, 1978.

Light, Alison. "Harnessed to a Shark." *London Review of Books*, 21 March 2002, 29–31.

London and National Society for Women's Service. Junior Council. Reports, lists of members, 1930, 1931. Women's Library, London Guildhall University.

Lovelace, Mary, Countess of. "Fifty Years: Society and the Season. The Chaperoned Age." *The Times* (London), 9 March 1932, 13, 14.

Lushington, Frank. *Portrait of a Young Man.* London: Faber and Faber, 1940.

MacCarthy, Desmond [Affable Hawk, pseud.]. "Current Literature: Books in General." *New Statesman*, 2 October 1920, 704; 9 April 1921, 18.

——. "The Intellectual Status of Women." *New Statesman*, 9 October 1920, 15–16; 16 October 1920, 46–46.

Majumdar, Robin, and Allen McLaurin, eds. *Virginia Woolf: The Critical Legacy.* London: Routledge and Kegan Paul, 1975.

Marcus, Jane. "'No More Horses': Virginia Woolf on Arts and Propaganda." *Women's Studies* 4 (1977): 264–89.

———. "Putting Woolf in Her Place." *Women's Review of Books*, March 2001, 4, 5.

Marcus, Laura. "Virginia Woolf's Feminism and Feminism's Virginia Woolf." In *The Cambridge Companion to Virginia Woolf*, ed. Sue Roe and Susan Sellers, 209–44. Cambridge: Cambridge University Press, 2000.

Marder, Herbert. *Feminism and Art: A Study of Virginia Woolf.* Chicago: University of Chicago Press, 1968.

———. *The Measure of Life: Virginia Woolf's Last Years.* Ithaca, N.Y.: Cornell University Press, 2000.

McLaren, Christabel. "The Book of Beauty." Letter to the editor. *Nation and Athenaeum*, 20 December 1930, 373.

McWilliams-Tullborg, Rita. *Woman at Cambridge: A Men's University—Though of a Mixed Type.* London: Victor Gollancz, 1975.

Meneghel, Meg A. "'Dear Mother': Ray Strachey's Role in Feminism and the League of Nations as Seen from the Lilly Library." In *Women in the Milieu of Leonard and Virginia Woolf: Peace, Politics, and Education*, ed. Wayne K. Chapman and Janet M. Manson, 87–94. New York: Pace University Press, 1998.

Monk's House Papers. University of Sussex Library, Brighton.

Mootham, Dolf. "Appendix A: The Comparative Values of the Pound." In *The Interior Castle: A Life of Gerald Brenan*, by Jonathan Gathorne-Hardy, 611. London: Sinclair-Stevenson, 1992.

Morgan, Robin. *The Demon Lover: The Roots of Terrorism.* New York: Washington Square Press, 2001.

Newbolt, Henry. *My World as in My Time.* London: Faber and Faber, 1932.

Nicholls, C. S., ed. *The Dictionary of National Biography: Missing Persons.* Oxford: Oxford University Press, 1993.

Nicolson, Nigel. *Virginia Woolf.* London: Weidenfeld and Nicolson, 2000.

Offen, Karen. *European Feminisms, 1750–1950: A Political History.* Stanford, Calif.: Stanford University Press, 2000.

Oldfield, Sybil. "Margaret Llewelyn Davies and Leonard Woolf." In *Women in the Milieu of Leonard and Virginia Woolf: Peace, Politics, and Education*, ed. Wayne K. Chapman and Janet M. Manson, 3–32. New York: Pace University Press, 1998.

Olsen, Tillie. *Silences.* New York: Delacourte Press/Seymour Lawrence, 1978.

Ozick, Cynthia. "Previsions of the Demise of the Dancing Dog," 261–62; "Justice to Feminism," 263–83; and "Literature and the Politics of Sex: A Dissent," 284–90. In *Art and Ardor.* New York: Knopf, 1983.

Pawlowski, Merry M. "Toward a Feminist Theory of the State: Virginia Woolf and Wyndham Lewis on Art, Gender, and Politics." In *Virginia Woolf and Fascism: Resisting the Dictators' Seduction*," ed. M. M. Pawlowski, 39–55. London: Palgrave, 2001.

Peach, Linden. *Virginia Woolf.* London: Palgrave, 2000.

Pethick-Lawrence, Emmeline. *My Part in a Changing World.* London: Victor Gollancz, 1938.

Phillips, Kathy J. *Virginia Woolf against Empire*. Knoxville: University of Tennessee Press, 1994.

Pugh, Martin. *The March of the Women: A Revisionist Account of the Campaign for Women's Suffrage, 1866–1914*. Oxford: Oxford University Press, 2000.

Radin, Grace. *Virginia Woolf's "The Years": The Evolution of a Novel*. Knoxville: University of Tennessee Press, 1981.

Rantavaara, Irma. *Virginia Woolf and Bloomsbury*. Helsinki: Suomalaisen Kirjallisuuden Seuran Kirjapainon Oy, 1953.

Rathbone, Eleanor. "Changes in Public Life." In *Our Freedom and Its Results*, ed. Ray Strachey. London: Hogarth Press, 1936.

Raverat, Gwen. *Period Piece: A Cambridge Childhood*. London: Faber and Faber, 1953.

Rendel, Margherita. "The Contribution of the Women's Labour League to the Winning of the Franchise." In *Women in the Labour Movement*, ed. Lucy Middleton, 57–83. London: Croom Helm, 1977.

Rice, Thomas Jackson. *Virginia Woolf: A Guide to Research*. New York: Garland Publishing, 1984.

Rich, Adrienne. "Disloyal to Civilization: Feminism, Racism, Gynephobia." In *On Lies, Secrets, and Silence: Selected Prose, 1966–1978*, 275–310. New York: Norton, 1979.

———. "Notes towards a Politics of Location." In *Blood, Bread, and Poetry: Selected Prose, 1979–1985*, 210–31. New York: Norton, 1986.

Ritchie, Anne Thackeray. *Letters*. Ed. Hester Ritchie. London: John Murray, 1924.

Roe, Sue. *Writing and Gender: Virginia Woolf's Writing Practice*. London: Harvester Wheatsheaf, 1990.

Roe, Sue, and Susan Sellers, eds. *The Cambridge Companion to Virginia Woolf*. Cambridge: Cambridge University Press, 2000.

Roof, Judith. "Hocus Crocus." In *Virginia Woolf: Turning the Centuries. Selected Papers from the Ninth Annual Conference on Virginia Woolf*, ed. Ann Ardis and Bonnie Kime Scott, 93–102. New York: Pace University Press, 2000.

Rose, Phyllis. *Woman of Letters: A Life of Virginia Woolf*. London: Routledge and Kegan Paul, 1978.

Rosenbaum, S. P. "Bloomsbury Letters." In *Aspects of Bloomsbury: Studies in Modern English Literary and Intellectual History*, 60–67. New York: Macmillan and St. Martin's Press, 1998.

———. *Victorian Bloomsbury: The Early Literary History of the Bloomsbury Group*. Vol. 1. London: Macmillan, 1987.

———. "Virginia Woolf and the Clark Lectures." *Charleston Magazine* 22 (autumn/winter 2000): 5–10.

———, ed. *The Bloomsbury Group: A Collection of Memoirs and Commentary*. Rev. ed. Toronto: University of Toronto Press, 1995.

Rosenberg, Beth Carole, and Jeanne Dubino, eds. *Virginia Woolf and the Essay*. New York: St. Martin's Press, 1997.

Rosenfeld, Natania. *Outsiders Together: Virginia and Leonard Woolf*. Princeton, N.J.: Princeton University Press, 2000.

Rover, Constance. *Women's Suffrage and Party Politics in Britain, 1866–1914*. London: Routledge and Kegan Paul, 1967.

Rubin, Elizabeth. "Down the Dark Hole of Chechnya." *New York Times Magazine*, 8 July 2001.

Sandbach-Dahlstrom, Catherine. " 'Que Scais-je': Virginia Woolf and the Essay as Feminist Critique." In *Virginia Woolf and the Essay*, ed. Beth Carole Rosenberg and Jeanne Dubino, 275–93. New York: St. Martin's Press, 1997.

Shaw, Marion. "From *A Room of One's Own* to *A Literature of One's Own*." *South Carolina Review* 19.1 (1996): 58–65.

Silver, Brenda R. "The Authority of Anger: *Three Guineas* as Case Study." *Signs* 16.2 (1991): 340–70.

——. "*Three Guineas* Before and After." In *Virginia Woolf: A Feminist Slant*, ed. Jane Marcus, 254–76. Lincoln: University of Nebraska Press, 1983.

——. *Virginia Woolf Icon*. Chicago: University of Chicago Press, 1999.

——. *Virginia Woolf's Reading Notebooks*. Princeton, N.J.: Princeton University Press, 1983.

Snaith, Anna. "*Three Guineas* Letters." *Woolf Studies Annual* 6 (2000): 1–168.

——. *Virginia Woolf: Public and Private Negotiations*. New York: Palgrave, 2000.

Sontag, Susan. "Looking at War: Photography's View of Devastation and Death." *New Yorker*, 9 December 2002, 82–98.

Squire, J. C. *Reflections and Memories*. London: Heinemann, 1935.

Stavely, Alice. "Name That Face." *Virginia Woolf Miscellany* 51 (spring 1998): 4–5.

Stephen, Leslie. *Selected Letters*. Vols. 1 and 2. Ed. John W. Bicknell. London: Macmillan, 1996.

Strachey, Jane Maria. "Some Recollections of a Long Life," part 4. *Nation and Athenaeum*, 30 August 1924, 664–65.

Strachey, Ray. *The Cause: A Short History of the Women's Movement in Great Britain*. London: G. Bell and Co., 1928. Facsimile edition, Cedric Chivers, 1974.

——. *Millicent Garrett Fawcett*. London: John Murray, 1931.

The Suffrage Annual and Women's Who's Who. Ed. A. J. R. London: Stanley Paul, 1913.

Thomson, Sir J. J. *Recollections and Reflections*. London: Macmillan, 1936.

Tinker, Chauncey Brewster. *Young Boswell*. London: G. P. Putnam's Sons, 1922.

Tomlinson, Barbara. "The Politics of Textual Vehemence, or, Go to Your Room until You Learn How to Act." *Signs* 22.1 (1996): 86–114.

United Nations. *Report of the World Conference of the International Women's Year*. E/CONF. 66. New York, 1980.

Villeneuve, Pierre-Eric. "Modalités épistolaires chez Virginia Woolf: Vers une économie politique de l'aveu." Ph.D. dissertation, Université du Québec à Montréal, 1996.

Warner, Eric, ed. *Virginia Woolf: A Centenary Perspective*. London: Macmillan, 1984.

Webb, Catherine. *The Woman with a Basket: The Story of the Women's Co-operative Guild*. Manchester: Co-operative Wholesale Society, 1927.

Wells, H. G. *Experiment in Autobiography: Discoveries and Conclusions of a Very Ordinary Brain (since 1866)*. London: Victor Gollancz and Cresset Press, 1934.

Whittick, Arnold. *Woman into Citizen*. London: Athenaeum with Frederick Muller, 1979.

Willis, J. H., Jr. *Leonard and Virginia Woolf as Publishers: The Hogarth Press, 1917–41*. Charlottesville: University of Virginia Press, 1992.

Women's Employment Federation. Annual report, 1938. Women's Library, London Guildhall University.

Woolf, Leonard. *Beginning Again: An Autobiography of the Years 1911–1918*. London: Hogarth Press, 1964.

——. "Co-op Topics: The Women's Congress." *Labour Leader*, 9 July 1916, 5.

——. "A Democracy of Working Women." *New Statesman*, 21 June 1913, 328–29.

——. *Downhill All the Way: An Autobiography of the Years 1919–1939*. London: Hogarth Press, 1967.

——. *Empire and Commerce in Africa: A Study in Economic Imperialism*. London: George Allen and Unwin, 1920.

——. "A Parliament of Mothers: Working Women and Their Problems." *Manchester Guardian*, 24 June 1914, 10.

——. *Quack, Quack!* London: Hogarth Press, 1935.

——. "Social Types: A Parliament of Women." *Nation*, 21 June 1913, 456–57.

——. "The Women's Co-operative Guild," *Ius Suffragii*, 1 September 1916, 171.

——. "Women's Wages." *New Statesman*, 4 December 1915, 199–201.

——. "Working Women and the War." *New Statesman*, 26 June 1915, 275–76.

——. "Working Women's Parliament: A Striking Assertion of Feminine Democracy." *Daily News and Leader*, 25 June 1914, 6.

Woolf, Virginia. "The Book of Beauty: A Protest." Letters to the editor. *Nation and Athenaeum*, 29 November 1930, 291; 20 December 1930, 373.

——. *Carlyle's House and Other Sketches*. Ed. David Bradshaw. London: Hesperus Press, 2003.

——. *The Collected Essays of Virginia Woolf*. 4 vols. Ed. Leonard Woolf. London: Hogarth Press, 1966–67.

——. *The Common Reader*. Ed. Andrew McNeillie. London: Hogarth Press, 1984.

——. *The Complete Shorter Fiction of Virginia Woolf*. Ed. Susan Dick. London: Hogarth Press, 1985.

——. *The Crowded Dance of Modern Life: Selected Essays, Volume 2*. Ed. Rachel Bowlby. London: Penguin Books, 1993.

——. *The Death of the Moth*. Ed. Leonard Woolf. London: Hogarth Press, 1942.

——. *The Diary of Virginia Woolf*. 5 vols. Ed. Anne Olivier Bell, assisted by Andrew McNeillie. London: Hogarth Press, 1977–84.

——. *The Essays of Virginia Woolf*. 4 vols. to date. Ed. Andrew McNeillie. London: Hogarth Press, 1986–88, 1994–.

——. *Flush*. Ed. Elizabeth Steele. Oxford: Shakespeare Head Press for Basil Blackwell, 1999.

——. *Flush: A Biography*. Ed. Alison Light. London: Penguin Brooks, 2000.

——. "The Intellectual Status of Women." *New Statesman*, 9 October 1920, 15; 16 October 1920, 45–46.

——. "Introductory Letter to Margaret Llewelyn Davies." In *Life as We Have Known It: By Co-operative Working Women*, ed. M. L. Davies, xv–xxix. London: Hogarth Press, 1931.

——. *The Letters of Virginia Woolf*. 6 vols. Ed. Nigel Nicolson and Joanne Trautmann. London: Hogarth Press, 1975–80.

——. *The London Scene*. London: Hogarth Press, 1975.

——. "Memories of a Working Women's Guild." *Yale Review* 20 (September 1930): 121–38.

——. *Moments of Being*. Ed. Jeanne Schulkind, introduced and revised by Hermione Lee. London: Pimlico, 2002.

——. *The Pargiters*. Ed. Mitchell Leaska. London: Hogarth Press, 1977.

——. *Reviewing*. London: Hogarth Press, 1939.

——. *A Room of One's Own*. London: Hogarth Press, 1929.

——. *"A Room of One's Own" and "Three Guineas."* Ed. Morag Shiach. Oxford: Oxford University Press, 1992.

——. *"A Room of One's Own" and "Three Guineas."* Ed. Michèle Barrett. London: Penguin Books, 1993.

——. "Thoughts on Peace in an Air Raid." *New Republic*, 21 October 1940, 549–51.

——. *Three Guineas*. London: Hogarth Press, 1938.

——. *Three Guineas*. New York: Harcourt Brace, 1938.

——. *Three Guineas*. Ed. Naomi Black. Oxford: Shakespeare Head Press for Basil Blackwell, 2001.

——. *The Virginia Woolf Manuscripts: From the Henry W. and Albert A. Berg Collection at the New York Public Library*. Microfilm. Woodbridge, Conn., 1994.

——. *The Waves*. Ed. James M. Haule and Philip M. Smith, Jr. Oxford: Shakespeare Head Press for Basil Blackwell, 1993.

——. "A Woman's College from the Outside." In *Atalanta's Garland: Being the Book of the Edinburgh University Women's Union*, 11–16. Edinburgh: T. and A. Constable, 1926.

——. *A Woman's Essays: Selected Essays*. Vol. 1. Ed. Rachel Bowlby. London: Penguin Books, 1992.

——. *"Women & Fiction": The Manuscript Versions of "A Room of One's Own."* Ed. S. P. Rosenbaum. Oxford: Shakespeare Head Press for Basil Blackwell, 1992.

——. "Women Must Weep," and "Women Must Weep—or Unite against War." *Atlantic Monthly Magazine* 1621.5 (May 1938): 585–94; 1621.6 (June 1938): 750–59.

——. *A Writer's Diary*. Ed. Leonard Woolf. London: Hogarth Press, 1953.

——. *The Years*. London: Hogarth Press, 1937.

"Working Women in Conference." *Common Cause*, 23 June 1916, 138.

"A 'Working Women's Parliament.'" *Common Cause*, 30 June 1916, 150.

Zappa, Stephanie. "Woolf, Women, and War." In *Virginia Woolf: Texts and Contexts. Selected Papers from the Fifth Annual Conference on Virginia Woolf*, ed. Beth Rigel Daugherty and Eileen Barrett, 274–79. New York: Pace University Press, 1996.

Zwerdling, Alex. *Virginia Woolf and the Real World*. Berkeley: University of California Press, 1986.

Index